G000244609

SATAN'S GUT, SAUSAGE BOATS AND ICE KISSES

The adventure travel notes of a nervous Man

TONY FOSGATE

*Down Cataract Canyon. **Photo: Wayne Ranney***

CONTENTS

"Take risks: if you win, you will be happy; if you lose, you will be wise." – Anonymous

Introduction

This is not a 'how to' guide to adventure sports, which is just as well, otherwise it would simply be wasting everyone's time. The author after all has no particular skills or ability when it comes to adrenaline activities, is not especially brave and frequently gets lost.

Instead this book simply relates some tales based on a few personal experiences of 'adventure travel', together with a bit of background on the people and places you find when you get there. At no time did the author really know what he was doing. That is a fact.

But then competency can be so overrated. The truth is that increasingly we live in a world where the more intrepid traveller has access to the kind of places and experiences that were once a preserve of the pioneering elite, all without necessarily needing a high degree of technical nous. Explorers spent centuries of icy deprivation finding the North Pole-now we can fly there with a Selfie Stick. Until the middle of the twentieth century only a handful of people with smashed up boats had ever braved the rapids of the Colorado's Grand and Cataract Canyons. Today many of us bounce through its wild water on large inflatable rafts like giant ping pong balls, our thrills made possible by the introduction of neoprene and the air pump. And at the

Cresta Run, the world's most infamous ice track, we too can try to emulate the Bob-Skeleton speed freaks: all it needs is a down payment of six hundred francs and we are all set for the toboggan ride to end all toboggan rides.

So go for it! That is not to say of course that these things aren't risky: along the Colorado people disappear into whirlpools while in the Arctic, Polar bears tuck into tourists. The Cresta Run, not to put too fine a point on it, can be carnage: a number of riders have died on it over the years and there is always the possibility of losing fingers and roughing up internal organs. That strangely seems to be part of its appeal.

So why gamble life and limb when you could be lazing by the pool? That's what people ask. While this book doesn't pretend to have the answers it does seem that we like to challenge and even frighten ourselves on a regular basis. Mostly we just get bored.

It is said that travel is a subjective thing, an interior journey that tests your preconceptions not only about the world but also about yourself. Add the adventure element and it becomes even more difficult, asking questions about what sort of stuff you are made of and even how brave you are. Most of the time you don't want to know the answers.

Such is the joy of adventure travel-that and the sheer weirdness that can often be found along the way. So come on a trip to a place so blank that you see visions and dream in Technicolor, where the cold snaps rubber, compasses fall over and time disappears. Or visit an ice track that is run by what must be one of the most eccentric institutions on earth: The St Moritz Tobogganing Club. Here its upper crust patrons regularly injure themselves and get served champagne when they arrive at the local clinic. Some of them keep their heads on with metal pins. Instead of trophies they give out Barbie dolls. Once they even had a horse as a member. Then there is the mighty Colorado with its billion gallon gush providing the ultimate roller coaster ride before being sucked dry by a burgeoning desert population that demands fresh vegetables and gambling. Don't fall into 'Satan's Gut' or you may never get out. Try not to stretch out in your sleeping bag when there is a scorpion in it. But most of all don't pee in the river. You may not live to tell the tale.

These are just some of the adventures you can go on: the world is your oyster and it is a very strange shellfish indeed.

Of course if you don't like it you could always stay at home or just lie on the beach instead. But then who seriously wants to do that?

Please note: everything in this book is undoubtedly true, although some names have been changed to protect the innocent and even the guilty, while some characters and their voices are based on a number of people the author met on his travels. They and the situations described are however faithful to the spirit of everything that happened.

SOME TRAVEL TALES

1

Satan's Gut and Sausage boats: Whitewater Rafting in the USA

You feel mighty free and easy and comfortable on a raft. (The Adventures of Huckleberry Finn.)
Mark Twain

BROWN BETTY

'There are three rules to white water rafting,' Pilot Pete tells us from the back of our sausage craft:

1. Stay on the boat.
2. Don't leave the boat.
3. Don't even think of getting off the boat.

His feet are firmly planted on a narrow plank at the aft of our inflatable from which incredibly he will steer us, still standing, through the maelstrom yet to come, hand on the tiller like an Ahab battling with the waves. All we have to do is hang on. Unlike Ahab, we do have the benefit of a four stroke outboard motor to power us through the rough, but should it fail we will be at the mercy of the currents. According to Pete, on one occasion the engine flooded and he had to strip it down and change the spark plugs in mid rapid. 'How is that possible?' I ask him. 'Adrenaline,' he tells me.

Never mind, best not think of these things right now. It is another beautiful June day in the canyon. The sun is hot and the Colorado flat. In the distance, around the next bend in the river is the first rapid but that is not for us right now. At present we are anchored close to a Jurassic cliff- flanked shore, drifting lazily in circles as we munch on lunch time burritos and listen to Pete prep us for survival. For two days we have travelled downriver like pioneers in the wilderness, serenely floating on calm water and watching the landscape unfurl from our sausage home as we look forward to the river turning wild and what it will mean for us. In that time our little group have remained just one happy family.

But then suddenly Pete comes up with a fourth rule: 'If you see a loved one, or indeed anybody go overboard, don't try to save them.' He is looking pointedly at one of the women in our group, a pleasant soft hearted American apple pie mom who clearly adores her two teenage kids, even as they recoil in embarrassment at her doting. They listen to the do or die lecture with a bored, 'whatever' expression on their faces.

I decide that if anyone is going to be a rule breaker it will be this protective mother hen. Hell, if the family owned a loveable flea bag mutt, which no doubt they do, and it inadvertently slipped into a raging torrent of death, she would jump in like a flash. That's the sort of Mom she is.

'There is no point in jumping in as well,' Pete tells us, as if reading her mind. 'If that happens then we will have

River running thrills: the Colorado and Cataract Canyon

two people in the water rather than one and neither of you is getting back on.' I doubt if she is even paying attention.

'So, how often do people come off?' I ask, wondering what it would be like to be a human cork riding up to a third of a million gallons of water, (In the Springtime, particularly after the snowmelt, that can be the amount of cold Colorado river that comes crashing downstream every second).

Worse still is the thought of the boat flipping over and me being under it, fighting my way out of a neoprene nightmare while choking to death.

'It does happen,' Pete admits but then tells me that this is rare on the motorised 'J-rigs' like ours where there are no oars to wrangle. Trying to paddle while concentrating on the more serious task of keeping your death grip on the boat would seem to me to be pretty much impossible anyway. It would just be asking for trouble.

Last trip he did have one raft capsize. How did that go I wonder?

The trick apparently is to 'walk out' from under the boat with your hands until you surface and then catch it as it goes by. Should the raft be leaving you like the last bus home, start swimming towards it as hard as you can. Should that fail, try striking out for the riverbank- there is after all two of them for your convenience.

Above all, don't panic-apparently this is a waste of time, although in my experience it has often been an integral and necessary part of pretty much any activity I have undertaken and found to regret afterwards. I am beginning to wonder about the wisdom of this latest adventure, now that the sound of the wild water is in earshot.

If your boat has truly sailed and none of the above has worked, you are, as Pete tells us encouragingly, 'Pretty much on your own,' and you and your lifejacket are about to embark on the biggest roller coaster ride of your lives. If that is the case the best you can do is to relax and pretend you are at home in your favourite armchair. The 'down river swimmers position' is the recommended technique for running a rapid solo, involving as it does tipping your head back, bending you knees and pointing your toes skyward so that you face the direction of travel and can use your feet as shock absorbers on the unforgiving rocks. It is best to, 'Keep your butt up,' so as to avoid any interesting bruises and gentlemen in particular should keep their legs together so that they do not fall foul of what river runners call 'romancing the stone', thereby finding that true romance is out of the window for anything up to the following month. I am not even going to think about that.

Pete tells us that it if you find yourself in this position it is important to get your breath under control and establish a rhythm. In the first place the snow swollen Colorado is likely to be a bit of shock after a sunny day's dry temperature in the canyon which can reach ninety eight degrees. In any case quite a lot of your ride will inevitably be underwater, as you are sucked down by the eddying currents before being released again as if on the end of a spring. Should you fly by the Park Authority's jet rescue boat at the bottom of the first rapid don't necessarily expect to be hauled out unless you are in deep distress: the name of the game in whitewater is 'self rescue', although this may mean shooting the whole set of twenty eight rapids on your own before finally idling in the smooth water downstream and waiting for everyone else to catch up.

Generally, he says, although some people do this sort of thing for fun, (for fun!), he wouldn't recommend it.

Pete concludes his briefing by reminding us that, all in all, the best thing is.....,'To stay on the boat?' I finish for him, almost shouting. 'Uh huh, you've got it.'

It is advice I am destined to take to heart; later, when the lovely Mom starts to pirouette acrobatically over my head I will continue to hang on for dear life and just let her get on with it. After all, I am just following instructions.

They say that water rafting is a white knuckle ride and so it will prove. At the end of it they will have to prise my fingers off the loops of rope that serve as hand holds on the bucking bronco that is our raft. My knuckles will literally be white with the effort of staying on and not being tossed into the broiling, bubbling water. Leave the boat? Who me? No way, no Siree.

Our boat is made out of sausages, or that is how it appears to me. Actually, it is made of three welded fingers of synthetic rubber, pumped up for a big splashy ride, half as long again as a family saloon and as broad as a Navajo warrior lying full stretch with a tomahawk in one hand.

Across its middle marches a row of containers as neat as a line of soldiers. Lockable and firmly attached to our floating home, they contain all the personal gear we want to take on our trip, the usual survival kit of the tourist: camera, sun screen, water bottle, sand encrusted towel, sunglasses, floppy hat that blows away. At the back there is a big container for the tents we pitch every night on the 'beaches' that fringe the shoreline of the sliding river and the sleeping bags we snuggle into, hoping that we are not sharing them with a petulant scorpion or any critter with more than two legs. There is also a fresh water butt and water coolers for our celebratory beers together with a tank full of mild lemonade which is encouragement for us to drink often so that our pee is just the right colour of straw. A large chest weighs the raft down, containing as it does everything we will eat by the end of the tour. The entire provisions sit on two huge blocks of ice so that throughout our four day trip the burritos and steaks will remain fresh and the salad crisp under a fierce Utah sun.

Remarkably, none of this will be unpacked to lighten the load in deference to a few rapids- the whole shebang is going with us for the wild water ride. If the worse happens and we flip, it will be a case of finger tipping the floor of our house while all our worldly goods and half a ton of meat roll above our heads, not to mention the celebratory beers going for a swim. If we weren't able to salvage any of it downstream that would be a hell of a waste.

Luckily the J-rig has a reputation for being stable: it has, after all, some fifty years of use behind it on the river. When Jack Curry, an early river man and founder of Western River Expeditions took delivery in 1965 of two boxcars of surplus rubber tubes used by the military in the Korean War, glued them together and built a frame to keep the whole thing in check, the J-rig was born. It has changed very little since, apart from modern developments in the plastics and materials used to build it, and is now pretty much standard for tourists joy riding the river. We have come a long way since the leaky wooden boats of the early river runners. Some idea of how far may be gathered by the fact that happily we are a hundred times less likely to die on the water than in our grandparent's time, although in those days some of their river based exploratory antics were close to suicidal.

Still, everything is flippable in the rafting world. This is an endeavour capable of any number of mishaps for which there is a whole vocabulary. These include a 'Tube stand', (when the whole raft balances upright on one pontoon before it keels over), 'Pancaking', (where the front flips back so the whole thing becomes like a taco, (hence also being known as a 'Taco'), and 'Dark siding' where the rafter tries to pre-empt being tossed out of the boat by jumping over the side voluntarily. The latter is rarely successful. Should the worse happen and you find that the raft has 'Dump trucked' on you it is likely that you and all your fellow passengers are bowling down the river with the brightly coloured flotsam of your gear floating with you. If that is the case you have just been invited to a 'Yard Sale'.

On the plus side our J-rig is a sexy thing. According to the tour operator it is the boat equivalent of riding, 'A luxury sports car,' instead of an old camper van. In addition it has one extra feature that makes it particularly hot: its central pontoon reaches out over the river so that it is the perfect place to ride, if in the words of the brochure, 'You want to go for the gusto,' (although, 'For a more secure feeling ride, select a spot in the center.') Best of all, from the front the raft looks like it is giving the middle finger to anything that the Colorado, tumbling in this stretch of Cataract Canyon, would care to throw at us.

Cataract Canyon: the words themselves conjure up hardcore white water thrills that are enough to give you some bragging rights at least. *I once met a girl with whom I was swapping travel stories and mentioned I had run Cataract Canyon. For a moment she looked at me in a totally different light. 'Respect,' she said simply.*

And its white water is the real thing, no doubt about it, a ballsy III-V on the international scale of river difficulty which aims to score rapids according to the turbulence of the water and the risk of injury and even death that they may bring. V is the tops- anything above that and it is pretty nigh impossible to come out alive.

There are twenty eight rapids to run in Cataract Canyon, all compressed into a fourteen mile stretch of the Colorado between its confluence with the Green River and Lake Powell downstream. These are run in quick succession so that the adrenaline doesn't stop flowing until you finally glide into the smooth waters of the lake, a huge canyon-swallowing reservoir some 186 miles long and 25 miles wide at its greatest extent. This body of water is entirely artificial and created by plugging the mighty Colorado downstream with the Glen Canyon dam. Its backed up waters are peaceful after the extreme turbulence of the rapids and offer a brake to your mad dash along the river's natural course. At this point you effectively come to a halt.

Some idea of the impact of the rapids on the early river runners can be gathered from the fact that many of them have been given specific names, often as a result of bitter or fearful experience. Among the most famous are 'Brown Betty', 'The North Seas', 'Ben Hurt', the self explanatory, 'Capsize rapid', and the enigmatic 'Powell's Pocket watch', (named after John Wesley Powell, the Colorado river explorer, whose timepiece did not fare well on his expedition down Cataract and the Grand Canyon).

However the best known are the notorious 'Big Drops' where the floor of the Colorado falls over thirty feet in less than a quarter of a mile and is littered with boulders, some the size of railway wagons, that break and twist the water flow to create the kind of eddies and whirlpools that test the most experienced river runner. The 'Big Drops' set of three rapids is generally regarded as the most dangerous place on the Colorado. Of the fourteen deaths recorded in recent times within the Canyonlands National Park that encompasses Cataract Canyon and the Green River sections, eleven have occurred in the 'Big Drops' and mostly through rafts flipping. The names given to these sets of rapids tell the story: 'Little Niagara', for example and 'The Claw'. The most famous though is 'Satan's Gut', a spinning, sucking vertical 'hydraulic' formed when the water meets a jumble of boulders and its sheer force creates a vacuum downstream. Essentially the river Colorado has a big hole in it.

Boat men and women will tell you that what goes into Satan's Gut rarely comes out and if it does, it is not in good shape. Every few years it claims a victim. Particularly dangerous are the times of 'Peak Flow' in May to June when the snow melt high in the Rockies swells the river, doubling or trebling the volume of water cascading along its choked bed. Some years are extraordinary. In 1997 when the water exceeded all expectations some 134 rafters were spilled from their boats in the six weeks between May and June alone, with thirty rafts flipping, mostly in the Big Drops around the Satan. According to Steve Swanke, the Park River District ranger interviewed at that time, the river was, 'Heavy with debris. (It) was carrying everything-tires, trees, dead animals. Shoot, I even saw a refrigerator float by.'

In 2008 the river levels were again exceptional, leading to tales of 'Whirlpools the size of football fields.' Just one year later Michael Don Carlos, thirty-seven, of Nederland, Colorado, was thrown from his raft and into Big Drop Two in peak water. According to the National Park Authority's River Report of the time, 'He was able to hold onto the raft at first, but let go for unknown reasons. Without the raft's high flotation, he was pulled under the surface of the violent rapids and drowned.' Just a few years earlier another day tripper had also lost his life when the raft he was travelling on flipped just ahead of the Gut and was left wedged on an overhanging rock with the boatmen and his fellow passengers dangling over its maw. In the words of the River Report of the time, all five occupants were then, 'flushed' into the feature. When he was finally retrieved the victim was suffering from cardiac arrest. 'CPR was initiated,' the report went on, ' .. With difficulty owing to the victim's clenched jaws and clogged airway. At 15.08 the victim was pronounced dead.' The report concludes that, 'This accident occurred in spite of strict adherence to safety considerations and depicts the inherent danger of rapids.' No kidding-it has happened before and it can happen again.

So, is it safe, this little river adventure? And how safe is it? That is what we on our raft are secretly asking ourselves now that *Brown Betty* is around the corner and Pete has finished his survival talk; as safe as houses?-probably not. Bowling perhaps?

Some years ago it was alleged that a state commissioned report using the latest statistical analysis had come to the conclusion that bowling was actually more dangerous than the supposedly extreme sport of whitewater rafting.

Of course the commercial river runners seized upon this immediately, wanting to emphasise the thrills while not wishing to scare the customers, and started to mention it on almost all of their websites and in their FAQs on safety:'..... Statistically, you're safer on a raft than in your car! One state government found in an investigation that the injury rate for whitewater rafting is similar to that for bowling!'

What this shows of course is that statistics can probably be made to prove anything. Still, Ten Pin bowling is not without its hazards. During the period 1990-2008, it was estimated that this seemingly innocent pastime actually resulted in over 376,000 accidents in the US alone. Worryingly, a fair number of these were what were called 'soft tissue injuries' from dropping the ball.

Practically the most dangerous activity a woman can undertake is cheerleading. The *US National Center for Catastrophic Sport Injury Research* has reported that statistically speaking this Pom-pom based enterprise is probably the most hazardous you can undertake. Not only has it resulted in a number of deaths and numerous cases of permanent paralysis but it accounts for 66% of injuries that are termed 'catastrophic', (i.e life changing), as well as more minor trauma including concussion, broken arms, busted collarbones and countless sprains. It is worse than American Football in this respect; in 2013 all that tumbling and pyramid building resulted in 26,000 admissions to the emergency room.

Then there is golf. This led to 50,000 admissions to A&E in the same period, 16,000 of which involved the use of electric carts, while roller skating accounted for some 46,000 accidents a year, (in-line skating had its own share of a further 12,000 reported injuries).

If you have a death wish, get on a bicycle. In the same period there were a reported half a million cyclists who suffered some injury while out on the roads. Nor are you safe in your own home: over 18,000 people die and a whopping twenty-one million people require medical attention each year in the US from home related accidents. 30,000 people alone leave a finger or part of it behind in a door jamb, while back in the UK some 3,700 men and women attend hospital each year as a result of an accident with their trousers and of those over 500 men a year require emergency treatment over eye-watering mishaps with their zips.

By contrast boating appears to be a rather sedate and low-risk pursuit with just over 4,000 recreational watercraft accidents reported in the US in 2013. Of course far more people own bicycles than boats and a gentle trip downstream is not the same as dicing with death in a raging current. Perhaps there is an inherent problem with trying to compare apples and oranges. Whitewater rafting is not bowling, nor is it cheerleading. In any event the statistics around Ten Pin leisure pursuits are prey to being skewed by the odd but mercifully rare bizarre accident, such as that which tragically befell David Geiger in November 2014 when he was crushed by the pinsetting machine while setting up the skittles at 'Northwest Lanes' on Happy Valley Drive, Butler, Ohio.

Every year millions of people go whitewater rafting in the US alone and in recent times on average up to fifty people have succumbed to the water on an annual basis. The majority of these are private river runners; the actual fatalities on commercial trips are more likely to be between 6-10 souls every year. The truth is that commercial river operators have an enviable safety record. The commercial element has, after all, provided the professional expertise and discipline that mad or drunken people who decide to have a go on their own inevitably lack.

One of the most significant factors in determining the number of deaths on the river is in fact the inherent stupidity of some people. In their excellent book, *Over the edge: Death in Grand Canyon*, Michael Ghiglieri and Thomas Myers, who are both veterans of whitewater, record in meticulous detail practically every mishap that has occurred along this stretch of the Colorado and find much human frailty.

Take Glen Rollin Hyde and Bessie (nee) Haley, two newly- weds who decided in the early days of river running to find fame by being the first husband and wife team to run the Colorado. Hyde, who was described by contemporaries as, 'Surly, conceited and stoopid,' insisted on two things that were guaranteed to seal the couple's fate: one, he designed and built the most unsuitable boat for the trip, (in the words of a local Green river man, 'It looked like a floating coffin,') and two: he would not be persuaded that they should don life jackets, eschewing what he called, 'artificial aids'. 'I am going to do it without life jackets or else,' he told all those who begged him in vain. In the end it was 'or else', and Glen and Bessie finally went down somewhere in the Canyon after travelling over 400 miles along the Green river and through Cataract with all its rapids. The remains of their boat were found on Christmas Day 1928.

Alcohol can explain a lot when it comes to inviting disaster. According to the US Coast Guard authorities, having even the legal limit in your system can render you ten times more likely to be killed in a boating accident. Sometimes it is not even to do with the control of the craft but simply being so uncoordinated that you fall in.

Even a supposedly properly planned and resourced expedition is not immune to a complete lack of common sense. in the late 1800's, long before Glen and Bessie took their suicide trip, Frank Mason Brown, a Colorado real estate and mining magnate, decided to finance an early scouting expedition down Cataract and Grand Canyon without the benefit of any sturdy boats, (most split end to end before they had even started), professional river guides, or even life preservers. The first mishap occurred at the start of Cataract's turbulent water when Brown capriciously decided to cross the river to camp for the night. The boat that was hauling their provisions lost control in the current and most of their stores went barrelling down the very first rapid. The name of the craft happened to be *Brown Betty.*

All in all the Colorado has had its fair share of misfits, drunks and madmen who have come to a watery end exploring the river. But that is not going to be the case with our trip: we have a sturdy boat and a capable team. Apart from myself there is the American mom with her teenage boy, (a thirteen year old kid embarking on his first real adventure together with his older sister), a father and son from Germany bonding in the adventure, and a brace of Californian doctors who are buddies. One of the medics has brought along his college son, for whom every last detail of our epic trip is worthy of the description: 'Awesome.' Sometimes even that is not enough and then the whole wilderness thing can only be adequately summed up as, 'Totally awesome.' Then there is Pete, who in his checked shirt and with his wild hair and backwoodsman's beard looks every bit the river runner, with some ten years under his belt of steering tourists through choppy waters and occasionally hauling them out. If he has ever lost anyone, he is not letting on.

Ten random people on a raft a hundred miles from civilisation and not just one but two of them happen to be qualified medics. What are the chances? Even better, one is a neurosurgeon and the other a neurologist, so that if there are to be any head injuries along the way we not only have the finest, (and probably most expensive), clinical expertise currently floating in the Southwest but also a second opinion to boot. Later this will prove particularly fortuitous. But that is in the future. Tonight as we pitch our tents on the sandy shore of the Colorado with *Brown Betty* whooshing in the distance the real challenge is yet to come; so far it has been a lazy glide downstream from the town of Moab on a deceptively laid back river. Now things are about to get wild.

Some of us have come a long way for the pleasure of meeting *Brown Betty* and her turbulent companions. In my case it has taken me a couple of days in cramped, pressurised purgatory to reach this kind of rough water. Others have endured even worse. In the process we have swapped aircraft like Russian Dolls, from the smooth wide bodied Atlantic jets that lumber into rainy Chicago O'Hare, to the sleeker in-country versions that whisk commuters west to the High Plains city of Denver, and finally a baby turboprop for the last bouncy hop over the snow capped Rockies and on towards the western slopes city of Grand Junction, gateway to the Canyonlands. The last leg is somewhat informal in keeping with the more intimate scale of about thirty passengers all escaping happily to big sky country. Our one stewardess is called Darlene and she treats us as if we were friends of hers, which no doubt some of us are. This is a regular service. Welcome to Darlene's bus.

And she is comic too, with a good sense of timing that cheers everyone up during the well worn trudge of the safety announcement. She treats this with just about the amount of respect it deserves. After all if this raft goes down I wouldn't fancy our chances, even if statistically speaking flying is the most non- lethal method of travel. 'If you are sitting next to a small child, or someone who is acting like a small child, please do us all a favour and put your own mask on first,' she tells us, or something similar. She gets a round of applause; and so too does the choppy ride in the turbulent air over a spectacularly twisted and deeply rutted landscape. After the unruffled float of the big jet's saloon car, this is like riding a bicycle over pot holes in the road. For some of us that feels gloriously real at last and we greet each bump with a certain perverse relish. Why, it is difficult to explain.

What is it about being bounced around that we like so much, from literally our time in the cradle through to rocking horses when we are five and then on to teenage birthday bumps and finally the ultimate theme park ride? Add the possibility of drowning and we are even more enthusiastic about the prospect. There is something in us that likes to embrace danger, at least within limits. No one can really say why that is, it's just part of what makes us human.

Whitewater safe?-of course it's not safe, that's the point. And even when you have stripped away all the fucked up personal element and have buttoned down as much of the risk as you can with professionalism and technology and all the rules and regulations that bureaucracy can devise, you are still left with the primeval wilderness of the canyon and above all the river with its unpredictability and random violence.

None of us should have any illusions about this, it is going to be a rollicking ride on some of the wildest water in the US or perhaps even on the planet, a visceral, heart in the mouth, seat of the pants thrill ride that is both exhilarating and scary as hell, with the wind in your face and your mouth full of water as the little rubber boat falls beneath your feet like an runaway elevator before cresting a wave so epic you can't see its summit, while all around you the billion gallon rush of the Colorado is tossing and spinning the raft and maybe even dangling it on the lip of the devil's plughole so that for one heart stopping moment it seems you are about to enter its corkscrew Hades, a fast track helter-skelter ride that would undoubtedly leave you kicking and screaming into a watery oblivion. I'm not exaggerating. That's pretty much what whitewater rafting is like in these parts.

Of course, you could always go bowling instead.

MOAB

Moab is my kind of town, a one street Mecca for all adventurers and adrenaline junkies, stuffed with every type of outdoor activity outfit you can imagine, ranging from paddle craft suppliers to base jumping specialists. Its population of just over 5,000 live to service the needs of hikers, off- roaders, dirt bikers, rock climbers and of course whitewater thrill seekers, over a million of whom pass through its tiny drag each year on their way to the nearby Arches and Canyonlands national parks.

Before tourism there was the bomb. Back in the Fifties Moab was known as the, 'Uranium capital of the world,' after a deposit of the stuff was found south of the town. When the Cold War folded so almost did Moab, forced as it was to exist on the scrapings of its remaining potash mining industry and some oil and gas reserves. More glamorous was its occasional film extra work, serving as a backdrop for such movies as, 'Stagecoach', 'Once upon a time in the West', and 'Rio Grande'. It was only in the seventies with the rise of the leisure industry that Moab finally achieved its destiny. Now, thanks to its position near some of the best water and epic wilderness that the US can provide, it has become the adventure capital of the Southwest, the gateway to whatever big country fun it is possible, (for desk bound urban folks in particular), to devise.

Every adventure starts in Moab and ours is no exception. It is but a half hour's drive away to the 'put in' or launch point on the Colorado which in honour of the town's dirty past is known as 'Potash Ramp'. But first there is the paperwork, which is why we are in the offices of our tour operator scribbling in a hand like a spider's trot on triplicate paper pads, claiming that we are not only sane and understand the risks involved but also that whatever happens to life and limb we will not be suing anyone. We are also being eyed up for a proper kit- out which most importantly consists of a heavy duty US Coast Guard 'Approved personal flotation device' and less vital to our safety a complimentary drinking mug with the operator's logo on it. The mug has a top and a spout to suck on. It reminds me of the kind given to babies or those who have lost all their teeth.

Speaking of having the right gear, I have in fact brought a Rain Mac with me in preparation for the might of the Colorado. This is undoubtedly one of the funniest and stupidest things that a naive tourist from the mild English Home counties has ever done. But to everyone else's credit none of them laugh. One hard bitten veteran who is wrangling with the guide about using her own bespoke gear which she claims has, 'Served me on the river for over ten years,' stops and looks at me as I fish out the thin plastic. 'Aaaaaah!' she coos, like I am a stray kitten.

I love Moab. It is a veritable treasure trove of outdoorsy stuff most of which I will never use or understand: gleaming karabiners and candy striped nylon climbing ropes jostle with oily dirt bike rentals while lightweight polyethylene Kayaks with funky designs and which boast, 'Effortless eddy hopping capabilities and smooth carving wave surfing on the river', are stacked up to the ceiling next to all the hiking gear you could imagine. If you want to step out into the big outdoors you have got to be dressed for the part and that means mostly in NASA developed brightly coloured fabrics which protect you from the heat and cold, wet and dry, and which wick away your sweat as you run, jump and stumble in a landscape that in some respects is more akin to the moon. All of this stuff is packed in numerous outlets, many of which are decked out in wood with verandas and swinging painted signs for that folksy frontier town feel. It is a bit like Dodge, only with 'Starbucks' and 4X4s.

Red tape over, we all pile into a jeep and fly along the main strip, waving goodbye to Moab. As we pass its city line it is a bit like crossing an invisible boundary. After all, this is the last bit of civilisation we will see before we are swallowed up by the high desert, a mostly empty elevated chunk of the US known as the Colorado Plateau which is half the size of Texas but with a permanent population roughly equivalent to the Queens District of New York. There, no one can hear you scream, except perhaps your travelling buddies and your cell phone is often useless. You are, (as hiker Aron Ralston found when he became wedged in Blue John Canyon in 2003 and could only escape by breaking the bones in his arm and then amputating it with a small knife), pretty much on your own.

Potash road, a dusty track, leads out of Moab towards the Potash evaporation ponds and hence to Potash ramp, a concrete-lined landing strip for boats on a bend of the river where the walls of the canyon step back to allow access to its waters. This is the main entry point for rafting expeditions and the place where we first see our J-rig. Our resident neurosurgeon or Head doc 1#, who up to now has been remarkably quiet and kept his own counsel, suddenly informs us that, 'For the purpose of this trip I will be the designated nervous passenger.' 'Don't get pushy,' I tell him, 'That's my job.'

Still, The Colorado is wide and sluggish at this point, not at all threatening. Today it is the colour of tea. At various times it can be like chocolate, pea soup or a rusty nail, depending on the season and what it is carrying. 'Colorado' means red in Spanish after the colour of the silt and sediment it bears away as it carves into the plateau; until recent times that was over half a million tons a day, causing early settlers to bemoan the fact that the river was, 'Too thick to drink but too thin to *plow*.' Cattlemen regularly lost livestock when crossing the river at fordable places, not because of the depth of the water but the sheer volume of the gunk it contained. Sheep were particularly susceptible, the sediment clinging to their woollen coats until they sank under its sheer weight.

Nowadays, the big dams downstream create huge man-made lakes that act as 'settling pools' for all the mud and silt that used to go all the way to the sea and therefore spill out water at the other end that is unnaturally blue or algae tinged green. Here though, above Cataract Canyon, the Colorado is still in its natural state, mostly reddish brown or in the rainy season when the sludge really gets going, the colour of a mud pie.

On the opposite shore of the river red sandstone cliffs step up into the sky. The same rusty hue, brought on by the oxidisation of iron in the stone, infuses the whole landscape; you don't have to ask what the Canyonlands looks like: this is 'Red rock country'. Every conceivable shade is here in its meaty bluffs and towers and in the folds and layers of the canyon walls there are constant changes throughout the day: a kaleidoscope of orange, tan, lilac, peach pink and vermillion- these colours all make their appearance. In the morning the tops of the Canyons are golden in the early sunshine. At sunset the broad flat topped mesas and their sides have a colour as deep and dark as blood.

From the air the Canyonlands territory looks a bit like a hard baked brownie, cracked down the middle where the Colorado and its tributaries have cut deeply into the heart of the cake. it is bone desert dry: less than ten inches of rain fall annually, squeezed as the area is in the 'rain shadow' of two great mountain systems: the Rockies and the Sierra Nevada. The surface is mostly bare rock or a sugaring of sand. Its flat topped surface is occasionally peppered with scrub.

Down in Horseshoe Canyon and in other parts of the park dinosaur tracks can be found, testament to a particular period in its geological history and a clue to the formation of the landscape we see today.

In fact the process started much earlier than the Jurassic. Some 300 million years ago the whole area was under a huge tropical sea which gradually dried out leaving thick deposits of sediment that came to form the base of the geological 'layer cake' that is exposed today. In its chequered rock building history what is now the Colorado Plateau has at various times been the bottom of a sea, a coastal plain and a desert, the ooze, silt and sand from each period adding another layer of lime or sandstone. By the time the dinosaurs arrived much of Southwest America resembled the Sahara, with the occasional waterhole left for them to drink from and leave prints in its mud. Consequently they have left a lasting impression in the stone that tops much of the canyons, evidence of the most recent episode in the endless time it has taken to bake a rock cake.

It is the river that has revealed much of this history: the Colorado has been the knife that has sliced right through it. Around seventy million years ago in a major mountain building exercise the whole region started to lift up in one block, gradually raising it thousands of feet above the rest of the American continent. While the Colorado is not the biggest river in the world, it does have one thing on its side: gravity. From its source 13,000 feet up in the Southern Rocky Mountains the river hurdles down the western slopes and is propelled over the Colorado Plateau before turning south and exiting in the Gulf of Mexico. In the millions of years it has spent flowing over the Plateau it has carved prodigious canyons out of the soft sedimentary layers. In fact it has cut so deeply that at river level in Cataract Canyon we will come face to face with rocks that were formed some hundred million years before any dinosaur padded about the earth.

'Let's go,' Pilot Pete commands us and we launch into the murky river, all agog at the sheer scale of the scenery but needing to make a start, to begin the float towards *Brown Betty*. Our trip will be in the nature of a sandwich, two easy slices of bread and an intense serving of meaty rapids in between. For the first two days we will drift without engine power over the placid forty seven miles that will take us to the confluence of the Green and Colorado rivers. There we will camp for the night. The next morning we will scream through the fourteen miles of rapids in one go, all before lunchtime. That leaves a day for a sedate trip into the calm if artificial waters of Lake Powell where we can swim and relax; a hundred miles of river-no problem. At least, that's the plan.

We all begin to settle on the raft, to unpack and repack our stuff. The American mom makes sure that no one has been left behind or is in distress. Head doc 1# eyes the spot in the centre of the boat, made more stable by the weight of dinners to come, while the kids take it in turns on the big finger as a substitute sun bed, stretching out to catch the merciless rays. The sun is hot and we slap on the biggest factor we can find. The sweet buttery smell of suntan lotion mixes with the crisp waft of the chilly water as we are borne along by the river's current at a stately but brisk five miles an hour. A light breeze ruffles our hair. This part is plain sailing, about as gentle as it gets on the Colorado.

After a few minutes of watching the canyon walls slide by and inspired by the requirement to sip as much weak lemonade as will keep our kidneys going, the conversation turns, as it sometimes does between guys, to higher things-in this case the art of pissing.

Head doc 1#'s college son, (who has the chunky physique of a football jock and something of the locker room exuberance that goes with it), informs us that he recently won a 'whizzing' contest. 'Straight over the bough of a tree,' he tells us proudly. Head doc 1# looks sad. 'I used to be able to do that,' he says from his perch in the centre of the raft, while his buddy Head doc 2# nods in recognition. The seventeen year old college student looks nonplussed.

This is not just idle chat: In the Canyonlands urinating is not only an important skill, it is also a matter of life and death. Getting it wrong can be deadly. In their book *Over the Edge: Death in Grand Canyon,* Michael Ghiglieri and Thomas Myers estimate that no less than six people have expired in the Canyon directly as a result of relieving themselves. On July 16th 2006, nineteen year old Iryna Shylo from the Ukraine disappeared while hiking in the Grand Canyon after taking a 'bathroom' break. Earlier she had been told by a Park Ranger that regulations only allowed peeing in the river and not on its banks and as a consequence had waded in to comply. Her body was found two weeks later floating some ten miles downriver. Add some beers and the situation can get even more risky. In July 1981 Charles Robert Hunter most probably died as a result of the unsteady act of emptying his bladder from the bow of the boat he was using to crash out in, (apparently he had been drinking heavily during the day and had taken a full case of beer and a back up supply of vodka on his trip).

It is all too easy to topple into the Colorado and for its current to take you under. Women are particularly susceptible, having a disadvantage when it comes to keeping their balance during the act. So serious is the problem of pee related drowning and near fatal accidents involving comfort breaks that Ghiglieri and Myers recommend the use of a 'Pee Bucket' so that that you don't have to go near the river. They claim that at a dollar per plastic bucket this represents, 'Incredibly cheap life assurance.'

Later, both American Mom and I will each have our own 'whizzing' incident. She will suffer a mental block while hanging half submerged in the river between the two rafts and attempting to let go, (her difficulty made worse by the fact that the whole expedition, including her stony-faced children, are looking on), while I will take the opportunity to "whizz" off the back of our raft just as it swings round in a lazy arc and exposes me in full view of the rest of the flotilla with everything hanging out. It will be a golden moment.

The college kid is still looking puzzled, so Head doc 1# explains that as you get older things change: your body slows down and stuff works less well than it used to. He doesn't go on to say that at the same time the sheer bravura of youth can also slip away, so that over the years we become a bundle of adult anxieties, many of which are just ghosts in our heads. 'I didn't know that,' the Jock says, no doubt wondering what it would be like to one day fumble the football pass or end up dribbling beneath the bough. For a while he is quiet and seems lost in thought. It is probably the first time he has been told that he is not immortal.

The fact is of course that none of us are. With age we become more careful. Once I would have vied for a spot on the middle finger as 'scout' with my feet swinging in space and a fuck may care attitude. Now I am more content to watch the scenery unspool sedately from the back of the boat. At the moment the view is all a slow tumble down of stone due to the eons of wind and water that have hammered the rock that surrounds us. In some places the brown bluffs of the canyon have crumbled like stale cake, leaving gaps where an impossibly vaster landscape beyond is revealed. Distant flat topped mesas stride across it, their sheer faces rising from its baked dust floor. It looks so dry that you can't imagine anything living in it.

A little further along, the walls of the canyon again close in on us and now soar high above our heads, all bare rock apart from the vivid green shrub at its base that sucks at the margins of the chocolate river. Occasionally fish flash in the cold water by our boat and a bird wheels in the sky, but mostly there is just the lazy drift of the current and everything else is still. The whole scene is eerily quiet.

Time for some hollering: American Mom cups her

hands to her mouth and gives it her all. 'Hello,' she shouts, 'Anybody out there?' Her voice comes back to her in a satisfying but empty echo. No, it appears not, it seems that in this vast and unkind wilderness we are presently very much alone.

Head doc 1# looks nervous and retreats even further into his comfort zone in the centre of the boat. This seems to cheer the College Jock up. 'Embrace the fear!' he tells his father, 'You gotta try to live in the moment!' The doctor does not look convinced.

About ten miles into our journey the Colorado begins a couple of large turns, the last a tight three and a half mile long 'gooseneck' that encompasses some of the most dramatic and photographed scenery in the US, or indeed the world. As we enter the double switch back we are dwarfed on our right by sheer flat topped cliffs of undulating striped red and white sandstone, ending in a pulpit promontory before they step down towards the bend in the river. From the top there is a God's eye view of the river's winding progress through the park. The drop is in fact over two thousand feet at that point and from that dizzying perspective we would look as insignificant as ants floating on a leaf, the creamy wake of our boat no more than a tiny zip in the brown ribbon of the Colorado. What is amazing is that you can drive up there and park on the queasy edge. In fact this part of the park is quite accessible and much visited and if you wish you can roll on the entire length of the scenic state route 313 from North of Moab right through to where it ends in empty space, all in air conditioned comfort.

The top of the first reach of cliffs is basically a flat surface of sandy scrub with the bulk of the next tier of sandstone bluffs at its back. The road is pinched to the east by the drop on one side and the sheer rock face on the other, but then the land opens up to a roomy jutting overlook, a wide flat expanse of scrub large enough for a parade or a phalanx of cop cars with lights flashing in pursuit. Cut off in both directions there really would be no escape out of here. If you were fleeing someone the only way out would be to go over the edge. Nowadays couples go there as a kind of pilgrimage. They like to park right on the limit and take selfies of themselves at the wheels of their breezy soft tops with the screaming drop right under their bonnet. Later they post them on Facebook. That sort of thing is quite iconic.

'No way!' the College Kid tells me. 'Yes way,' I tell him, it really did happen. Well kind of. In Ridley Scott's famous 1991 'Neo-feminist' road movie, 'Thelma and Louise', starring Geena Davis, (Thelma) and Susan Sarandon, (Louise), the two protagonist fugitives end up just above our heads trapped in a 1966 Ford Thunderbird convertible, having been on the run since they gunned down a would be rapist who attacked Thelma at a roadhouse. The film charts their odyssey across the wild desert landscape until they arrive at the edge of the Canyon, caught by what seems to be an army of state troopers. Not wishing to give up their freedom, they decide to just, 'Keep going.'

Ridley Scott filmed the ending on this spot because it looked like the edge of the Grand Canyon and offered one of the few places along the river where it was possible to chuck a whole vehicle over the side without presumably too much red tape. 'Right,' the college jock says, '...But that was not real life, nobody died did they?'

I tell him that In fact for the final sequence the director used a number of motor 'body shells' that were fired from a ramp, (or so I have read). The actress Geena Davis remembers that when one of them went off accidentally and flew over the edge, 'My stomach went oooo.' Luckily there was a spare and while the two actresses sat in the actual T-bird for their close up, the final shell with the Thelma and Louise dummies in it was shot over the side and tumbled endlessly before it finally crashed at the bottom of the canyon, quite possibly at a spot just in front of our raft. I look for it but of course it isn't here today: modern park regulations require quite rightly that all litter is removed from the backcountry before you leave the area.

'Awesome,' says the Jock, clearly impressed by the idea of a flying car whizzing into space and causing so much havoc. But we are not done with tragic demise: there is more around the corner. A little later we are sailing through the throat of the goose when we learn of still more death in the Canyon. Past the end of 'Thelma and Louise Point' and round the next bend the cliff ends in a dizzyingly high promontory that juts towards the far bank. Pete gestures towards it and tells us that this is 'Dead Horse Point'.

'Up there?' we ask, craning our necks. 'Yes,' says Pete. 'How do they know?' 'Bones,' he tells us. Apparently it was once a huge graveyard littered with carcasses licked clean by the sun, the remains of wild mustangs roped by the cowboys from the range but perhaps untameable or not fit for riding and so left behind. For some reason they never found their way back. They died within sight of the Colorado, an endless drink beyond their grasp.

It does beg a lot of questions, the most important of which is who to blame. We do not like to think it was the cowboys-we think of them as the good guys.

The cowpokes loved this place, mostly because it was a

natural corral for horses and cattle. 'Dead Horse Point' is actually a fat stubby finger of scrub, large enough in itself to hold a decent herd but connected to the main Mesa top by a narrow neck of land only thirty yards wide. Since there was a sheer drop on each side and the neck of the 'bottle' could be plugged with a fence of brushwood to prevent escape, this was the perfect place to pen and examine the herd and select those who would be taken to market. As for the rejects: they would be set free and could return to the wild plains they had come from. That was the idea anyway.

Legend has it that either the cowboys forgot to remove the fence or the animals for some reason hesitated at the exit and wouldn't go back. Many people's money would be on human stupidity. It is a certain fact that human beings are sometimes the dumbest of animals. Once when I was hiking with a group in the outback of Australia we came across a tourist without a drop of water on him. He had simply woken up that morning and decided he would,'Go for a stroll.' That particular day it was more than forty degrees centigrade in the shade. I remember that our guide did his best to dissuade him and to give him some of our supply. He asked him how far he was going and it seemed like he was planning on a long walk, particularly without any liquid in that furnace heat. Our leader was straight with him. 'In that case,' he told him matter-of-factly, ' You are almost certainly going to die. G'day mate.'

To expire through lack of water is not a particularly pleasant way to go. We can only really speculate about how awful it is but given that humans and other mammals are essentially bags of liquid, there cannot be much more than skin and bones left after the agonising days it can take before we finally expire. During that time it is likely that your tongue will swell up and plug your mouth and that your eyes will shrink back into their sockets. Your brain will recede from your skull. Long before it is all over, you will in all likelihood have gone mad.

In desert landscapes where the temperature can top a hundred degrees and there is little shade to speak of, the average hiker is encouraged to take along a gallon of water a day to stay out of trouble. Larger animals of course need more. A horse for example may need five to ten times that much.

Luckily for those who make the journey today either in air conditioned 4X4s on the top of the Mesa or on foot or bike along the trails that run on the rim, there is the 'Pony Expresso' coffee shop which offers not just water but, 'Assorted juices and fresh fruit smoothies,' as well as, 'Baked goods and ice cream,' in fact everything you need for a little, 'Pick me up.' From the visitor centre it is a short hike along paved trails that loop around the tip of the finger where there are overlook spots and signs promoting the mystery of what happened here.

The views are stupendous. From this eyrie in the sky, the whole travelled trail of the winding Colorado is set out before you, all the way back to Moab in one direction and towards the rapids to come in the other, a table top model of stone with huge chunks missing- bitten, gouged and chiselled into impossible shapes, its reds and browns stretching into the blue haze of the horizon.

The vista is changing constantly throughout the day. The rock can be on fire at sunrise, honey at midday and then orange at sunset; in the afternoon deep shadows bloom from the bottom of the canyon. The sandy trails of the overlook are fringed with low juniper and pine, the same brush wood that the cowboys were supposed to tangle into a fence. The edge can be treacherous for the absent minded, disorientated, or just plain reckless. Occasionally, just occasionally, someone slips over the side, an event that is mercifully rare but which inevitably makes the news, a source of concern to the Park Authorities. But then the sheer feeling of being suspended above such a vast echoing space is enough to make anyone light headed. Distances become almost meaningless up here so that a point that looks within reaching distance is actually tens of miles away. On a clear day you can see far further than that, over a hundred miles distant.

From our raft that is beached below the jagged rock face, we trek sweatily from the mud of the river bank up along a boulder strewn and scree infested trail, at least part of the way up to the point. The American Mom is fully engaged in her hiking shorts, the German Father and Son offer solid support from behind, while the College Jock just bounds ahead followed by the Kid who cannot quite keep up and ends up exhausting himself with his enthusiasm. Undoubtedly one of the signs of maturity is learning to pace yourself. Both me and Head doc 1# take it nice and easy. After a few hours we are rewarded with a view of the winding river below and the mesa opposite that is caught in its lasso. But it is tiring work. To the college jock that unlike the lanky kid has weight and muscle behind him, it may be just another work out, a training session for the field. But still, he is clearly parched after his climb. I hand him a spare can of sugary cola which he glugs down greedily. I like to think he is drinking in the memory of the fate of the unfortunate stallions on 'Dead Horse Point'. 'Thanks man,' he tells me, 'I was dying of thirst.'

THE ART OF SURVIVAL

Day two of our trip down the Colorado starts with the echoing sound of teenage screams filling the canyon. A scorpion has been found in American Mom's tent. It is not as large as you would expect from the movies, (about as long as your thumb), and is a light brown colour. It is just sitting in the corner, not doing much.

To prevent American Mom jumping on to it to save everyone, Pete sticks a bucket over it. 'Looks kind of sleepy,' he tells us, as are we. Eventually he removes it and sets it free at a safe distance, its adventure pawing through the Mom family's underwear now over.

It is some comfort to know that of the numerous scorpions, rattlesnakes and black widow spiders that inhabit the canyonlands, none have ever been known to kill anyone. That is not to say that they desist from biting. In fact the record number of stings on a single occasion is thirteen suffered by an unfortunate hiker as she struggled to get out of her sleeping bag with a nervous scorpion tangled up in it.

'How poisonous is it?' asks a worried American Mom. 'Well...,' says Pete with characteristic understatement, 'If you're stung you won't feel that great.' In fact Ghiglieri and Myers cite the case of a one hundred and eighty pound college jock whose encounter with just such a three inch critter incapacitated him for a full thirty-six hours. But then he had gone padding around in bare feet and therefore had only himself to blame. Of the ninety or so species found in North America the worst is probably the Arizona Bark scorpion which has a cocktail of toxins in its venom some of which are 100,000 times worse than cyanide. On the face of it that does not sound good, but the thing about this clever creature is that it controls just how much it injects, so as to stun its victim, no more, no less. For a healthy adult this means a couple of days of nasty pain coupled with numbness. That is probably the worst that anyone will experience.

A rough estimate by rangers of the inner Grand Canyon is that one in two hundred of summer overnight camping visitors get stung and that is usually because they like dancing bare foot on the river bank and leaving their gear in the open so that it becomes a temporary refuge to any crawling thing.

In the wilderness you have to use your head. Life here is pretty much squeezed into a narrow ribbon of survival along the edges of the Colorado. If you pitch your tent on a beach of sandy scrub next to the river's slide, expect to share it with everything else. That's if it hasn't run away from another load of tourists.

In the end when it comes to encounters on the river bank, prevention is better than cure. 'Remember to shake all your clothing and check your foot wear,' Pete tells us. It is also a good idea not to unroll your bag until you are about to get into it. Above all though, it is important to keep a sense of perspective. You are in fact far more likely to die peeing in the canyon than by being attacked by any of its wildlife.

So we say goodbye to the scorpion, wishing it a long and happy life. A couple of hours later and we are all packed up and ready to go. By the time we launch into the river the sun is already in our faces and the shade rapidly disappearing from the cracked surface of the bluffs that rise from the opposite bank. It is another hot and thirsty day in the canyon, one which will send everything but us heading for cover.

After a while Head doc 1# joins me on one side of the raft. He dunks a towel in the cool river and then proceeds to wear it as a hat. He repeats this process several times in the space of one morning. The little craft eats up the river miles, deeper and deeper into the dry and broken backed country it goes and we don't see another soul. On the right bank is the area known as the 'Island in the sky', a stepped up mesa that shoots to a height of over six thousand feet in the middle of the wedge between the Colorado and Green rivers, tapering to a lofty point at the confluence of their waters. Its base is a wide sandstone 'bench' that drops another thousand feet to the river itself, so that all we can see from our vantage point is a sheer cliff face towering above us, the top of which is just the first rung on a ladder that climbs into the sky. Above the cliff the bench or broad 'White Rim' contains a road running around the edge of the island. It is about a hundred miles long and takes two days to drive, even with a four by four. This is the road that Thelma and Louise used before they hit a dead end. Built by uranium prospectors who found no uranium, the track is a relic of the atomic side of the 'Cold War' between East and West. Nowadays it is possible to drive along it but the rugged terrain and campsite incapacity mean that its use is rationed. There is not a drop of drinkable water along the route.

On the other bank of the Colorado is the 'Needles' district, named after the fantastically carved candy striped rock pinnacles it contains along with its other equally strange natural formations, all sculptured by wind, frost and the chemical alchemy that takes place in the beds of stone over millions of years. In such a harsh and unremitting landscape you could be forgiven for thinking that no one could ever have lived here, let alone thrived. But that would be untrue. Just outside the 'Needles' park boundary there is something as equally fantastical as the natural stone spires but it is not a product of nature- rather it is made by human hand. It is in fact a rock with over six hundred and fifty designs scratched into the dark patina of its surface. These include animals such as buffalo, deer and antelope, men on horseback and numerous symbols, some of which may be magical, some astronomical, while others may simply be reliving past events. The earliest carvings date back over two thousand years, and these have been added to over the centuries by the subsequent waves of people who made the Canyonlands their home. To the Navajo, who were relative latecomers in the 14th century AD and who contributed their own native art, this is 'Tse' Hone' or the 'Rock that tells a story'. Modern settlers have christened it, 'Newspaper Rock'.

Newspaper Rock is far from unique. There is plenty of evidence throughout the park of a human presence that spans millennia and traces of it can be found all along Cataract canyon. Had we looked more closely we would have found one example just downstream from our launching point two days ago. There on the right bank, suspended high on the rock face, is a structure of clay and twigs that has the rounded appearance of a shell. This is a 'Turtle Back Granary', a storehouse for grain and seeds built by the Anasazi or Ancestral Puebloans, who began to inhabit parts of what are now Utah, Arizona and New Mexico as early as some twelve centuries before Christ and who were themselves the likely descendents of the hunter gatherers who began visiting the Grand Canyon some six thousand years earlier.

The name Pueblo actually means town in Spanish.

When they arrived in the sixteenth century the conquistadors gave the settlements they encountered this name and the people who lived in them became known as 'Pueblo people'. Their descendents, the modern Puebloans, prefer the term 'Ancestral Puebloans' to that of Anasazi.

The Ancestral Puebloans were virtuoso dry land farmers, cultivating corn, beans and squash on the mesa tops above the canyons and storing the grains in their specially built granaries. Most of these were constructed from sandstone blocks plastered with adobe, (a mix of sand, clay, water and sticks), and were made airtight by starting a small fire inside to consume the oxygen and then sealing the opening up. This ensured the preservation of the contents within.

Any society that masters the basics of food production and storage has a head start on their competitors and this group became dominant in the area over the centuries, forming ever larger settlements which boasted well planned community spaces and complex structures not unlike the multi storey apartments found in modern cities today. They built these out of stone and adobe. Some of their vast buildings were more than five floors high and contained hundreds of rooms.

In their heartland, (the 'Four Corners' area of the Southwest where the states of Utah, Arizona, New Mexico and Colorado now meet), a population of more than 30,000 lived in towns and cities linked by over four hundred miles of roadways cut into the rock or formed by levelling the terrain.

These were highly sophisticated people with a well developed culture. They had knowledge of celestial movements, as indicated by the alignment of some of their buildings, and are likely to have had some form of calendar necessary to anticipate such events as feast days and solstices and provide an ordering of everyday activities. Pictographs left on the rock in various sites are said to show the movement of the sun and moon. Many of them are highly detailed.

Despite all this sophistication, life was still hard for the average Puebloan. Generally they were married at twelve and dead at thirty. The sand in their diet usually meant that their teeth were worn down well before they reached that age. After that it might not matter how much grain you were able to store.

In fact these people and their civilisation always lived a precarious existence, forever on the brink of disaster. They were continually at the mercy of one thing: lack of water.

Around 1100 AD North America entered a period of prolonged drought. Rainfall patterns became less stable and the water table dropped, leaving areas that could no longer be farmed. Competition for resources became more intense, probably leading to an era of worsening social strife and conflict. The response of the Ancestral Puebloans was to abandon many settlements and adopt new defensive positions, sheltering for example under rock faces. In some cases they decided to literally go up in the air.

In the northern section of the Grand Canyon above a place called Nankoweap creek, there are a number of slot like openings in the canyon walls that look down on the Colorado over six hundred feet below. These granaries were built into the cliffs around the time when the climate began to change and were used by the Puebloans to store grain where it could be kept safe from their enemies. Even today corncobs and pumpkin shells can still be found on the floor of these structures. To get to these larders involves negotiating a hair- raising trail from the beach below to some precarious rock ledges. Once there, intrepid hikers can get a great view of the river while swinging their legs in thin air. Official guides tend to warn that, 'Those uncomfortable with heights and exposure may choose to stay just below.' They go on to say that for the more adventurous there are even more precipitous places for a better peek, although these, 'Must be traversed very carefully!' This is particularly true in the case of one of the paths as it has a three foot section that is missing, raising the possibility of simply stepping into space.

Imagine then hauling a full bag of grain up to the top. That the Pueblo people actually constructed the homes they lived in so that they dangled just below the cliff top is even more remarkable. Sometimes they fashioned these using the overhangs in the rock face, other times they actually punched through and created chambers in the canyon walls themselves. What is still uncertain is how they got in and out of such places. Even contemporary rock climbers with all their modern gear and rope work tend to struggle. It is thought that they used nothing more than log ladders cut by stone axes to form footholds, although these in themselves would not be enough to reach some of the dizzying heights. Some of the ladders can still be found today, propped on ledges hundreds of feet above the ground. What does seem certain is that the paranoia from living in such troubled times outweighed any fear of slipping into the abyss. It must have taken intense concentration. One false move and they would have been done for. Their lives were literally on the edge every time they went outside their front door.

Eventually these people were overcome by the effects of climate change and began to leave their homeland for wetter areas. It is thought that they then merged with other groups, the descendents of whom are the 'Modern Pueblo' native Indians such as the Hopi and the Zuni.

Meanwhile other tribes began to arrive in the Canyonlands such as the Utes, Pauites and also the Navajos who gave the Anasazi their name, (literally 'Ancestors of our enemies', perhaps reflecting a history of rival groups in the region in the past). Initially hunter gatherers, the new influx of peoples eventually began to adopt many of the ways of the Pueblo people and their culture. However the era of the 'Ancestors' together with their civilisation and architectural brilliance was well and truly over by that time.

Today the ghosts of the Anasazi are found all over the area, including at Lathrop canyon, an offshoot of Cataract, the trail into which winds from the top of one of the Colorado's characteristic one hundred and eighty degree loops some fourteen miles downstream from Dead Horse.

Here it is possible to hike from the riverbank up to the white rim and even the Mesa above should you wish to. However, much closer to the Colorado, through a landscape of rock, sand and tamarisk shrub, Indian relics can be found including granaries, dwellings and rock art.

We walk among the artefacts and peer into the dark cool spaces of the grain stores cut out of the blazing sandstone. 'Amazing to think what these people achieved,' Head doc #1 comments. Indeed the legacies of the Anasazi are everywhere. One rock in the area depicts a number of human hands, probably created by blowing pigment to leave an outline. They wave at us in greeting down the centuries, a message from people who lived in a complex society like our own, who worked and fell in love and raised families just like us, and who above all managed to survive and even flourish in such a harsh place.

There is nothing formulaic or generic about what has been left on that rock: someone pressed their palm to the surface and made an actual impression of their own hand at that time, a record of a living breathing human being from their era which has endured through the ages. This is an intensely personal and unique statement. The hands are different sizes. One has a finger missing.

Later we drift past Indian Creek, an outlet which itself drains past *Newspaper Rock* further out in the Needles area. Here there are more ancient relics and indeed along the remaining lazy path of the meandering Colorado the messages are pretty much all native Indian. That is until we run slap bang into a metal danger sign that is genuinely twentieth century.

First though there is 'The Loop', a final prodigious twist of the Colorado before it meets the Green river. Here it doubles back on itself in a long bow whose ends are almost pinched together so that you can hike over its neck, thereby shortcutting some four miles of its course. Pete of course stays on the raft and we bid him farewell as we start to scramble up what is called 'The Saddle', a gap in the Canyon wall that bridges the two opposing channels of the river. From the top we can see Pete and the raft sail away, its wake a small zip in the water below. Before long he will round the loop and come back to meet us on the other side. It is not an easy climb over the hump of the Saddle-the paths can be treacherous if you don't watch your feet. The Kid charges ahead. 'Careful, ' says his Mom, 'Let's stay together.' The kid pretends not to hear. He is trying to break away.

The sign when we reach it is difficult to ignore. 'Danger!' it shouts at us from the bank. In big red letters it says, 'Hazardous rapids two miles.' And then in a more bureaucratic tone, 'Permit required for boating.' After all if you are going to do something reckless and needlessly dangerous, the least you can do is get the paperwork right. There is something slightly incongruous about it, stuck as it is on two posts in the middle of the natural beauty of the canyon. It is undoubtedly a twentieth century artefact and late twentieth century at that: up until the last years of the second Millennium no one had even thought to get a permit-the idea hadn't yet been invented.

In fact no one had seriously taken to the river until the United States acquired the Southwest and the Colorado basin from the Spanish in the middle of the 19th Century. It is not known if the Ancestral Pueblo people ever navigated the waters, certainly the Navajo weren't that much bothered.

The first known white man to run the rapids was Major John Wesley Powell in 1869. He had come down the Green River and had found that a torrid enough experience. Little did he know that the 'Big Drops' then lay in wait. They so terrified him and his men that he named this stretch of river, 'Cataract Canyon'.

Since that time innumerable people have passed the spot where the warning sign is now planted, (some eight thousand a year currently), many of them on the kind of motor powered sausage raft that we are travelling on. In the early days however it was wooden boats that went down the river and there were many mishaps. Those shaken and sometimes broken by the rough water have left their own signs, just like the ancients, often on rocks along the way, although the messages tend to be more straightforward: *JULY 7 1952 BILL & FERN DAVIS WENT OVER UPSIDE DOWN CARRIED 300 FT. UNDER WATER*

UPSET HERE,' is one inscription at rapid number sixteen, all in silver paint.

In fact Bill and Fern were both serial river runners and silver paint sprayers, as the rocks nearby bear witness. They made trips in 1952, 1953, 1954, and 1964. In the first one they came off twice. They also set the record for the smallest boat to ply the waters of the canyon: it was just over eleven feet.

There are others, some much earlier: the disastrous Stanton- Brown expedition of 1889 left one of the most mournful carvings on the rock face: *'F.M.Brown, president DCC & PRR, [Colorado Canyon and Pacific Railroad Company] was drowned July 10th 1889, opposite this point,'* it says; so ended Brown's part in the history of Colorado exploration and his dream of running a railroad through the bottom of the canyon. Naturally he didn't wear a lifejacket. Naive he may have been about the dangers of the river but he was nevertheless well liked as a man: while the inscription is not neat and hardly a headstone, it is heartfelt.

The Best Expedition of 1891 undoubtedly fared better in that no one died, but it suffered its own calamity. After overturning and wrecking their boat, its members scratched some self explanatory words on the matter in the boulders opposite rapid number fifteen: *'CAMP #7, HELL TO PAY, NO.I SUNK & DOWN.1891.'* Today rapid fifteen is better known under the name, 'Capsize'.

The modern age has also left some larger relics behind in Cataract Canyon, many of which bear evidence to the stupidity and general foolishness of some. These include the remains of the Frank Shafer No 1 oil test site which in 1925 caught fire and for six months released a thousand barrels a day of crude into the river. It never actually produced a drop of oil that was sold to anyone.

An entire aircraft is still stuck in the eddy below rapid twelve, (or at least the wreckage of one), courtesy of a supply drop to a camping trip that went awry in the summer of 1985. The plane made a number of passes over the river before hitting the water and breaking up before sinking. The pilot and passenger were rescued and then evacuated. The reason for the drop: someone fancied some ice cream.

Such human vulnerability is doubtless not just confined to our times, but it is rather better documented now. Thankfully we have not left much worse in the canyon, at least to date. The metal sign is an intrusion but it does serve to focus our thoughts as we drift towards the main business of our trip. And we can sense that the river itself is changing: for almost fifty miles the Colorado and its tributary have been zigzagging towards each other through the deep groves they have carved in the landscape until now finally they have met at the tip of the Island in the sky; its point hovers above us, a chunky thousand foot high slab of white sandstone topped with an edge of red. The Colorado is broader now and has a stronger current. It has more of a dirty look, courtesy of the load of silt that the Green River carries with it. Up to now it has barely been awake but all that is going to change. In a few more bends it will come alive and then it will go on a rampage.

Head doc 1# is looking nervous; American Mom is fidgety, while the College jock is hyper. The other teenagers just don't know what the fuss is about. They think that this is going to be so cool. Me, my anxiety has just stepped up to a new level. *Brown Betty* is just around the corner and who is Brown Betty?- nothing less than the unfortunate President

Brown's cook boat that eventually got sucked into a vortex and gave the rapid its name.

THE RAPIDS

It all starts peacefully enough, another lovely day on a placid river. The sun is sparkling on the deceptively smooth water and there are fluffy white clouds sailing in a blue sky when we launch from the shore. All is calm in this stretch, scarcely a ripple in the Colorado. But appearances can be deceptive. We may not be able to see it yet but about a hundred yards down the road the action is about to begin and when it does it will be sudden and take us by surprise. In this place you go from zero to a hundred miles an hour all before you can catch your breath.

It is early morning but already we are hot and sticky in the bulky kit we have to wear to keep us alive in the event we become detached from the mother ship. Like an astronaut going for a space walk, (albeit unscheduled), we will need an independent survival outfit. In our case this consists of a neck to toe dry suit to protect us from the cold shock of the Colorado water together with a personal flotation device on top made of a blown up foam core covered in nylon. The other kinds of materials used to keep us buoyant in this satellite system are related to the neoprene used in the raft itself or the sort of stuff used in non stick frying pans and electric wiring insulation. It is all very high tech and in a screaming red colour so that we can be easily picked out on the dirty river.

Still, at the moment we are safely on our raft and remain so, cooking in our gear. The anticipation is making us sweat while we wait for *Brown Betty*. We sit to attention in three rows of three each astride one of the pumped up pontoons. Head doc 1# nervously bags the centre spot at the back and is flanked by Head doc 2# and the German father who is looking implacable in his Teutonic will to see this out. I take the middle left hand side next to American Mom and her daughter. The rest of the kids are of course at the front where the fat pontoon fingers point to the sky making the whole raft a bit like a cupped hand. They are told to remain back on the fingers, especially the raised middle one on the basis that should anyone somersault over them and slip under the raft their journey would likely end in the chopping blades of the four stroke motor, after which the prospect of drowning is fairly academic. 'Why don't you stay back with me?' a concerned American Mom asks, but the kid who later will vie with the Jock continuously for the stick it to them middle finger and its bronco ride is not listening. For the purpose of this expedition he is doing his own thing.

Pete steers us out into the centre of the river and we start a leisurely progress downstream towards the first rapid. For the moment nothing happens and to me the river still looks the same: smooth and indolent, the small tangles of brushwood it carries floating lazily around us in its mud coloured drift; but all that is about to change. The first sign that anything is up is when the Colorado gives a burp. On our left side a single circle of belched water briefly blooms like a smoke ring before evaporating, an indication of the rumbling indigestion that is going on below. More liquid hiccups follow littering the increasingly ruffled surface that swells and dips under our boat. Dribbling wavelets meet the raft, gently rocking us. 'Aaaaah!' we sigh at our first taste of baby whitewater, just wondering though where this is leading. We don't have to wait long. Suddenly the tangle of tamarisk stems and cottonwood twigs that have been drifting sedately in front of us shoot forward and disappear into the distance, tumbling downstream. We follow them, hard on their heels. At which point the river which has been simmering nicely comes to the boil and breaks apart like water on the stove. Whatever 'Ooohs' and 'Aaaahs,' there may have been in the nursery slopes of rapid number one, these are long gone. Now it is time for some full throated shouting.

Oddly, one of the best ways of experiencing *Brown Betty* is actually not to run it at all but view it from afar. On either side of its channel the canyon walls slip down into a jumbled field of boulders, pebbles and scree, the hot brown stones offering a conveniently dry perch from which to watch the water based mayhem. From this vantage point the rapid is nothing less than a dirty chocolate slide topped with cappuccino foam. It whips past the spectator on the shore, carrying with it a continual parade of kayaks, dories, oar craft and motor rigs as one by one they grapple with the smashed up mill race that is *Brown Betty*. It is very entertaining, at least for those watching from the sidelines.

Yet for all its lively floor show, Cataract Canyon's first rapid does not usually end in too much drama- at least for those who see it coming. It is a remarkable fact that over the years quite a few people have stumbled upon it unawares, happily ignoring among other things the screaming red danger sign just a few miles upstream. In 1982 a group of gentle boating enthusiasts took their pleasure launch through *Brown Betty* after taking a wrong turning at the Confluence of the Colorado and Green rivers, (which they failed to notice), following which they sailed on downstream despite the hazard warning. Ten rapids later they were rescued by the park service who in their report noted that the remaining equipment salvaged from the party consisted mostly of empty beer cans. Under 'type of incident,' the report came to a conclusion of, 'Impaired judgement'.

Three years earlier rapid number one had claimed a fatality in an expedition that came armed only with a fairly redundant road map, inadequate life preservers and an even more unworkable sense of direction. The lone survivor escaped drowning by clutching on to a plastic bag.

On the Colorado it is important to pay attention. The endless miles of flat water lull you into a sense of false security. At this spot everything suddenly changes and then the rapids begin, an alchemy that starts in the ledges of soft rock that are found here in the canyon walls; when mixed with sand and water these run like toothpaste into the river, carrying with them the boulders that layer its bed and make it turbulent. Although in the words of one river runner, 'Brown Betty speeds the heartbeat and shortens the breath,' it is not the wildest water we will come across, just the first. The fact of it being the introductory serving of turbulence for many a tourist gives it a kind of notoriety along with its almost comic historical part in swallowing most of the Brown-Stanton Expedition's provisions. The cook boat *Brown Betty* was named after a popular dessert of the time, a sweet toothed fruit cobbler made with layers of sweetened crumbs that had echoes of the baked strata of the canyon cliffs. If such a pudding was made for President Brown it definitely ended up at the bottom of the Colorado. In both cases add water and you get mush.

As we enter rapid number one Pete steers the sausage boat towards the left bank, perhaps to avoid the 'Hole' that sometimes opens on the right side of the river, (after all, at this stage there can be such a thing as too much excitement). In front of us we can see choppy waves crest and then spill over, the whisked air bubble heads of foamy water lurching and then collapsing like rollers on a beach. Our raft runs to meet them and then the bucking ride begins through a deeply and eccentrically ploughed patch of water, a churn up of swells and white tops that slice the river at every angle, courtesy of the erratic topology of the submarine bed and the boulders that poke just below the surface. In the bobbing mess of foamy water we bounce our way through *Brown Betty*, hurdling past the shoreline and any figure that might be sitting on the stones and enjoying the show. The cold Colorado bombs under our raft and kicks spray into the air. Now we are really shrieking and hollering over the rush of the river, as well we might: this after all is our first whitewater and any initiation to the river wild requires whooping and then some, although the more serious incantations like, 'Oh my god!' 'Jesus Christ!' and, 'Fuck me!' should be saved until later. Rapid number one is not a push over but there is far more prodigious screaming material to come. In fact our first ride does not take long. One minute we are surfing head high crests and being drenched and then all of a sudden the river starts to subside, its energy dissipating within itself until all that remains to rock us are some limp wavelets and dribbling runs of liquid. A final hiccup of bright water and the Colorado is at peace again. It is as if none of that turmoil had ever happened.

This is the way with Cataract Canyon: it provides a continual succession of rapids stitched together with Zen like moments of calm flat water that are all too brief. Before long you lose count of how many you have been down-they all begin to run literally into each other.

Now that the river has anointed us we allow ourselves a bit of whooping self congratulation. Strangely for the moment we seem to have forgotten Pete who at the far back of the boat behind the locked boxes and water coolers glistening in the sunshine, has kept the four stroke running and steered us successfully through the pinball machine that is Brown Betty.

There is however little time for us to catch our breath. A few seconds pass and then the river becomes agitated once more, a prelude to another fit of rage. Rapid number two, or perhaps 'Lower Brown Betty', or even 'BB2', is one of those rare things: a sequel that is probably better than the original production. Not only is it longer and wilder but it begins to hint at some of the scarier 'Hydraulic' features that we will encounter as we progress down all twenty eight rapids and which are apt to spin, stall, flip and even swallow rafts. This is a bouncy liquid world where stream piercing rocks and jutting underwater ledges create swirling eddies and mini-waterfall 'Pour-overs', and where reverse breaking 'Stopper waves' collapsing under their own weight hit your boat like brick walls. Ask any whitewater Kayaker about this-they know. At this point it is not a good idea to mention whirlpools but given the right conditions of energetic swirl these can get going until they revolve like a watery drum with a hollow centre and produce the same kind of vortex you get when you pop out the bathplug and water disappears down the plughole, although of course of a rather bigger scale.

These can be powerful enough to suck a raft down into them and pin a swimmer to the river bed. John Wesley

Powell almost lost his life to one when he was thrown from his boat the *Emma Dean* in his second expedition up the Colorado. According to Frederick Dellenbaugh who was one of his party and the author of *The Romance of the Colorado River*, the Major and his cork lifejacket were, 'Sucked beneath the surface,' although after a moment or two Powell, 'Shot up like a rocket.' Dellenbaugh added wryly that Powell, '... Had tried to make a geological investigation of the bed of the river, and this was not advisable.' The Major probably did not find it very amusing at the time.

The truth is that the sheer variety and complexity of fun and deadly features that can be crafted out of water is mind boggling, and while Cataract exhibits these in various measures according to the ebb and flow and height of its water, it is all an endlessly shifting river landscape that never fails to amaze. While low water may uncover more of the boat shredding and bone jarring boulder garden and make for a trickier blunt trauma ride, rising streams mean fast action and the kind of water features that can only hint at what lies below. In our case there is no doubt the river today is high and swift and keeping everything buried: It is even more dangerous for that.

Most rapids announce themselves with a clearly defined milky 'Horizon line' of dancing liquid that marks the point where all that water starts to slip off into space. *Brown Betty 2* is no exception. You just follow it, falling into big scooped out masses of swirling brown stuff that carry you downhill. We pitch and roll in the mad swell, cresting its tops in a cloud of spray while we are tossed and turned and sideswiped by the waves that rebound off the shore only to be struck again as they are batted back by the submerged rocks. It is all a holy wonderful mess. Suddenly two curling waves fold together in front of our boat and we smash through the crown of the zipped up water as it buoys us up into the sky; we navigate it in precisely the way I suspect that Pete wants us to, all in the cause of added entertainment. It is not over, even then. At the end of this rapid as in all the others there is more mayhem as its fast jet crashes into the sluggish water downstream. Such a pile up creates what are called "Tail waves" and sometimes they have a ridiculous amount of energy. When constantly replenished by the stream of the river these may bob up and down without going anywhere. Such 'stationary waves' may include 'haystacks' where the water leaps pyramid like into a resemblance of a harvest bundle before collapsing into the river again. On the other hand at the bottom of a drop you may be confronted with a large curling roller that resembles nothing more than an ocean swell breaking on a tropical shore. Unsurprisingly this is known as a 'Hawaii 5-0', after of course the famous TV cop series. In the course of our river running we will have any number of trips to the tropics, each brief but certainly memorable.

After about five or six rapids we hear a disembodied voice from the back of the raft. 'How are you doing?' it asks us and the answer as it happens is pretty fine. We are shiny and wet and elated. American Mom is smiling. I have a more relaxed death grip. Even Head doc 1# seems to be enjoying the ride. We are pretty much old hands at this now and a lot of our initial nervousness has disappeared. In fact there is an air of confidence on our raft, dare I say it cockiness even; all that is about to change. At this point we hit something called 'The North Seas'.

The North Seas may well be the closest you can get in the desert to an ocean voyage, a short one granted but while you are there that's what it feels like. Anyone who lives in the British Isles will recognise why this particular patch of water has such a suitable name. The North Sea on Britain's east coast has a reputation as a grey and stormy place, its procession of cold rollers pitching and tossing the largest ships as they cross its sometimes treacherous surface. And while along the Colorado it is sunny and hot and there is a blue sky, rapid number seven does whip up an uncanny resemblance to this sea in miniature, lining up its swells one after the other as they roll towards us in rapid succession, each crashing and ending in surf that threatens to drown our boat entirely. These waves are up to twenty feet tall or more and would not disgrace the real thing. In the unlikely event that you live in a three storey apartment block and perch a rubber boat on its roof with you in it before launching into space, that is pretty much what it is like to run rapid number seven. I stare into the impossible pit of each succeeding trough and wonder how we are going to get to the bottom before the climb to each mountainous crest leads to the same question. Walls of water leap at us; at least part of the time we fly submerged. It is like having buckets of cold Colorado constantly tipped over your head.

When it is all over the College Kid declares it to have been 'Totally awesome' and that is praise indeed. Personally I have resumed my white knuckle grip; Head doc 1#, who it has to be said is still struggling a bit with his sea legs, has all the wide eyed look of a startled rabbit, one which inexplicably has just taken a trip through a very big car wash.

Three miles downstream and much torrid water later we come across the rather more tranquil site of the ice cream delivery that went spectacularly wrong. Unfortunately there is not a lot to see. At this point Cataract's waters are at their deepest, between sixty and ninety feet, and have swallowed the six- seater Cessna whole, all thirty six feet of it. The plane now lays beneath our raft on a quiet stretch of the Colorado between rapids 12 and 13, still in the eddy where it lazily spun while sinking over thirty years ago. This is actually a lovely spot for a crash. The water is smooth and calm here and remains so for over one and a half miles, an uncharacteristically long 'pool' that is dubbed, 'Cataract Lake'. This however is just the calm before a storm. A couple of river bends later the whitewater begins again and when it does so it is in full on fashion, an uninterrupted chain of six mostly full throttle rapids all squeezed into less than two thousand yards. This is 'Mile Long', and is perhaps second only to the *Big Drops* in its wild water notoriety.

At large flows the rapids tend to merge into each other but each generally maintains its own individuality in some way. Together they represent an assault course of boulders, ledges and other assorted debris that the boatman or woman has to weave between in order to make it safely out the other side.

While the first is no more than a riffle, the tail of the second rapid is energetic enough to give you a firm push towards where the fun really starts: the 'Rock Park' of 'Capsize rapid', or 'Hell to pay'. Here there are many opportunities to flip or smash your boat as the Best expedition of 1891 found out. In order not to follow their example generations of river runners have established their own system of negotiating the rapid in a swerve between the three main boulders that stick up from the river bed. This they liken to a home run in baseball, aiming to make it past the rocks that constitute second and third base and on to

'Home plate' which in this case is *Capsize rock*. Contrary to popular belief the Best expedition only got as far as third base but *Capsize* has been responsible for catching many others out. In the 1990's during one summer a boat wrapped itself on the boulder and spent the entire subsequent winter at *Home Plate*. Some people just don't get to complete their home run, at least not in one piece.

In our case however we manage to play the game successfully. Pete steers us through the mountainous waves that slap and pour over the rubble and on through rapid 16, the site of Bill and Fern's watery adventures and their expressive spray painted messages left on the dusty stones that litter the nearby shore. Rapids 16-19 are known collectively as the 'South Seas', although there is nothing particularly 'Pacific' about them. They run out into a widening channel of smooth water split by a pebbly slick of land, bald apart from a few sparse tufts of tamarisk shrub. This was the final resting place of a motor boat which in the late fifties made an epic voyage down Cataract Canyon with no one on board. Its owners, Joe Baker and A.C.Ekker hadn't tied the craft properly at *Brown Betty* and it went sailing away, running all 19 rapids on its own until finally breaking up, the last piece with its name inscribed on it clattering onto the wastes of this mid stream island as a kind of epitaph. The boat was called 'Ben Hurt', and the rapid nearby is named after it, although over the years various alternatives have been used like 'Been Hurt', and even, 'Ben Hur', presumably on the basis that running it had a passing resemblance to the thrill of a chariot race.

For us however it holds no fears; at high water in any case it is not that threatening. There is however a certain tension on the raft as we bounce over the remains of its tail waves and into the still water beyond. Downstream the river starts its prodigious fall of over thirty foot in under a quarter of a mile creating a ride which in comparison to what has gone before, (and that has been hair-raising enough), is in another league entirely. We have now reached the most anticipated stretch of the Colorado on our tour, a place responsible for more spills and accidents than anywhere else in this territory, where the water can bend and twist the metal on rafts and gobble them whole before spitting them back out some hundred yards downstream. In front of us are the *Big Drops* of Cataract Canyon, the apogee of its whitewater and ultimately the thing to record for posterity and post on social media as long as your hands are free. After all, it would be terrible to go through all that and not be able to show you were there.

The big drops are particularly scary because of the 'Holes' in them. *Holes* are undoubtedly the most treacherous hydraulics of all and the most respected and feared among the river runners. Imagine water spilling over a ledge or boulder just below the surface of the river. Given enough flow and energy the water dives down creating a depression in the river's surface and then rebounds back towards the obstacle at the opposite lip of the crater. *Holes* can be 'keepers' or 'flushers'. If the water just re-circulates back and catches the pour over there is an endless cycle in which anything trapped in the hole just goes round and round. In that case the advice is sometimes to actually ditch your life jacket and make for the river bottom where the current is still heading downstream. A flushing hole is one in which the re-circulating water has an exit and can spill you back out into the main river. Rafters are advised to know which is which. One way of telling is that the lip of the depression looks different in each case. Viewed downstream a hole that won't let you go inevitably looks like a downturned mouth, i.e. it frowns, while one that spits you out has a happy face. It is not a good idea to mix these up when you are about to get sucked in to something that could swallow an entire house. These hydraulics can be massive and here along Cataract Canyon are found two of the biggest: 'Little Niagara', an epic spillover emanating from a ledge the size of a Greyhound bus and the legendary 'Satan's Gut', a huge sucking pit that has been the nemesis of more whitewater runs than anything else in this stretch of the Colorado. The Gut is always at the back of anyone's mind when embarking on the water slide ride that is Cataract Canyon. It may be some twenty rapids down the line but in the fast track race through all this wild water it comes closer with every minute. When we meet it, it is unlikely to smile at us. You don't have to ask what sort of 'Hole' *Satan's Gut* is. It is of course a *keeper*.

Before tangling with the Big Drops however, we first have to embark upon a ritual which every river runner and boating crew are obliged to perform before passing through. Pete steers the raft to the shore and from a sandy beach above *Big Drop 1* we take a well trod path that winds downstream for about half a mile, climbing through the scree and shrub until it ends in an overlook topped by a chunky boulder which commands the heights above the river. This is 'Poop Rock.' Generations of Colorado guides have made the trip to this rock, just so that they can work out the way the river is going and the best 'line' to take through the rapids. Not to do so would be negligent if not suicidal. In the words of the river authorities, *Big Drops 1-3* require a, 'Mandatory scout.'

We gaze at the scene and then look at Pete. I am waiting

for him in stereotypical fashion to spit on his finger and trace a route in the dust on the rock. That I am sure is what river guides do. Instead he is looking thoughtful. The *Big Drops* are tricky, that's for sure. For one thing they are stuffed with every kind of liquid trap that is the river runners' nightmare and joy, from the big *Holes* of Gut and Niagara and their associated stacked up waves to numerous smaller hazards all liberally scattered along the way. Negotiating this is difficult, especially since the river current tends to chuck you out of one stage only to throw you in the path of the worst thing possible in the following section. At the entrance to *Big drop 2* there is a 'marker rock', splitting the stream which invites the rafter to make a choice. Going right may be a high risk strategy: that is where you find *Little Niagara*. Taking a left is often better but it has its own consequences. Here a huge 'ledge wave', bounds off the shore and meets the re-circulation of the falls, causing at high flows a pile up of some thirty feet of water that has the rather ominous title of the 'Red Wall'. On the other hand at certain times something called 'The Window' appears, a ribbon of water between the rock and *Niagara* that allows free passage through the turbulent water. This is particularly sought after by paddle craft enthusiasts who want to live, but the only problem is that 'window' means precisely what it says: when it is open everything is fine, but should it suddenly close then those with oars and without an engine on the back must be pretty much aware that they are totally fucked.

While the left hand approach may be initially successful, it does have drawbacks further down the line. At the end of the rapid it pushes you into some meaty tail waves that will knock you around and maybe off, and then the current aims you right towards *Satan's Gut* which naturally is on that side of the river. It would be, wouldn't it?

Occasionally some new major feature makes its appearance and complicates matters even further. In 2009 river runners were surprised to find a new *Hole* in the *Big Drops*, a huge thrashing pit with a giant back wave that looked like it could rip your boat apart. They called it 'The Claw'. Created when a giant boulder plopped uninvited into the Colorado as part of the rock falls that have taken place over eons, *The Claw*, (or more controversially the 'Mother-in-Law'), is a testament to the changing dynamics of the river even in our lifetimes. Sometime in 2017 it disappeared entirely as the boulder was washed downstream. According to one River Ranger this was a good thing. 'Without the *Claw*, Big Drop 2 has gone back to its full painfulness', he says. 'That rock backed up the flow and ..... [made] the run a lot more forgiving. We are back to the [earlier] version of *Big Drop 2*.'

While we wait for Pete to make up his mind we look at the view. It is magnificent if not terrifying. A hundred and fifty feet below us the river churns and foams with an urgency that surpasses all we have yet seen. In the distance is *Big Drop 2*, a bubbling cauldron of waves and froth tumbling down a steep incline, its raw power eclipsing anything else along this river. The sound of the water is deafening, and its speed prodigious: A whole Olympic swimming pool slips beneath our feet every second.

Clearly, any decision on the route for our raft is not an easy one to make, and Pete takes his time coming to a conclusion. Once he has seen enough we start the trudge back to our boat leaving the boulder for the next expedition and their obligatory scout. And so we exit *Poop Rock*, apparently so called because of the affect it has had on river runners throughout the ages, particularly the early pioneers. Essentially they came here for the best view of the river and to witness the wanton exuberance of the drops they were about to run. At which point they shit themselves.

Well, that's the story anyway, and who are we to deny that on occasion this may have been true, at least figuratively? Wesley Powell like many others avoided running the river at this point and preferred to haul all his supplies around the water that terrorised him. We on the other hand are going down them for fun.

For the uninitiated, the *Big Drops* are undoubtedly disorientating, a smashed up train wreck of water sliding down the side of a mountain which just carries you with it. At least that's what it feels like. While *Big Drop 1* is a relatively gentle introduction, *Big Drop 2* starts with a bubble line of rough water ahead of us, with Little Niagara exploding in the distance. Before long the 'ground' seems to give way from under us and a series of huge cascading waves smash over our raft as we start our racetrack journey downhill. The Kid and the Jock are thrown up into the sky still attached to the middle finger as we bounce around in the swirling water, buffeted and side slapped by the surf racing from the left shore, while the rest of us at the back just cling on madly. Up we go into a rising wall of mashed up foam while a monster hydrant bears down at us from the right. At low water *Little Niagara* is a curtain that resembles its namesake, but when the river is swollen as it is today, it takes on a different appearance: an angry pulsating kick up of frothy violence and curling rebounding waves that sends spray trampolining high into the air. It looks huge, a bubbling tear up that seems to devour one side of the channel- a place you definitely want to avoid. We head right for it. Pete smashes through its outskirts and for a moment we are in cloud world of white effervescence before our sausage boat veers back to the left, bucking, shuddering and tilting with the effort of climbing up the remains of the stacked up water that rushes from the left bank. We fall off the wall into the tail waves of *Big Drop 2*, greasy thirty foot rollers that we scale and then pitch into in quick succession until their train throws us into the final bumpy descent of the last of the *Big Drops*. At which point something seems to be slightly awry with our raft.

At first this is barely noticeable in the race through the buffeting first waves of *Big Drop 3*. But then it occurs to me that our sausage home has become a bit unstable, an impression confirmed by the fact that the occupants of the far side of the boat, Head doc 2# and the teenage daughter of American Mom, seem to be slowly rising above our heads. It is as if a giant unseen hand is slowly pushing us over. The Kid and American Mom do not help the situation. The Kid, who has been whooping and hollering his head off with exultation throughout the giant water park ride, now seems to have lost his grip, (whether by accident or because he has decided to adopt the bucking bronco rodeo cowboy position so beloved of the College Jock), and therefore is flapping around like a lost baby bird. In her consternation American Mom lets go with one hand and reaches out to him, throwing herself off balance. As the boat begins to turn over she leans into me as if she wants to shout something in my ear which could be, 'Abandon ship!' but in fact there is simply a wild look in her eyes as she scrambles for a purchase. One leg has become detached and is in the air.

Like a stack of dominoes, the rest of the crew follow, tipping towards an exit on my side of the raft.

There is no doubt in my mind that we are about to flip. At this moment of course the river opens up on our left hand side into what can only be described as a giant pit, an actual depression in the river surface that spews up great clods of foam and spray from the depths of its bowels. It is a violent and malevolent thing to see; the whole river seems to be pouring into it, everything around it warped and twisted by its gravitational pull. It looks like it is only a few feet away.

I decide that when it comes to it I for one am not letting go of this raft. I am not going to be dunked in the water, finger tip my way around a ceiling of neoprene, dangle on the lip of the *Gut*. I am not going to become a statistic, adopting the 'Down river swimmers position' before getting picked up by the Ranger's boat downstream for a river report. I am definitely not joining a yard sale. While everything around me is unravelling and everyone is in the process of flying off our sausage home, I just dig in deeper, turning on my death grip. I tell myself that whatever happens I am going to follow the rules: there is no way I am getting off this boat.

Sometimes you reach a tipping point when you just know you are going over and we have surely reached ours. We are now at a very odd angle indeed. The river foams around our raft but there is just one focus of attention and it seems to be getting closer. The milky fringe of its mouth opens before us, ready to swallow anything that comes its way. We look into its bubbling entrails and it frowns back at us, pulling us in. The next moment I am sure we are going to go over and slide into the *Gut*. For a second this seems a certainty, at least to me. But then time reverses itself. The *Gut* seems to stare at us and we stare back. Then it closes its big eye and turns its face away from us. Slowly, at first imperceptibly, our raft begins to right itself until we are once again on some sort of level. I don't look back, at least until we are far from that spouting monster, by which time it is lost in the turbulent mash up of riverscape which is currently shooting us out of *Big drop 3*. Eventually the river begins to slow and finally subside until little rippling traces of its power are all that are left. And then they too disappear. At which point we can safely say that we have run the rapids of Cataract Canyon.

Well, almost. After the big drops there are still a few stretches of whitewater, including 'Repeat', (as many times as you wish in fact by back tracking up an eddy on the side), 'Powell's Pocket Watch' and 'Imperial', but while these are all quite worthy they cannot match what has gone before. Downstream we find ourselves amongst the ghosts of rapids past, all drowned by the encroaching waters of Lake Powell, the push back from which restores the river once again to its indolent crawl. From here it is a thirty mile drift to the Hite Crossing Bridge, a steel arch construction slung over the Canyon just above the northern entrance to the Lake. This pretty much marks the end of the wilderness as we know it. But that lazy run on smooth water is for tomorrow. Tonight we make camp just beyond the whooshing of the last rapid in an empty echoing canyon. We break open the beers that did not after all succumb to the Colorado and pretty soon there is a party going on. Tomorrow we will glide into the placid aquamarine waters of Lake Powell and it should be a breeze. What could possibly go wrong?

Later we ask Pete if he thinks we really were about to capsize and spill into the biggest *Hole* down these parts. As ever he is enigmatic about it. 'Could be,' he tells us, 'then again- maybe not.' It's just another example of the mystery of the river.

LAKE POWELL

The first thing to say about Lake Powell is that it is a lake, well sort of. To be more precise, a better description would be to say that it is more like a liquid snake, one that has swallowed a whole crack in the earth, a long sinuous body of water stretching from the Hite crossing bridge to the city of Page at the eastern end of the Grand Canyon. In places it is over five hundred feet deep and has a shoreline longer than the entire US Pacific coast. Beautiful it is, with its deep crystal blue waters sparkling in a bowl of orange and white canyon walls, but there is nothing natural about its formation: it is entirely man made.

In fact the lake was created in 1966 when the Glen Canyon dam was constructed downstream causing the waters of the Colorado to back up all the way to Cataract Canyon. In the process Glen canyon disappeared together with ninety six side canyons and a half of the Cataract rapids that Major Wesley Powell rode on his original epic journey; all of these are now submerged together with the original settlement of Hite under hundreds of feet of water.

The other way of describing Lake Powell is that of a big tank, part of a very large water storage system. Once the Glen Canyon dam had plugged the Colorado and the water began to back up, it took seventeen years to fill it. One of the main purposes of the dam apart from electricity production was to create a reservoir which together with Lake Mead at the western end of the Grand Canyon would ensure the survival of the American Southwest. You could argue that by rights no one should live here, let alone farm here, at least not a population of over forty million which is heavily dependent on the Colorado for its water supply and which likes gambling and lettuce. As the Anasazi found out, the key to the American southwest is water and its sustainable use, and they were in many ways more canny farmers. In recent years the snowmelt from the Rockies has not been what it was and the cistern has been at times only a third full. You can tell where the high water mark used to be: there is a white ring running along the surface of what used to be the canyon walls that is caused by the chemical reaction of the hard minerals in the water and the sandstone from the bluffs. It is colloquially known as the 'Bath Tub Ring'.

Lake Powell is in fact one big splashy tub that attracts over four million visitors a year for boating, paddling and jet-ski fun. It is Utah's number one attraction. It is also the end of the journey for the river runners like us who have spent the last three days in the wilderness and have finally made it back to civilisation, one with hard surfaced roads and steel bridges slung over the river. Here there are marinas where you can service and fuel up your seventy five foot 'Odyssey' houseboat, or rent out ski tubes, wakeboards and kayaks. The houseboats are like floating apartments: the Odyssey for example comes with a convertible dinette with double bed, 3 bathrooms, a flat screen TV with satellite and stereo as well as a hot tub.

Along the lake there are spots where you can go golfing or sample fine dining at water front restaurants. There are facilities for RV camping and shopping centres where you can top up on groceries, ice creams and souvenirs, including 'Native American' items.

After a long day splashing in 'The Tub' you can relax at the 'Anasazi Restaurant' on 'Bull Frog Marina'. Here you can stare at the red butte scenery as you sample the, 'Delicious dinner entrees from fresh fish to pasta to steak.' Or you can just drop in for a coffee and dessert. The ancient ones would be amazed.

All in all the lake is still the big outdoors, wilderness country for sure, only not quite as we have known it during the last three days. For one thing it is not the same as drifting through the narrow slot of a canyon with only your own company. Here there is the growl of speedboats and the bustle of people. It is a sky wide panorama of water and stone that is in complete contrast to the funnelled rock enclosure of the natural river. It is also likely to give you vertigo if you think about it. Drowned mesas which used to soar to giddying heights above the canyon floor now just peep above the surface of the lake, islands around which people can swim and paddle and look down towards a fathomless bottom. Occasionally a drop in the water level uncovers features that have been drowned for decades by the artificial lake. At some spots buried waterfalls that have been lost for decades have simply sprung back to life. Lake Powell it has to be said is something else.

Still, its northern shores are more isolated and away from the centre of action. Here it is relatively quiet and when we beach near 'Hite Marina' we find a sign saying that due to dropping water levels it is currently closed. There is little point in a launching ramp if it doesn't actually reach the water.

A little way from the shore, beneath the calm surface of

the lake, is the original town of Hite, with its convenience store and post office now under two hundred and fifty feet of water. Born out of the gold rush of the 1880's and sustained by the uranium boom, its fate was sealed in 1960 by the first pouring of the concrete for the massive dam upstream. Today there is a campground, convenience store and restrooms inland. It is not quite the 'City of Hite' as it was known in its glory days.

For us it is time for a brief period of relaxation after all the turmoil of the last few days. We flop down on the shore or take a dip in the waters above the drowned city. Tomorrow we will fly out over the Colorado and back to Moab. We will retrace the entire river journey that has taken us over three days, all in the space of an hour. Our extraction point will be Hite airport, but when we say airport we actually mean a single concrete strip on the top of the cliffs nearby where the little Cessnas queue like shuttle buses to launch the river runners into space. Somewhat worryingly it is actually quite difficult to tell it apart from the black topped highway 95 that runs nearby.

But the view from the air will be magnificent; the park set out below us like a map, with the canyon a little crack in the baked earth and the green strip of the river winding at its bottom. From that height it is possible to get a sense of the scale of the whole thing, the striding flat topped mountains and deep clefts in the earth, the whole broken backed brown desert stretching to the horizon. We will all be sorry to say goodbye to such a monumental, if at times lethal, place.

But first there is one more challenge, one more chance to immerse ourselves in this country of bare rock and water, to get to grips with its scenery at ground level and below. Pete announces that we are going on a hike. Not just any stroll in the park though, it is going to be a 'wet hike'.

I have never been on a wet hike before- I'm not sure what it means. But then this sounds like a gentle wind down after the excitement of the last few days, a bit of a scramble that cannot surely compete with the danger and excitement of the *Big Drops*. I mean, after facing those odds what is there to worry about?

We begin near Route 95, the access road for tourism in the northern part of the lake. From the airstrip it continues its journey over the Hite crossing bridge, the same steel arch that we ducked under on our way into Lake Powell. From there it goes south of Hite and crosses 'White Canyon' which is just one of the 'slots' or ravines in this area that tend to be partially drowned, particularly when there has been heavy rainfall, or at its most extreme, 'flash flooding'.

The starting point for the *White Canyon* hike is just off the highway, from where it is possible to descend into the inner gorge. This is a place where the walls close in at various locations and the floor is flooded. There are rocks to scramble over and pools to wade through. In some parts benches or ledges above the waterline are available for a careful foothold and handhold to avoid a dunking. At other times it is just a question of paddling or even swimming through.

Dressed in our bathing costumes we squeeze ourselves into the ravine. According to local sources, 'The canyon makes a great semi-technical adventure hike. Access is easy and permits are not needed. It has become popular with families and youth groups. However, it is a challenging route carrying an element of danger.' I looked that up afterwards.

There are some rules for our walk, not three this time

but for all practical purposes just one. Pete tells us to try to follow him and use his hand and foot holds in the more tricky bits. Essentially we are being advised not to stray from the path and do ourselves a mischief.

Most of us are exemplary at taking this advice. The Germans are particularly scrupulous in matching Pete's lead, while the American Mom and the Head docs gingerly pick their way along the polished stones that I keep slipping over. Only the Kid seems to want to go off-piste.

The sensible thing of course is to take great care, even to the extent of looking at your feet rather than the scenery. The terrain ranges from the flat to the uneven and twisted, at times a dry pebble scattered streambed, at others a wet plunge if you tread carelessly. The water is breathtakingly cold where the mesa sandstone walls narrow and box the sun out. Further into the canyon there are jumbles of boulders to climb over and tangled brushwood to negotiate. For the even more adventurous there is a place downstream with sheer ravine walls where there is nothing for it but to swim. It is called, 'The Black Hole'. Thankfully we are not going that far.

About a couple of hours into our walk, there appears to be a bend in the gorge and the safest way to negotiate it is by traversing a ledge around the top. There is a more exciting path, a short cut over a slick choke stone boulder hanging in a cleft in the rock, but then why would you? Pete takes the safe route- undoubtedly the standard vanilla crossing, and we all follow him; all of us that is except the Kid. Exuberant at our adventures he thinks he is Spider Man. We watch as he clings to the rock, suspended in mid air for a moment as he paws at it for a purchase, hoping that sheet momentum will take him to the other side. But then he is unlucky and begins to slide and then drop. This of itself is not a disaster: it is after all a fall of no more than ten feet into the cushion of a water hole below. However as he begins his descent the curve of the boulder rises to meet him. He cracks his head open on the rock.

Pete shouts, 'Nooooooooo!' but his cry is not one of angst or even lamentation that he has steered a bunch of tourists through some of the most dangerous rapids in the world only to have one of them killed on a walk. It is in fact directed at American Mom who even now is aiming to launch herself after her son from a ledge another ten feet up, an acrobatic feat that will undoubtedly result in more broken bones and her being airlifted out of the Park.

The Kid is conscious and he is weakly thrashing about in the water looking dazed. Pete fishes him out and gets him on dry land. There he is joined by not one, but two neurologists who have spent sixty years between them learning to deal with just such a situation, and who normally charge a thousand dollars an hour consultation fees. The Kid is very lucky.

He gets sized up with fingers held up to his eyes and is asked a bunch of questions. He allows his Mom to cuddle him while the head doctors consult about medication and whether it is safe to move him. Eventually they decide that he is going to live but needs to rest awhile. 'How are you feeling?' I ask him later and he looks goggle eyed and proceeds to throw up over some of the most starkly beautiful landscape on the planet. 'That's perfectly normal,' Head doc 1# says knowingly.

And so ends our water rafting odyssey and our trip down the mighty Colorado. But it is not the Kid's fault. In fact all hail to him. He slipped all right but maybe he knows something some of us have forgotten. Follow the rules of caution and you will be totally safe, that's what we are told throughout our lives. Perhaps not as safe as houses, (errant underwear aside), but at least we will be more secure than freewheeling on a bike, line dancing or joining a cheerleading parade. But no one really wants to follow the rules to the letter; no one really wants to be safe if is at the expense of feeling alive. That's what whitewater rafting is all about, taking a calculated risk against the odds. You would be mad to do it but do it anyway. Swirl around in the water; take the chance of capsizing and running the rapid on your backside. Piss in the Colorado, ride the express elevator of the Big Drops, dangle on the lip of Satan's Gut. It is one hell of a ride and you will never feel anything quite like it again. It is after all very, very dangerous and you would be lucky to survive. You need to let everyone know that if you have been down Cataract Canyon. You need to boast about it.

You can push things too far though. I haven't been bowling in a while.

There are numerous tour operators who offer rafting expeditions along the Colorado, in Cataract Canyon and in the Grand Canyon. The best time to go:

April to mid-May	*Chilly water but rapids are good.*
Mid May to Mid June	*Peak flow-the rollercoaster.*
Mid June to October	*Warm and calmer waters but still an adrenaline rush.*

Grand Canyon National Park, Canyon lands National Park, (U.S. National Park Service): www.nps.gov

Suggested reading

Ghiglieri, Michael and Myers, Thomas. 2012. **Over the Edge: Death in Grand Canyon**. *Puma Press, USA.*

Owen, David. 2017. **Where the water goes: life and death along the Colorado River**. *Riverhead books, New York.*

//

Hurry Up and Wait: A Trip to the North Pole

To know how to wait. It is the great secret of success.
Joseph de Maistre
philosopher

JUST WAITING

I was late, very late. I was way off schedule. You know how it is, you get some lousy weather and the whole transport system grinds to a halt: your flight gets delayed. It doesn't help if the runway has a crack in it.

'A crack in it?' I asked Alexi, who for the purpose of my grand Polar tour appeared to be the local Russian fixer. He shrugged. 'Of course, it happens,' he said, 'It's made of ice after all'.

I hadn't thought of that; the weather yes, notorious in the Arctic for freezing up your plans and screwing up the simplest timetable. But the logistics of an actual landing at an 'ice camp', just a snowball's throw from the North Pole, no.

Not in a twenty tonne jet anyway. How did that work

exactly? I mean its slippery stuff, ice. I guessed it was even worse with a hole in it.

'It's ok,' he said, 'They will fix it,' and went on to tell me that a landing strip in the Arctic pretty much involves some guys going out with a snow plough and shovels and clearing a path picked out with bin bags. By the time they had liberally sprayed it with water a few times it would be smooth and slick and polished. Like an ice rink in fact. That thought alone was not reassuring.

'Of course,' he continued, 'they might have to make a new one. That may take some time.'

Back home no one had mentioned that the ice moves around up here. I had pretty much assumed that when you are this far north of the equator everything is frozen solid and locked down. I didn't know that it went for a walk.

But then I was learning that the Arctic is a crazy place. Nothing here is as it should be. For one thing this is the 'Land of the Midnight Sun', that insomnia producing phenomena of twenty four hour daylight in summer that can make the locals so desperate for some shut eye that they smother their windows with tinfoil and wear shades indoors. For ten weeks from the end of May nowhere in the Arctic Circle experiences proper darkness-even the stars don't pop out in the sky until mid August. And the further north you go, the greater the number of days of continual sunlight. At the North Pole the sun just rolls around the sky like a fuzzy roulette ball for six months between each solstice and never drops below the horizon.

The opposite of course is true in winter when the night can last for several months and a blue twilight linger before the sun shows its face again. That sort of thing can seriously mess with your body and your head. It is not wise to assume

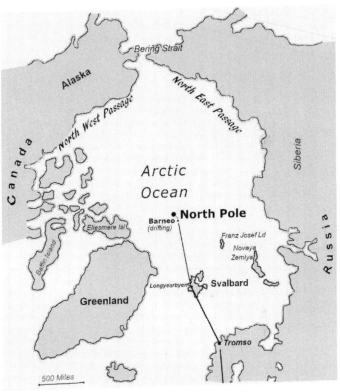

The way North: up the Arctic basin

that what little light there is makes much difference. In Murmansk, northern Russia, the authorities once tried to economise by switching off the streetlights from 11am to 2pm, in what they optimistically called the 'brightest' part of the day. Needless to say many smash ups ensued and by the time the city had become the traffic accident capital of the world the practice was abandoned. Winter can be a melancholy time for the people who live here: many of them hit the bottle and suicide rates climb. Some of them may be affected by SAD, (Seasonal Affective Disorder), due to the lack of sunlight. On the plus side however Santa Claus is alive and well and living in the small town of Ilulissat in Greenland, (population 4,500) where there is an actual mailbox for the delivery of wish list correspondence. Sometimes he even writes back.

The weirdness of the Arctic even extends to our perception. The pure cold air focuses the most distant object, flattening depth and making it impossible to determine how far away everything is. This can lead to some startling misconceptions. In his book, *Arctic Dreams* the American nature writer and environmentalist Barry Lopez relates the story of a Swedish explorer who lovingly wrote down a detailed description of a craggy headland he could see together with its two symmetrical glaciers and a larger island beyond. It turned out to be a walrus.

Even more disconcerting are the mirages that appear on the horizon. These are the result of light being bent through the warmer layers of air above those squatting on say a cold patch of ice. The illusion of something being there can be so detailed and convincing that it is difficult to dissuade yourself that the coastline, mountain range or even city you think you see doesn't actually exist. In the Arctic it is literally possible to see ice castles in the air. The term for such phenomena is 'Fata Morgana' an Italian phrase that alludes to sorcery and witchcraft.

Even when you can trust your own eyes, it is all too easy to get lost. The landscape is often featureless, a huge blank expanse of white snow and ice. Compasses simply don't work here. This is because they align to the magnetic pole where the lines of force exit the earth, not the actual geographic one. In any case the compass becomes increasingly erratic at such high latitudes, wandering about drunkenly and sometimes just spinning on its axis, so that it is impossible to tell which direction is north or south.

For a long time Polar exploration was seriously hampered by these difficulties and the problem of using the Sun or stars as a guide when they were often absent. Remarkably, the Norse seafarers used a navigation aid that overcame some of these issues centuries before any attempt was made to reach the Pole. Where the day was overcast or the sun was just below the horizon so that no celestial bearing could be made, they used a 'Sunstone' or crystal that polarised light when pointed to the Sun's source. For many years aircraft flying over Polar Regions used a 'sky compass' that employs an artificial lens instead of a crystal but the principle is the same. They were using a technique that the Norse men employed over a thousand years earlier.

Clearly nothing is straightforward about the Arctic. Unlike Antarctica which is a continental landmass, the North Pole lies beneath fourteen thousand feet of water, so that there is nothing solid about it: on the contrary, the drift and pack ice are restless and continually on the move, propelled by the wind and sea currents so that they circulate the Polar basin, sometimes for years on end. Eventually they escape by being shunted down the side of Greenland or end up getting stuck down the throat of some inlet in the extreme north Canadian coast.

The Arctic Ocean is huge, as big as Russia in fact, only restricted to the south by the landmasses of Europe, Asia and the Americas. In winter the sea is almost entirely frozen, although in the summer melt between March and September the ice cap can shrink by about a half to a third, (a process that appears to be accelerating due to global warming).

The various challenges thrown up by the Arctic environment were to severely hamper early explorers. Such obstacles made reaching the Pole by a surface route a difficult proposition and were one of the main reasons why in contrast to the South Pole which was attained in 1911, no one reached its northern counterpart until the comparatively late year of 1968 when the world was more pre-occupied with the Vietnam war and civil rights marches than the delayed conquest of a spot at the top of the planet. (This assumes that all disputed claims were void-[see 'A History of Arctic Exploration']). Even then it was achieved not on foot but by using snowmobiles which were promptly abandoned on arrival. Such a first excludes of course flying and parachuting in or even using icebreakers or nuclear submarines, but then these might be regarded as a bit of a cheat. The fact is that no one had even seen the North Pole until the Norwegian explorer Amundsen sailed over it in 1926 in an airship which to the consternation of the local Eskimo peoples looked like a 'flying whale'. In the meantime, the 'Cold War' of the 1950's between the West and the Soviet Union gave both sides the excuse to slide their own bath toys under the ice cap. In 1959 the nuclear submarine USS Skate actually popped up at the North Pole, followed by any number of soviet craft. The first surface vessel to get there was the Russian ice breaker *Arktika* which carved its way into the history books in August 1977.

Until then there had been a long history of failure, of explorers drifting past their objective, their ships stuck fast in the ice only to be eventually crushed like matchsticks. The Norwegian Fridtjof Nansen, one of the greatest Polar explorers, had the right idea when in 1893 he deliberately wedged a specially strengthened ship, The *Fram*, in the ice north of Siberia to catch a ride on the transpolar current. The ship was stuck for three years during which it achieved a new record for a northerly journey but never made it to the Pole. Nansen himself set out from the vessel with the idea of continuing on foot but was overcome by the southerly drift of the pack ice.

Undoubtedly one of the problems of striking out in the direction of the North Pole is that courtesy of the drifting pack ice you are more than likely to end up somewhere else entirely. This is still true today. In the case of any number of the early attempts to reach ninety degrees north they never got close. In fact many of them found themselves going backwards.

This world of ice is not only on the move, (it can drift several kilometres a day), but is in a state of constant flux, creating a landscape that is continually shifting. Ice flows ranging in size from a few feet to several miles across sail on their own or bunch together into pack ice, jostling or smashing into each other to create pressure ridges thirty feet high or tearing themselves apart under the strain and opening new reaches of water. The frozen sea squeaks, pops and booms with the stresses within it. Eventually the strain gets too much and something has to give.

'About the crack?' I asked Alexi, me still being green about the way the Arctic works so that the whole idea of the camp I am headed for just coming apart at the seams appeared bizarre. In fact at 'Barneo', a small settlement of half barrel tents screwed into an ice floe, there are any number of polite signs suggesting you do not go too far for a walk in case you drop through the white surface and into the underworld beneath; 'leads' or fissures that open up right to the ocean below are not that uncommon.

That happens even with ice of the best kind, the sort that has been around the Polar pin ball machine for a few circuits and has therefore matured to achieve a concrete hardness you can nail your home to. Every year the Russians build the base from scratch and that involves looking for a floe with the right qualities: big enough to accommodate an airstrip over a kilometre long and thick enough, (2-3 metres), to support a little village of tents. It also has to be drifting in the right direction. When they are satisfied they have the right spot, they drop in a heavy duty tractor by parachute and get to work. Even so, sometimes the landing strip is only a metre thick. This makes it prone to breaking up and me to worrying.

'It's fine,' Alexi told me. Alexi seemed quite laid back about it all and pretty much in control. He was one of the first people I met in the Arctic along with Eric, a bona fide Australian Polar explorer who arranged expeditions to the Pole. I would be travelling there with his company. I never did find out exactly what Alexi's position was but then the Russians seemed to run most things in this part of the world. After all, it was their ice camp I was going to and they operated the powerful Siberian- hardened Antonov jets that ferried the adventurous from Svalbard, north of

Norway, to Barneo just south of the Pole. From there it was possible to ski to the North Pole or be helicoptered in. Just for clarification, I made it clear to everyone that I don't ski.

'What should I do?' I asked him, not happy about being at the mercy of events but learning that this is the way things pretty much roll up here. 'Just be ready if I call you,' he told me, and of course I would, although I had not yet got to the stage of sitting fully clothed in my Polar gear while awaiting the summons. Later I would do just that, smothered in a parka that was so stuffed with thermal insulation that at room temperature with the heating off you broke out in a sweat. By that time people would be fighting for seats on that Antonov aircraft: I wanted to make sure I was first in line.

And then came the killer blow, the kind of comment that makes you certain that nothing, just nothing is going to happen soon and then not very fast, unless of course it does and then it is all a million miles an hour. 'Why don't you do some sightseeing,' Alexi added, 'You have time, as long as you don't go far. You could try snowmobiling.'

This is Arctic speak for your plans are screwed but just in case remain on high alert-you never know what is around the corner.

And this, I was beginning to realise, is what Polar travel is like: you can't really expect to be in command of the situation all the time, or even any of the time; here you just have to go with the flow. Above all you need patience. This after all is the land of 'hurry up and wait.'

SVALBARD

If you do find your Arctic odyssey on hold, Svalbard is not a bad place to be stuck in. This group of chilly Norwegian Islands, about the size of Ireland but a thousand kilometres off the tip of northern Europe, is not only a prime hopping off point for a trip to the Pole but an adventure destination in its own right. It is a mountainous, glacier carved wilderness that is both incredibly harsh and beautiful at the same time, all wrapped in a snow blanket so encompassing that you can ski from one end to the other pretty much without a break. Appropriately enough Svalbard means 'cold edge' in Norwegian.

People come here not only to ski but to try dog sledding, ice caving and snowmobile treks into the cavernous and empty interior, in fact any kind of snow based fun imaginable. They arrive sometimes by boat but more usually, as I did, on board the regular air service from Tromsø in Norway's far north. In recent years visitors have outnumbered the permanent population of around 3,000 by about fifty to one.

More than a half of Svalbard's inhabitants live in the capital Longyearbyen, a coastal settlement squeezed into a thin strip between sheer sandstone bluffs. To the north the town faces out towards the Adventfjorden, a wide breezy channel, its waters choppy and blue in summer and ice bound in winter. At the back its heels are licked by a couple of glaciers coming down from the mountains that rise beyond its outskirts. The whole place is no more than three kilometres long from end to end and apart from the waterfront area is mostly less than a half a kilometre wide. And into this boxed in space fits everything: the municipal buildings, the post office, shops, the most northerly Co-op in the world, and most of the hotels and guest houses that Svalbard has to offer, a scattering of chiefly wooden buildings stilted against the permafrost.

Longyearbyen is a pretty laid back town but it has its rules. For one thing, in a reversal of most inner city logic, it is actually mandatory to carry a gun, at least outside the municipal boundary. It helps if you can use it. One of the first things that the local school kids are taught when they are old enough is how to shoot straight, and not between the eyes, not when they might miss. When it comes to self defence against a 1,000 pound mammal there is after all a big body target in the bulk of the furry chest for them to aim for. Among the 'Common sense rules for Svalbard' laid out within the tourist office's guide to Longyearbyen I found that, 'Pursuing, attracting or enticing polar bears is strictly forbidden.' On the whole this seemed a pretty superfluous regulation as in any encounter I expected to be the one being pursued. There are after all plenty of them to do just that-at the last count they more or less matched the human population. Most of the bears live out on the sea ice on the eastern coast of Svalbard but they do wander across the islands to Longyearbyen, sometimes frightening the other wildlife on the edge of town. A sure sign that they are prowling around the outskirts is when the local stubby legged, pygmy like Svalbard reindeer take up residence in the city centre and refuse to budge, (That actually happened while I was there). Occasionally even the sanctity of Svalbard's capital is breached, as happened recently when a mother and her cub strolled right into town one day and spent the night there before checking out the next morning. Such things are rare however and firearms are not generally considered necessary within the city boundary itself. If you must go to the supermarket with a Mauser 30-60 you are obliged to stash it in a locker until you have finished your shop. Waving one around at the Co-op is definitely discouraged.

While Longyearbyen is not quite the ultimate wilderness, (it does have pizza, sells polar bear postcards and has some pretty good pubs for the tourists), it is still a frontier town of sorts, on the very margins of human northerly existence. This after all is a place without a tree or even a shrub, where the ground is frozen hard for most of the year and where you are in permanent darkness between October and February. In winter the average temperature is generally minus sixteen degrees and the town retreats under a snow cover that hides the cocoa coloured bare rock beneath. Ironically for a place where nothing grows, it is the perfect spot to bank a copy of all the world's crops in the underground global seed vault just outside town, so that in the event of a nuclear holocaust Svalbard is the go to place in order to re-boot the planet's entire agricultural industry. Here the cold preserves everything: in the graveyard on the outskirts of the city, originally established to bury victims of the 'Spanish' Influenza outbreak at the end of the First World War, scientists have retrieved samples of the virus from intact corpses. The lack of decomposition in the permafrost is a real problem. The graveyard closed for business some seventy years ago, refusing to bury any new bodies so that expiration means being shipped out to mainland Norway. In Longyearbyen it is against the law to die.

Why settle in such a harsh country in the first place? Originally the answer was coal; the relics of a tapped out industry are still strewn along the valley today, evidenced in the abandoned hillside mining stations and aerial tramways that at one time hauled buckets full of the rich seams to the harbour below. In recent years it is the tourist industry that has taken over and mined the pockets of numerous visitors instead. Early April, when the sun comes back, is particularly busy: At that time the days are lengthening and becoming lighter and the temperature rising but not yet enough to blunt the ice. This is a perfect time to indulge in snow based activities before the summer sun arrives and turns everything to slush. It also happens to be the only practical time to go to the Pole, while the weather is milder and before the spring thaw cuts everything up. That window of opportunity is slim: just a few weeks in April while Barneo is up and running and the planes fly north.

'Any news?' I asked Alexi when I next caught up with him on Longyearbyen's main drag, knowing that the answer would be no, that he would have called me if there was anything to say, or at least sought me out because in Longyearbyen a cell phone can be a pretty redundant thing: most people you might want to ring are probably just as easily found wandering about town.

I had been supposed to fly out on Monday and it was now the following Wednesday. Every day I had made the trek from my guesthouse, the Mary Ann Polarrigg, (a long eccentrically timbered building, not unlike a funky stretched log cabin), through the snow and to the east side of town just to see what's what. Today the main shopping street was busy, the locals and not a few tourists bustling past its parade of souvenir shops, provision stores and arctic outfitters, its buildings a jumble of multi coloured roofs under a slate sky. It was minus five and sleeting, not a bad day in Longyearbyen. Occasionally a reindeer wandered across our path.

'They are having a bit of a problem with the weather,' Alexi told me, and once again that was pure Arctic speak for something else. As I found out later there had actually been a full scale blizzard blowing at Barneo ice base, a sixty miles per hour humdinger that had destroyed the old runway and was hampering building a new one. At some point it had been necessary to screw the tents more firmly into the ice to prevent them from flying up into the sky. There were fifty three people at the ice base and they were going nowhere for the next few days. Eventually it would get so bad that rumours would start circulating that Barneo was sinking into the Arctic sea and a general evacuation was being called for.

Whether Alexi knew all this and didn't want to worry me with the specifics or was as blissfully ignorant as I was, I don't know. In any case nothing would be going north or coming back for some time.

'I'm thinking about going dog sledding or maybe snowmobiling,' I said innocently. 'I would do both,' he told me.

So, I did. That afternoon I turned up at the kennels outside town to wrangle some huskies and fall flat on my face.

'Here is how you attach the harness to the dog and the gang line for the team,' we were told and there followed a demonstration that left me clueless. Within ten minutes I had trussed up one dog entirely and there were still five to go. 'Pepper', 'Ask', 'Embla', 'Loke' and everyone's personal favourite 'Vodka', waited patiently for their turn, all watching my efforts with the cool detachment of a more intelligent species. Not that they were unhelpful. Seeing I was in difficulties one of them actually lifted a paw to indicate where I should place the loop in my hands. Swear to God that actually happened.

Eventually we got the team together and attached to the sled, at which point the huskies started bickering and got all tangled up again. 'Remember to show them whose boss,' were our instructions. 'Now stoppit,' I said in the firmest voice possible, as if I was talking to some naughty children, 'Just behave.' Needless to say they totally ignored me. Finally, peace restored thanks to the intervention of a member of the kennel's staff, we were ready for the off, at which point it was important to remember to release the brake gently if at all for the first kilometre: they really did go out of the traps.

The sled itself was shaped like a steeply curved bath chair with the passenger in front and the musher or driver standing in a more precarious position at the back. There actually was a brake: a metal bar to stand on which bit into the ice to slow you down. In times of desperation or when at a full stop there was also a snow hook, a two pronged metal device on the end of a rope which when thrown into the snow anchors the sled and prevents the dogs running away with it. That was the theory anyway.

For the first run I elected to be the passenger, a decision which although on the face of it prudent, did have its own consequences. One of the important things I had failed to realise was that the dogs had been well fed between outings and had probably just had time to fully digest their last rich meal of high carbs, fats and meats before we arrived. Their howling and pawing at the snow was not just in excitement at the prospect of running wild, but letting go generally.

Once we were off they let fly with their bowels and I found myself in the middle of a shit storm made worse by being so laid back in the seat of the sled as to be looking down the barrels of their arseholes. Amazingly I came out unscathed, probably due again to the smartness of the dogs which knew how to point themselves so as not to fire point blank at the customers.

Evacuation complete, it was then all about carving the pristine snow with the dogs yomping at a lick through a field of white that stretched as far as the eye could see. I had no idea where I was but that didn't seem to matter-they knew exactly where to go.

Afterwards I hitched a car ride back into town with one of the huskies whose paw merited a trip to the Longyearbyen veterinary surgery. This was a treat for both of us. 'Curry' sat next to me on the back seat for the entire journey, an inquisitive bundle of fluffy fur, craning his neck to get a better view as the scenery rolled by. He was obviously enjoying the ride. 'Pretty cool to have someone else do the pulling for a change,' I said conversationally. Curry had to agree.

The next day I went snowmobiling. While dog sledding had its challenges, this was a different proposition entirely, involving as it did playing keep up with a girl armed with a gun, while trying to master a wayward two stroke motor.

Boy did we go fast, or at least it seemed that way to me. Our tour leader, an Amazon blonde in a snug fur hooded parka with a lethal rifle at her back, flares in her pocket and a crackling walkie talkie at her belt, was in a hurry to get this expedition on the road : no sooner had we dutifully followed her in convoy on to the broad racetrack of the Adventdalen valley floor outside town, (our super highway to the east coast of Spitzbergen and the lair of the bear), than she sped off and we had to go with her or be left behind. In Svalbard you are either born on a snow scooter or are made to learn quickly. Before long my speedometer was touching fifty kilometres an hour. It seemed to stay that way for a lot of the trip.

In keeping with the billing of our tour as a 'safari' our machines were big felines, variously labelled, 'Snow cat', 'Panther', and 'Lynx', although to me they looked more like big black bugs with two spindly but go fast ski legs growing out of a squat bulbous body. They were all powerful beasts with a lively twist grip throttle. And they were heavy: weighty enough to bleed the speed to nothing if you took your fingers off the gas, so that you just rumbled to a stop. The brakes, we were told, were really for emergencies.

Having never ridden so much as a moped before, I spent the first few miles concentrating on learning to handle my snow mobile while the crisp white valley floor streaked under my skis and the distant snow capped mountains sped by. Occasionally I got a chance to glance at the epic scenery, but mostly I had to concentrate really hard. Eventually though, I began to relax, to find the whole wind in your face experience exhilarating even, as I felt increasingly confident that the scooter was obeying my commands. In fact it seemed that I had just got the hang of it when the world and everything in it disappeared.

Anyone who has experienced a white out will appreciate what it does to your brain. The pure white of the snowfield is bad enough but when it meets a fog bank all your points of reference are erased: you are a disembodied traveller in a cloud of your own and it is a freaky lost feeling. In the worst case scenario people lose all sense of orientation and balance-they have been known to get lost in their own front yard.

The ghost of a scooter in front of me kept appearing and then disappearing like a magic trick. Sometimes it wasn't there at all for what seemed a long time, a disconcerting prospect when you are bowling along at fifty plus kph. Worse still, I had visions of my shooting off from the main pack down some side valley, deeper and deeper into Svalbard's chilly heart, never to be seen again.

But of course nothing like that happened. When the fog lifted everyone was still there playing follow our leader in perfect single file, a neat line of bugs scurrying along the bottom of a huge channel which carved its way east through the plateau. Svalbard is like this: dizzying mountain blocks all cut up by interconnecting valleys and glaciers, sometimes miles wide, that in winter forms the only road network for the islands. The distances seem endless: miles and miles and yet more miles would fall under our skis until finally we arrived on the east coast, the blue ice cliffs of an enormous glacier at our backs while the snouts of our lined up scooters looked out over the sea ice.

When we got to the sea the girl with the gun scanned the horizon with her binoculars. No one could see anything. We had lunch and we waited, an hour or more. We carried on waiting as is usual in the Arctic for something to turn up: in our case it was for some bears.

They were nowhere in sight, but then anyone who goes on a snow mobile safari to the east coast of Spitzbergen, the 'Kingdom of Polar Bears', does need to be philosophical about it. Despite their numbers it is estimated that there is probably about a one in ten chance that you will see one. Their Kingdom is sometimes a shy one.

The lady with the entire bear proofing kit but no bears got on her radio to find out if any other tours out in our region had been more lucky but drew a blank. Before long it became apparent that short of waving our arms about and smearing ourselves with seal blubber, we weren't likely to get any attention-at least not today.

It would be a lie to say that the ride back was easy. It was a long day: nine hours in the saddle there and back with the blonde warrior at the head of our empty handed scouting party whipping us on through ever more lofty mountain passes and over dizzying ridges where you didn't dare look down. Inevitably I was headed for an accident. I finally lost control on the top of an icy rise where for some reason our single file of growling machines came to a halt. There we balanced on what seemed to be a knife edge or perhaps more appropriately a 'Cold edge' with a steep drop on either side. Inevitably I wobbled. Undoubtedly one thing you shouldn't do when you feel your Panther or Lynx begin to playfully roll over is turn it downhill in an attempt to right it. Gripping the handlebars in panic just makes it worse as the throttle opens and before long you find yourself accelerating to your doom. There were some particularly sharp boulders at the bottom which it would be good to avoid. In the end I simply bailed out, jumping into the snow while the machine carried on rider-less for a while before grinding to a halt. Back up on the ridge, the rest of the line swivelled their heads as one to look at the guy who had just broken ranks in a suicidal death leap. Being of a practical and taciturn nature, (and that is the Norwegians all over), when they saw I was not dead or severely injured they lost interest and just carried on. They even looked a bit embarrassed on my behalf. In Svalbard is does not do to let yourself go.

By this time I was starting to have enough of the winter wonderland assault course that was our trip to the bears. The grandeur of the scenery had not diminished but I had got to the point where the sheer concentration required in keeping on the road for over two hundred kilometres in one day had become exhausting. And I was in pain, courtesy of my predilection for falling over continuously in the icy conditions of Svalbard, particularly in the first few days after my arrival. One day I had stepped outside Mary Ann's and immediately flipped over, jarring my back. Now every lump in the snow and every wrinkle in the ice was a reminder of that slip. The pristine purity of the Cold edge was about to be sullied by bad language.

'Fuck,' I shouted as the scooter bounced over a ridge in the ice and then 'fuck' again as it hit the next little pressure ridge and the next one and the one after that. 'For fuck's sake, aren't we there yet?' I yelled. Finally Longyearbyen came into sight. I hobbled all the way to Mary Ann's Polarrigg. There I went to bed after downing a couple of paracetamol and more than two whiskies. That night I replayed the entire marathon journey of epic mountain grandeur and snarling bouncing bobcats on a continuous loop in my head, the scenery rushing by in booming hypnogogic images that I couldn't get out of my brain. No doubt I screamed a bit in my sleep. 'Shit,' I shouted into the illusory breeze as we sped across the white wilderness of Svalbard and rode on corrugated iron in my dreams. 'Aren't we there yet? Fuck, fuck, fuck!'

'How did the snowmobiling go?' Alexi asked the next day, it being a slow day for any other news.

'Great,' I told him. We met in the 'Kroa' bar down the high street, a snug place with a trapper's cabin sensibility: all polished wood, animal skins and satisfying high carb steaks and burgers on the menu. Built from the spare pickings of a Russian settlement elsewhere on the island, it had a rescued bust of Lenin behind the serving counter. Some things are a long time in passing.

Alexi had just got off a call on his cell phone which seemed to consist of someone squawking at him loudly for a couple of minutes followed by a blizzard of Russian from his end that lasted twice as long. 'Everything Ok?' I asked him. 'Fine,' he told me. 'I'm thinking of going to the ice cave outside town this afternoon,' I said. 'Good idea,' he replied.

I headed to the outskirts of Longyearbyen which took all of five minutes. Along the way I passed the tourist office with its list of diversions, many of which I had now sampled. Stay long enough in Svalbard's capital city and eventually even this winter wonderland may run out of things to offer you. Not quite yet though, I still had the ice cave.

A few kilometres outside town, half way up the Larsbreen glacier that overlooks it, there was a solitary shoulder wide hole in the snow marked out with a flag and a wooden board. I watched it swallow any number of people and then joined them.

To climb down into the belly of a glacier, the bit underneath its plain white wrapper, is to enter another world, a place of twisted polished surfaces, a whipped and folded air bubble crawl space of blue and white ice, sometimes glassy and smooth, sometimes opaque and rutted. It is a mad frosted ice box world that demands a degree of contortion to inhabit. Luckily no one got stuck.

The glacier that houses the cave is a tongue of ice over a hundred and sixty feet thick and three kilometres long, sliding down the valley towards Longyearbyen at the slow but inexorable pace of about four metres a year. If the snowfall in winter is greater than the summer melt it will continue to advance and each new season will bring another layer on top like rings in a tree. In summer the melt water carves into the ice, sometimes all the way to the glacier floor, and then in winter the opening is sealed again, so creating the cave. From floor to ceiling such spaces cut through the annual ice 'rings' and therefore expose them like pages in a history book. Some layers contain dirt and gravel that suggest avalanches in earlier years. At the bottom there are often seeds and plant remains from the time of the birth of the glacier. A thousand years in the making, the glacier and its ice caves are a lesson in the power of natural processes to shape the world, given enough time. The average tourist whisks through all this history in the space of about 2-3 hours.

Like snowmobiling and dog sledding, the ice cave was one of the three big visitor draws in Svalbard and now I had done them all. Within the safe boundaries of Longyearbyen my options were now diminishing for further entertainment unless I wished to pop down the remains of a coal mine or attend the 'Spanish/Mexican horror night' at the local cinema. All the bigger trips into the interior were strictly controlled so as to protect the environment from the visitors and the visitors from themselves. In Svalbard you couldn't just walk into the wilderness 'willy-nilly', or even go for a quick stroll outside the city boundary, unless of course you had the appropriate protection.

Longyearbyen was a lovely place but by Saturday I was beginning to think I knew every square inch of it. I had the urge to stretch my legs and do a bit of hiking beyond the cute Polar bear signs that guarded every road out of town and which forbade anyone to go further on pain of being eaten alive. On the water front there was a fingerpost with signs pointing wildly at the world's destinations, (New York, Rome, Moscow, London, [only 3,043 km as the crow flies]). All I wanted to do was go down the road but it felt just as daunting. In short I needed to escape. And to do that there was only one thing for it: that morning I marched into one of the licensed sports shops in town and asked if I could hire a firearm.

Defending yourself against Polar bear attack is a serious business. An adult bear may weigh up to 1,500 lb and stand between seven and nine feet tall. Their skulls are so thick that bullets literally bounce off them, (hence the advice to aim for the belly). At full charge it can cover the distance between you and it at about ten metres a second so that if it is less than fifty metres away you will not have time to even take aim, (five seconds being the minimal reaction span with your pump action shotgun, and that is if you have really good reflexes).

The situation is even more dangerous if there is more than one of them. According to one photographer and explorer, in the space of his two and a half months living in Svalbard in which he left his camp just once a week, he had five encounters with bears, two of which got closer than fifty metres. In 2015 three Kayakers who became the first to circumnavigate the islands spent an entire night fending off no less than nine bears, some of which chased after their boats. Like humans, bears can have different temperaments. Some of them are timid, others downright psychotic, so that despite flares at their feet and bullets whistling past their heads, they will still keep coming, deterred by nothing in their mission to basically rip your guts out.

The sports shop was a cheerful place, full of attractively coloured jackets, boots and snowmobile suits as well as useful survival equipment including your very own emergency beacon, ('Wrongful activation may result in a penalty.') There was also a rack of guns in a case behind the counter, sturdy weapons with weighty wooden stocks and lethally sleek barrels. They looked like the sort of thing I wouldn't have a clue how to handle.

The guardian of these machines of death was a not unkindly man but he did get straight to the point: 'Have you ever fired a gun before?' he asked me in perfect English. The answer to that was not entirely straightforward. Once in Cambodia I had handled an AK47 in one of those tourist shooting galleries that sprung up when the country was awash with ammo at the end of the civil war. It had taken two Cambodian guys to hold me down while I struggled with the recoil. In the end they had found a picnic table to rest it on and got me to sit down while I loosened off rounds like a bloody tea time massacre. I had not used so much as a pop gun since. 'No,' I prudently told him, 'I haven't.' The man with the weapons sighed. 'In which case,' he said, 'You are more likely to damage yourself than the bear.'

And that was that. In the evening I got a text from Alexi which said, 'Good news!' Apparently the weather had settled and they were making some progress in building a new runway outside Barneo. They had completed some three hundred metres of slick and serviceable ice, about a quarter of what the Antonov would need if it were not to plough into the snow and presumably explode. 'Maybe tomorrow?' I asked Alexi hopefully when I rang him back. 'Maybe,' he replied but didn't sound that certain. '... Or maybe the day after that.'

The Arctic 'giveth' and the Arctic 'taketh' away. It just dangles one promise after another in front of you before snatching it away, laughing. Its joker card is always the weather. Up in Barneo where they had already been through the worst storm for a decade, the air pressure was falling and the winds rising again so that Alexi's news was about to become old. In fact it was possible that what they had managed to build in the last few days would simply be trashed and they would have to start all over again.

It had now been almost a week since the flights to Barneo had ceased and in a season that may last little more than a month it was causing a significant logjam of skiers, adventurers and tourists who were anxious to get to the North Pole but had to bide their time in the waiting room of Longyearbyen instead. And every day the flights from the Norwegian mainland brought more of them.

Some of the arrivals happened to be Eric's team of skiers who would fly to Barneo and then cover the last degree of latitude to the Pole. Such an undertaking is not to be dismissed lightly, not when you are pulling a forty five kilogram sled over a shifting, drifting surface of ice ridges as large as houses and leads like small rivers, all in a temperature that with the wind chill can fall to minus forty degrees centigrade and below.

The energy expenditure in hauling a sled for eight hours a day in these conditions can be the equivalent of running three marathons on the trot, all fuelled by a daily intake of between 5,000 and 7,500 calories supplied by among other things plenty of freeze dried noodles, porridge and energy bars. Everything gets supplemented with butter and olive oil-in the Arctic there is no such thing as a low fat diet.

In such extreme conditions, and particularly once the

temperature falls below minus fifty degrees centigrade, nothing behaves as it should do. Rubber becomes brittle and nylon tears like paper. Metal tent poles just snap. It is vital for your survival that you have the right equipment for the job, from the GPS to calculate your drift during the night to the clothing that wicks away the sweat from your body so that once it freezes you are not glued to your layers. When pitching your tent at the end of the day it is important not to do so on thin ice, a requirement that is becoming all the more difficult with global warming. Above all it is not advisable to fall into the stretches of water that inevitably open up in the pack ice. It is not so much the water that is the problem, (that has to be above freezing to be liquid after all), no-it is the air temperature of minus forty once you get out that will kill you. In his book, *Going to extremes*, about his travels to the hottest, coldest, wettest and driest places on earth, Nick Middleton recounts his experience of joining the 'Walrus Club', a group of cold water swimming enthusiasts in Angarsk Siberia where it happened to be minus 38.6 degrees centigrade on the day he went for a dip. Fine while he was doing the breast stroke in the tub sized hole they had cut into the ice, once he emerged, in his own words he, '... Lost the plot very quickly along with all feeling in my toes.' Utterly baffled as to what was happening to him, he was only saved by the Russians drying and warming him, as he couldn't do it for himself. He remembered them waving his solid boxer shorts in front of him and the fact that his sock would not go on as it was completely welded to his foot. If it hadn't of been for his comrades' actions, he says that his cold- numbed brain would have shut down and left him sitting there, slowly freezing to death.

Eric told me of one incident in which a member of

his expedition team had fallen through the ice. Pulled out soaking, they had quickly put up a tent and dragged him and his clothing inside. While he had dried quickly, his kit had taken longer, several days in fact with the stove full on while a plume of steam had risen from the top of the tent like smoke from an Indian tepee. Eric reckoned they had used most of the expedition's fuel before the heavy Arctic gear was dry enough to put on again.

The skiers were not the only ones piling into Longyearbyen. People were here for a number of reasons. Apart from the expedition teams of varying nationalities that had now arrived together with their families to see them off, there were also loved ones waiting for news of intrepid husbands, wives, boyfriends and girlfriends who were somewhere between Barneo and the North Pole or on their way back and likely to get stuck until the weather cleared. Then there were those who just wanted to come here for a run. Each year the 'World's coolest Marathon' or alternatively 'The most Northerly marathon in the world' takes place close to Barneo ice camp, 26.2 miles of foot racing that is unusual in that the course itself is moving and the competitors may find themselves being chased by Polar bears. Where else would you be outrun by huskies and have to drop out not through exhaustion but because of second degree frostbite? Some of the runners are so serious they train in industrial refrigerators for the event. A common hazard is perspiring too much as the race goes on and then finding yourself welded to items of your clothing. One competitor recently discovered at the end that her scarf was stuck to her throat and wouldn't come off. It took a lot of heat to melt it and eventually peel it from her skin.

Finally of course there were those like me who had

come here with the express purpose of getting to the North Pole but did not want the inconvenience of dragging a sled or big plastic 'Pulk' over sixty miles while getting frost bite or having to remove stuff welded to our body parts. No, we preferred to be airlifted in. By Saturday there were quite a few of us, including a couple from New York, a gastroenterologist and his wife doing the planetary rounds, a high school teacher with a class to present when she got back and a guy with a fur trapper's hat and wild beard. I never did find out who he was but he looked like he would fit right into any wilderness situation. None of us had undertaken the sort of physical preparation or kit testing that the skiers or other expedition members had been so diligent about. The New Yorker looked like he had trained down at the deli, while the Doctor's most important piece of Polar equipment was a large Vodka bottle which he intended to use to toast our arrival at the Pole, if we ever got there. They had brought a large American flag, a small stuffed bear with a bib and a candy striped pole with a sign on it that said, 'North Pole'. By comparison I had travelled light. Just so that there was no misunderstanding we had all been supplied with badges to indicate our preference when it came to the journey north. Ours did not say 'Ski' but rather 'Heli'. We expected a lift to the Pole. That was the way we intended to roll.

Pretty soon we were seeing each other around town and rubbing shoulders with the other expeditioners in the bars around Longyearbyen that were rapidly becoming a bit of a crush. That evening Eric was having a welcome meal for his team and some of his adventurer acquaintances and seeing that I was at a loose end, asked if I would like to come along.

We met for dinner at Mary Ann's Polarrigg. Mary Ann's was probably the purest expression of character and eccentricity that could be found in Longyearbyen. It was wonderfully bonkers. At one time a miners rig or dormitory in the shadow of the coal bearing slopes to the west of town, it still had the same rough hewn quality, at least from the outside which appeared to be formed of irregular planks of timber like jagged teeth. Inside it was all warm polished wood, stone fireplaces and comfy sofas, awash with reindeer horns, animal skins and other hunting paraphernalia, while old miner's photographs stared down at you from the walls. In keeping with its idiosyncratic nature, you could not walk the entire length of the cabin like guesthouse without going out: the kitchen took up the middle bit and blocked access. Once outside there was an old red miner's bus that served as a smoking area and a wood fired tub if you wanted a soak.

Mary Ann's had a restaurant attached and a good one too. To get there from the guesthouse you encountered a sense of the dramatic, a dark faux rock tunnel with twinkling lights inviting you to step down a mine but which opened up into a greenhouse like space instead, full of gorgeous foliage. The whole place was flooded with Polar daylight, still bright enough at two pm for us to read our menus. In one corner a Polar bear stared out at us wearing the slightly surprised expression of one who has been stuffed.

I must admit I was a bit intimidated at the thought of the company. After all these were people who ski across Greenland for a laugh, and who tackle mountains and sail the Southern Ocean while the rest of us are tucked up in bed. Eric himself was a renowned figure in the Polar exploration community, having led numerous expeditions in the Arctic and Antarctic and was at the forefront of development in the kind of specialised high tech gear that is required if you are going to face such extreme conditions.

On a more mundane level he knew plenty of Russians with hats, or at least Russians who specialised in cold weather clothing and in the course of the trip I was able to acquire a small hat collection. They were excellent in keeping my ears warm. But In terms of gear that was about as technical as I got.

Eric introduced me to Rosina, an Italian woman whose husband was currently making his way back from the Pole on a skiing expedition. Like many others she was stuck in Longyearbyen waiting for his safe return while he no doubt was stuck somewhere on the ice.

Rosina shared her husband's taste for adventure and had spent the previous summer sailing a small yacht in the Southern Atlantic, a fact that she just casually dropped into the conversation. As the meal progressed the company traded further tales of their daring, each more hair-raising than the last. Eventually Rosina got round to mentioning that last year her husband had almost been decapitated.

According to Rosina, he and a fellow expedition member were trekking over some ice floes when her husband fell through a crack in the ice. With only his head above the surface, the two pieces of floe began to come together again. His friend had pulled him out by the hair, only just in time. 'Otherwise,' Rosina told us, and she motioned with the blade of her palm across her throat. 'He really owed him for that one,' she added.

By this time it was clear to me that these people were not like the rest of us. And they all seemed to know each other, a regular tight knit community of explorers and adventurers, ('Weren't you at the South Pole last Summer?'), who both supported and competed against each other, sometimes bickering, sometimes literally saving each other's necks.

Occasionally there was even the whiff of scandal as in a recent disputed claim by one such adventurer to have smashed a record for solo skiing to the South Pole. This had been rubbished by many of the Polar exploring community who considered that the selfie taken at a 'Welcome to the South Pole' sign had been simply photo shopped. In another incident, in 2010 Austrian Climber Christian Stangl who had many genuine achievements to his credit, admitted lying about breaking the speed record for a summit of K2, the world's second highest mountain and just about the most difficult to climb. Clearly the pressure to be successful had got to him on this one occasion. His comment was that, 'Fear of death is bad enough, but fear of failure in an achievement-oriented society is worse.'

Nevertheless the community did have many bona fide stars, people like Eric and also Victor Boyarsky, the Russian explorer and guide whose many achievements included crossing Greenland from top to bottom on skis and a successful 6,500 km traverse of Antarctica using only dog sleds and manpower. Chairman of the Polar Commission of the Russian Geographical Society (RGS), member of the National Geographic Society of the United States, full member of the National Tourism Academy and the International Academy of Refrigeration, Candidate of Science in Physics and Mathematics and member of the Union of Russian Writers, Victor was a busy man. He was however currently unavailable since he was stuck at Barneo in the midst of a blizzard. In the leaflet given to visitors to the ice camp there was a photo of Victor and he looked everything like a Polar explorer should be, with his broad face and rugged features. He even had snow in his beard. If we ever got to Barneo, as expedition leader to the camp he would be the first person to greet us when we arrived. To the Arctic travel world Victor Boyarsky was a hero. To the Russians it seemed he was a Polar God.

Why do they do it these people, why do they suffer such privations and danger to reach places that they could get to by air or by boat? Why in some ways do they seem to make it purposely difficult? The answer as with so much extreme sport and like activity is complicated and has engaged any number of psychologists over the years. Whether it is the need for the adrenaline rush or the urge to test our boundaries, research has shown that the people who trek into the unknown often have a particular mindset and one which on the face of it can be contradictory. For one thing they tend to have a positive outlook, not giving up the struggle just because they are hopelessly boxed in by ice ridges or cut off by breaking ice. On the other hand they may also have something called 'Productive paranoia', in which they meticulously prepare for the worst and try to conceive of everything that could possibly go wrong in order to have a contingency for it. This makes good survival sense. Successful Polar adventurers tend to go with the flow and not battle with nature. Sometimes they achieve an almost Zen like calm so that in the words of one explorer relating his travels, 'I seemed to cover great distances at a flash.' Undoubtedly they have a high degree of mental resilience and are good at creating coping strategies when in stressful situations. Faced with the same odds most of us would just as likely panic.

To be a good Polar explorer it helps if you like butter. This is a necessary supplement to your diet to provide the energy to haul those sledges twelve hours a day. According to the expedition leader Patrick Woodhead, 'It tastes revolting, but then your body just craves the fat content and you eat butter like blocks of cheese.'

It is also an advantage if you generally get along with people. There is a saying in the Polar expedition world: 'Choose your companions carefully, you may have to eat them.' Strangling someone because they snore in the tent or have a bad toenail clipping habit is not advisable, especially if you don't need the calories.

Even more difficult than facing up to the physical hardships of Polar travel are the mental challenges that have to be overcome to survive the sheer weirdness of the Arctic and Antarctic. For one thing these are places with very little visual stimulus, a blank and flat landscape of white with few shades in between which forces the brain to compensate for what is missing. Arctic explorers regularly report for example that at night they dream in full Technicolor.

One of the greatest difficulties of coming back home after a Polar expedition is adjusting to civilisation. According to the English Polar explorer Ben Saunders quoted in a recent online magazine article, once back, 'Everything is too noisy, too smelly, too colourful, too amplified – it's almost overpowering. It feels like you're watching TV with the brightness, colour and contrast all turned up far too high.'

He even found walking downstairs frightening: ' I'd spent ten weeks relying on the stabilising effect of two ski poles. Suddenly dealing with stairs, obstacles and slopes was really confusing. It took a week for my brain to make these activities fully automatic again.'

Clearly, the Arctic mucks about with your mind. In fact you probably have to be a little bit crazy in the first place to fully embrace it. That may or may not have been true of the people around the table that night at Mary Ann's, but it did seem to me that amongst the characteristics they shared one would have to be a really, really low boredom threshold.

I was therefore surprised when Rosina suggested I accompany her the next day on a walk within the confines of Longyearbyen. This seemed quite a mild proposition after sailing the Southern Ocean and almost losing your head. But both of us were twiddling our thumbs here and although I felt like I had seen the town many times over, it would be good to explore it again with company. We might even go up to the cemetery on the hill overlooking the town where the unthawed bodies lay. 'Wrap up warm,' Rosina told me, 'It's going to be cold tomorrow.' She obviously knew something I didn't. When you are told to wrap up warm at this latitude it seemed to mean something more than the usual three thermal inner layers and the fleece and parka that went on top.

There was no doubt that Svalbard's weather could be described as changeable. Courtesy of its position under the collision of the Polar and warm sea air masses, an atmospheric battle was always going on in the heavens above it and the town often caught the tail end of some Arctic squall. But since my arrival the days had been relatively clear and calm and the temperature a sharp but manageable minus ten degrees centigrade. I was not expecting much to change and the next morning when I awoke the little beetling flakes of snow outside my window didn't suggest otherwise. I and Rosina were both staying at Mary Ann's and I met her outside her room as agreed at 10 o'clock. She seemed to be dressed for a jewel heist. I laughed. Her brown eyes blinked at me through the peep holes in her face mask. 'It's not funny,' the mouth said through its own hole, 'You ought to get one.'

She did have a point. At minus twenty degrees centigrade human flesh can quickly freeze. Usually it is the wind chill factor that is responsible: a wind speed of fifteen km an hour can drop another ten degrees off the temperature. At that point you have about thirty minutes to keep your nose and ears. Frostbite is a perennial danger in the Polar environment-countless toes and fingers have been lost to it. But that is on the windswept high plateau of the Antarctic in a blizzard or on the ice in the Arctic surely, not in the centre of this town in April for God's sake. As usual, I would be proved wrong.

I covered my mouth with a buff and put on my mitts before stepping outside. The first thing I noticed was the chill-it was appreciably colder than yesterday. The second thing was that the snowflakes were no longer beetling, they were more cascading. When we rounded the corner of Mary Ann's the wind hit us. 'Where are we off to?' I asked over its howl. 'Let's see how far we can go,' shouted Rosina.

The answer was not very. The bits of Longyearbyen between the timber buildings were rough and uneven underfoot and as we bowed under the wind we made little progress. After a few minutes my hands and feet began to tingle. We had only gone a few yards when the hotel behind us disappeared. In front of us lay the town church or Kirke, a bright red building with a sharp snow protected roof and a spire that pierced the white sky. It was the only landmark I could see. 'Let's go there,' I said.

It seemed to take ages. At some point I lost all sensation in my feet and then my fingers went too. Eventually we staggered into the vestibule of the church. By that time there was a blizzard blowing outside. 'I can't feel my hands,' I told Rosina, starting to feel the edge of panic as one by one my body parts went numb. 'Put them inside your mitts on the radiator,' she told me. I tried to sit on that source of warmth and get my circulation going while the people of Longyearbyen filed past us in their Sunday best with not a hair out of place. I can't quite remember how we got back but some time later we fell through the door of Mary Ann's Polarrigg like survivors from an epic march, which in our case was all of four hundred yards. (The truth was that I could actually see the church from my room in the Rigg; it filled much of the window-it was that close). 'You really ought to get a mask,' Rosina said. 'I know,' I told her, once I had got my face to work again.

The next day the sky cleared, the Sun came out and for a couple of hours everyone went around town in shorts. The weather in Longyearbyen was not so much changeable as demented.

FRIENDS IN HIGH PLACES

About this time it became noticeable that Longyearbyen was getting pretty crowded. The flights from Norway continued to arrive, bringing with them ever more tourists who wanted to explore Svalbard as well as those trying to get to the North Pole. This was adding to a backlog already a week old.

On Tuesday the entire Malaysian national skydiving team arrived for an epic jump over the Pole. Dressed in identical orange parkas *come* jumpsuits they swarmed around like ecstatic bees at their first sight of snow, rolling and sliding in it, scooping up great handfuls and lobbing it in all directions. On the hill behind the Polarrigg they tobogganed on their stomachs, arms outstretched as if they were flying through the air. They went on like this for hours.

And every day there were more visitors. The town could not go on absorbing this influx of people forever. It had at most about three hundred hotel and guest rooms with about eight hundred beds in them. In the season in which Barneo operated it could expect two hundred and fifty or more tourists and skiers while the marathon attracted over three hundred and seventy runners. In addition Longyearbyen would be the host to all the other visitors staying there because they were either on business or had just come for a vacation in Svalbard. The place was now bursting at the seams; to all intents and purposes for the first time in its history it was a town that was simply full up. Something had to give.

I had already extended my stay at the Polarrigg once. Now I went back to Mary Ann again and asked to keep my room. 'I'm really sorry,' she told me, '...But I have run out of floor space.' She wasn't joking either. By the time I vacated my lodgings people were sleeping in the corridor. The Malaysian skydiving team had camped in the games room. Several of them were wedged under the pool table.

I rang Alexi. 'I have a problem,' I told him, 'I am about to become homeless. What should I do?' After all this was not a place where you could sleep in the streets or camp out, not without freezing to death. 'Get in touch with Eric,' he told me, 'He will find you a place.' And so he did, a 'company' house outside town close to the airport, a cosy stripped pine cabin of a place out in the sticks or at least just past the city limits. 'You will like it there,' he told me, 'some of the Russian guys are using it at the moment but there is still room for more.'

The cabin was part of an isolated scattering of buildings on a headland about four kilometres outside Longyearbyen, sandwiched between the long strip of the runway and the waters of the adventfjorden which flowed past the town. From the back it was just a few steps on to an icy beach on the channel's southern shore. From the kitchen window the massive white bluffs of impossibly stark mountains loomed across the water. They looked close enough to touch but were in fact several kilometres away. The front looked out over the perimeter fence of the airport. It was possible to see all the landings and take offs from the strip as they came in from the south or flew out towards the north. For the moment nothing was going in that particular direction.

This was our little house on the prairie. It was basic: there were no washing facilities to speak off and one unheated annex boasted a chemical toilet that put me in mind of the stories of soldiers on the Russian front in the Second World War whose bowels froze when they tried to relieve themselves out in the open. For some reason this place of contemplation and easement was furnished with what appeared to be vintage 1970's Swedish porn magazines just in case you came over all sexy in the sub zero temperature with a Polar bear prowling outside while you pooped the remains of you seal steak. I rarely did.

Still, apart from the toilet, it had a snug feeling about it, what with the Christmas card views and the snow banks that hugged its walls. On the kitchen window sill rows of bottles containing vodka and other spirits formed a cheerful and orderly queue. The lounge was welcoming with its big easy chairs and once the sleeping bodies were cleared from the floor surprisingly spacious. It was however pretty full up already.

Alexi and Eric had driven me outside town to my new home. When we arrived they seemed unsure where to put me. The lounge was being used by a number of people as their sleeping quarters and there appeared to be just a couple of private rooms, one of which I sincerely hoped would be mine. In the end they hovered over the threshold of a room no bigger than a closet which had one small electric bar fire in it. Alexi seemed hesitant and it was clear that he and Eric were pondering something. I had no idea what they were debating. 'Why not...?' Eric seemed to say. '...Here are your quarters,' he finally told me.

During my stay at the little house on the prairie a bewildering number of people came and went. Some of them looked askance at my little room but no one said anything. The mainstays of the homestead were Sasha who represented a Polar equipment and clothing company in Moscow and Grigory who was in St Petersberg real estate and who had come to Svalbard for the season.

What Sasha didn't know about winter hats was not worth repeating. Technical gear for the serious Arctic adventurer and its spin off into fashion is big business and he was part of it. This is a world of cutting edge threads and cut throat competition, where the budget for research and development into smart fabrics and interactive textiles is NASA sized and borrows from space technology. Such clothing not only has to provide the right amount of insulation and be windproof but must be hydrophobic, wicking away perspiration from the skin which if it freezes could lower the body temperature below that necessary for life.

That is the least it should do. Nowadays it is expected to push the boundaries way further. Some idea of how far the modern Polar outfitting industry has strayed into the realms of science fiction can be gathered from the arrival of the 'Moon Parka', not something that astronauts wear but in fact an unearthly winter jacket made from synthetic spider silk which is as strong as steel, light as carbon fibre, as elastic as cotton. Its manufacture involves culling protein strands from bacteria fed with sugar, (real spiders are too lazy and tend to eat each other). There has also been talk of genetically modifying goats to produce the same sort of 'silk' in their milk but progress has been slow on that one.

In my second day of residency Sasha was kind enough to give me one of his hats and although it wasn't made by robotic spiders or interlaced for example with the 'Gossamer combings of a Mongolian goat's chin', it was a perfectly serviceable wool hat with a polypropylene lining, enough to keep your head snug when kicking around Longyearbyen. It was a nice red colour, (to show up against the snow), with a white and green motif and a bobble on top, (the last being my only reservation about its design). Still, it is better not to look a gift hat in the mouth.

Unfortunately I was restricted in my opportunity to take my headwear for a walk. Out at the cabin we were in Polar Bear territory, at least in theory, and therefore I was not able to wander even down to the chilly beach overlooking the Adventfjorden. For getting into town I was reliant on lifts from Alexi or Eric and then unable to get back until they turned up with transport.

Evenings were probably the best time at the cabin: they passed in a semblance of domestic bliss, with Alexi coming round to chat and Eric sitting on the sofa while he repaired or tinkered with the equipment that his skiing party would need in their forthcoming attempt at the Pole. With the sun still in the sky, one of the bottles waiting in the kitchen would inevitably appear in the lounge of our little home and vodka toasts would be made. 'Here's to the North Pole,' (in the hope we would eventually get there). 'Vladimir Putin,' I proposed, whereupon Grigory raised a glass to the ghost of 'Margaret Thatcher.' Often we would run out of ideas before the booze ran dry. One evening everyone ended up toasting my hat.

While life was not at all bad at the little house on the prairie, (I did have my own room after all, a privilege that in the eyes of the many visitors to the house seemed to afford me an odd kind of status), by the time I had spent a few days in the log cabin this half way house to camping had begun to pall. However good the company was when it was conscious, I still had to wake up to the sight of any number of blokes littering the floor, parading their belly fluff above wrinkled leggings and snoring and muttering in their beards. I needed out. That however, would not be easy.

'What news?' I asked Alexi on more than one occasion and there was none of course. The airport remained eerily quiet. But then slowly things began to happen. There were rumours that the runway at Barneo had been completed and a second Antonov jet was flying in from Moscow so that four trips a day could be made in order to catch up with the schedule. Then one day we were having breakfast when we heard an unexpected sound: a low rumbling and then the scream of a jet as it roared down the airstrip outside our window. Then there was the unmistakeable silhouette of the Antonov as it climbed into the sky. We watched as it turned north. Everyone cheered.

'At last!' I thought, but not quite yet. First there was a backlog to clear. Well, no: in fact first there was a private flight out for one of Putin's friends who with the blessing of the Russian president had commandeered the aircraft for a picnic at the Pole. That was the story going around anyway. I had visions of a Vodka and cocaine fuelled party on board while the Oligarch in question surveyed the scene from his golden throne, surrounded by hangers on and a squad of Russian bunny girls in furs. That feverish vision may or may not have been true but at least Putin's favour probably speeded up the arrival of the second aircraft and that was no bad thing for the common people like me waiting to get our ride.

The other person I wanted to thank for my eventual liberation from the cabin and the chance to make my Arctic dreams come true was in fact the former US Secretary of State and presidential candidate Hillary Clinton.

It seemed that some strange stuff had been going on at Barneo in the teeth of the storm that had raged for several days. In particular it was said that some American tourists had put in a cell phone call SOS once it became apparent that they would not be moving on anytime soon from the weather besieged ice base.

The online *North Pole News and Guide*, a conduit for all manner of Arctic gossip, took up the story:

'Bored of being stuck in Barneo ice base and wanting to get out asap in style?' it asked, and then went on to say, 'Just call Hillary Clinton and the lady will send the cavalry along.' Apparently the tourists, alarmed by the howling of the wind and the groaning of the ice as it cracked all around them, had contacted Hillary's secretary who had in turn got in touch with the US Life Guards to get them out.

This in turn had sparked rumours that Barneo was sinking into the Arctic Ocean, leading to a frenzy of speculation in the Polar community and in the words of the online magazine, 'Firing all alarms and putting everybody in rescue mode.' In fact the only people not panicking by this time were Victor Boyarsky himself and the hundred other inhabitants of the base who were tucked up in their beds nice and dry and sleeping soundly, (as far as you can with the banshee screech of an Arctic gale going on outside).

Particularly affected by this kerfuffle was British helicopter pilot Jennifer Murray, then in the midst of her record breaking journey to both the South and North Poles and dependent on the very aircraft Hillary would have been commandeering, for her fuel drop. According to all accounts, she was not best pleased. Apparently Jennifer rang a surprised Victor Boyarsky the next morning only to be told that everything was fine thanks and that far from Barneo vanishing beneath the ice, it would be around until the 4th May, enough time to complete its usual tour of duty providing a refuge to the intrepid expeditioner, not to mention the occasional hysterical visitor.

Whether a squadron of Twin Otter aircraft did arrive to rescue the tourists from the dangers of a serviceable and secure camp and whisk them off to the dubious safety of the wilds of Alaska and thence to the equally dangerous gun filled streets of large North American cities, was in the end unclear, but assuming that they did manage to empty Barneo, the knock on affect for those trying to reach the base could only be favourable. All of which proves that it is not what you know but who you know. After all, it helps to have friends in high places.

Even so, the backing real or imagined of world leaders does not immediately get you to the front of the queue: you still have to get in line and wait. And as with all things logistical in the Arctic, there is always the tease; 'Get ready to go,' Alexi texted me a couple of days later, 'I will call you.' This sounded promising, so much so that it finally prompted me to sit for a whole day in the lounge of the snug little house on the prairie in full Polar proof kit in a sweat of anticipation. I had to wait until the evening before I was told to stand down. It was another false alarm.

By this time I had just about had enough. All my personal logistics were unravelling. I had a life to live, obligations to meet. I called Alexi. 'The thing is...,' I told him and was about to say that it had been an interesting experience this hanging around but now time was running out for me, and thanks for everything but at some stage I really would have to go back to civilisation where there were timetables and real clocks, where day and night were not the same and Polar bears didn't stroll into the centre of town. The fact was that I simply couldn't wait any longer, even for the North Pole. I didn't get a chance to say another word. 'Eight thirty tomorrow morning. Be ready.' This time I thought, he actually sounded like he meant it.

THE MONKEY EARS EXPRESS

The Antonov An- 74 is an impressive machine, although frankly it is also a bit odd looking. For one thing it has monkey ears. Not literally of course but its oversized engine ducts do resemble the saucer like appendages of a chimpanzee or perhaps more strictly those of a giant mouse. Perched as they are on top of its high wings and projecting above the nose of the cockpit, head-on they actually give it a bit of a Mickey appearance. So much so that the 74, workhorse of the Polar regions and serious bit of flying kit that it is has endearingly been given the nickname of 'Cheburashka' in Russia, after a children's cartoon character which sports large dish like lugs from its little rounded head. The popular comic book creature was in fact the original soviet equivalent of Disney's capitalist western mouse.

There is however nothing Mickey about the plane's performance. The huge exhaust its engines generate flows over its wings, helping to give it extra lift. It can take off and land on the shortest runway or really no runway at all, the kind found particularly on the ice flows that litter the Polar basin and which for most aircraft would end in a dunking. It is incredibly rugged, coping with temperatures such as minus sixty degrees centigrade on the ground, well below that at which jet fuel turns to jelly. It is ideal for arctic operations. It can even be fitted with skis. All in all it is not your conventional aeroplane.

Sitting on the concrete apron of Longyearbyen airport it was undoubtedly an odd thing to look at but then again it was not designed to be pretty. Inside, it was a functional stripped down tube, the faded faux leather seats of the passenger space vying with a cargo hold stuffed with skis, expeditionary kit and the basic supplies that kept Barneo from starving. On an Antonov 74 flight there is no cabin crew, complementary peanuts or in- flight movie. You simply buckle up and pray for good weather. That means doing what you do best north of the Arctic Circle: you twiddle your thumbs and wait.

There is good reason to take your time before flying anywhere in the Arctic. When you think about it, (and it is not always a good idea to consider the prospect in too much detail), quite a lot can go wrong. Apart from the vagary of the weather, with the problems of extreme winds, icing and turbulence, no magnetic compass really works here. In fact the closer you get to the North Pole the more likely it is to simply lock up. On reaching the convergence of all the lines on the earth's surface it is asked to about face in an instant: one second you are heading north and then it is south all the way. If it is enough to make the most sophisticated GPS software have a nervous breakdown, a mechanical gyroscope literally falls over.

Long before the days of GPS, the early Polar aviators had to rely on a sextant to establish their position, a piece of equipment first developed for sea navigation in the eighteenth century which relied on establishing the relative position of a celestial body with the horizon. This was difficult enough on the rolling deck of a ship, but in an aircraft moving at over a hundred miles an hour and buffeted by freezing winds, it was near nigh impossible. Consequently finding your way was all a bit 'hit and miss'. Getting lost in the Arctic is not a good idea. This is an area half the size of Africa in which there is no real practical place to land. Until as recently as 2011 modern twin- engined commercial jets were not allowed to fly over the Polar basin because they had to be within three hours of a proper air strip. Only with improvements in safety features were they able to take advantage of the so called, 'Santa shortcut', which can knock off considerable flight time to far eastern and pacific destinations from Europe and America.

One of the greatest hazards of Arctic and Antarctic flight is not being able to see anything at all. Probably the worst aviation disaster in the history of Polar air travel occurred in November 1979 when a McDonnell Douglas DC-10-30 carrying 237 passengers on a sightseeing flight slammed into Mount Erebus, one of the highest peaks in Antarctica. The pilots didn't even know it was there. Sometimes fog and blizzards can merge with snow to cause a complete, 'whiteout', in which visibility is zero. This can cause complications, particularly on arrival. In the words of one veteran high arctic pilot, ' If you can't see the runway, it can really put a damper on your day.'

But perhaps the most significant challenge that pilots face, including those of the An- 74, is that they are trying to hit a moving target, one in fact that is continually slipping away from them. Everything in the Arctic basin including Barneo drifts on the ice so that it is no longer in the same spot when you arrive. You really have to look into the future to decide where it is going to be, and how you do that I have no idea. It is like skaters jumping into the air and aiming for a place to land on the ice while the whole rink is being pulled from under their feet. It is a testament to the skill of the pilots that anyone actually gets to their destination. What sort of flight plan has to be filed, I can only imagine.

And so we waited, all comfortable in our squeaky plastic coated seats, the Doc, me, the high school teacher and the bearded wild man along with many others, while our jet was given clearance. Those like us who would be airlifted to the Pole sat in special blue and grey parkas with our 'Heli' badges pinned on. The 'Heli' team was generally recognisable by the amount of stuffed toys and other mascots that would accompany it on its way to the end of the earth and which would feature heavily in the kind of photographs that would later appear proudly in various social media. Generally the skiers and other expedition members on board eschewed such frippery, fiddling constantly instead with highly technical equipment full of zips and bindings which they trusted would keep them alive during their frozen ordeal. They looked pretty serious about everything, more serious it has to be said than we did.

Finally the skies cleared and there was the unmistakeable high pitched whine of the engine start up. Slowly and with unexpected grace, the Antonov An-74 began to roll off its stand at Longyearbyen airport. We passed the airport hanger, permanently frozen into the ground, along with a scattering of other buildings including the most northerly departure lounge and baggage reclaim on the planet. Having done with the snow, holiday makers were waiting to board the sleek commercial jets that would take them back south to the crush of civilisation. We were going somewhere else, an empty place of nothingness. With us, it was pretty much going to be snow all the way.

Until the 1970's, Longyearbyen's airstrip suffered from the fact that in summer the earth underneath it melted and consequently on an annual basis the whole airport erupted in big chunks of tarmac. That rather precluded flying at any time other than winter when the ground was as hard as iron. The infrastructure was pretty primitive in those days in any case, with the inhabitants of the town periodically lining up their motor vehicles along the strip so that the car headlamps could serve as landing lights for the planes. These at least supplemented the paraffin lamps that they used to use. In 1973 however construction of a proper airport started and the runway was insulated from the permafrost that had an inconvenient habit of turning to mush in April and heaving the ground into small hillocks. Longyearbyen's runway is in fact the last serviceable all year round commercial airstrip this far North. Anyone who flies in the opposite direction to the commercial flights going south to Tromsø and Oslo should note that from here on, there really is no proper place to land.

Longyearbyen's state of the art runway was probably lost on the Antonov though: It simply ate it up and leapt into the sky. Below us the little settlement shrank into nothingness, a narrow strip of brightly coloured toy bricks dumped in the snow, the ghostly outline of its miniature streets still just visible from the air. In the next moment it had disappeared entirely, obscured by the vertiginous white bluffs that hemmed it in. Somewhere beneath us was the peephole of the ice cave, the huskies yowling and shitting along the frozen Adventdalen river floor, the girl with the gun and walkie talkie scouting on another fruitless mission to the Kingdom of the Bear, (or perhaps she had got lucky this time round). All this was quickly swallowed up by the epic scale of Svalbard's wilderness. You just wouldn't have been able to tell that any human being had ever set foot down there.

We sailed across the crisp blue waters of the Isfjorden and then turned north, the archipelago's soaring peaks glittering gold in the sun, its valleys deep in purple shade. When we reached the northern coast of the islands the last icy ridges of this remote outpost simply halted and tumbled into a flat frozen sea. After that there was a lot of nothing, a vast plain of mostly featureless white that from 30,000 feet up looked as flat as a pancake. It stretched to the coast of Alaska in one direction and between Greenland and Siberia in the other. There was enough ice down there to smother Europe and yet at most it was no more than six to nine feet thick, riding on an ocean about fourteen thousand feet deep- a very fragile skin on an extremely big tub of water, all chilled in a deep freeze. In places a spider web of cracks opened up leads of black in its surface, the sun flashing off the liquid like a polished mirror. Occasionally the shell broke completely and formed separate islets that slowly drifted with the sea currents, not unlike the ice Barneo was pegged to. From up here the floes looked tiny, though actually they were probably tens of miles across, if not more. Some of them would have been the prowling territory of Polar bears.

It took the Antonov two and a half hours to cover our journey over the seemingly endless and monotonous ice desert. Then the jet began to descend, apparently skimming over the tops of the pressure ridges that carved up the landscape like ghostly hedgerows fringing a patchwork of white fields. Suddenly Barneo base came out of nowhere and sped beneath us, a striking collection of blue half barrelled tent like structures neatly arranged to form a perfectly pleasant if isolated community at the end of the earth. On closer inspection it would even have a civic quality, the whole place surrounded by a low city wall of piled snow into which various flags and welcoming signs were planted, giving our arrival a ceremonial feel. Outside its entrance, someone had ice carved in giant shoulder high letters the word 'BARNEO', just to make it perfectly clear where you had ended up. The whole thing was coloured in the same sky blue that the tents wore in their stand-out fashion against the field of white. It poked you in the eye.

The Antonov made its pass and then began to descend again, banking and switching back towards the base and its blue ice runway. Helpfully, to prepare first time visitors for their experience of touch down outside Barneo, the authorities had provided us in advance with an official leaflet which included some tips on the landing procedure. 'You *MUST* fasten your seatbelt before landing and keep it fastened until the aircraft comes to a complete halt,' it told us. So far, so holiday flight to Malaga. However it then went on to remind us: "*REMEMBER* that you are not 'landing' in the usual sense of the word but doing it on an ice floe in the Arctic Ocean. Landing on ice can be rough and braking can be jerky. The plane can shake more than usual, [more than usual?]. Please....stay cool and calm.'

While this was worrying enough, the main concern about landing on ice remained the question of staying in shape and also importantly, being able to stop before it was too late. For this reason it is not a good idea to apply the brakes until you are rolling below five kilometres per hour, as twenty tonnes of metal fishtailing is a bad prospect. Instead, cutting your speed from over a hundred miles an hour on landing to walking pace is reliant on the big buckets of the Antonov's reverse thrusters being full on, and then it takes a while. In the insensitive words of the science of physics, the runway we were about to use was one with, 'A low co-efficient of friction.' It pays to make such touch downs roomy and long. In fact to be sure it probably needs to be over three times longer than your average landing strip.

One characteristic of ice that may be surprising is just how hard it can be. In fact high Arctic and bush pilots know that there is not just one type of ice but many such surfaces, ranging from a 'slick candy coating' to 'smooth glass', to tough 'blue ice' with all the air bubbles squeezed out of it so that it is, 'Like concrete.' In April 2015, in one of the few incidents recorded at Barneo over the years, an Antonov jet hit the deck harder than anticipated and snapped its landing gear. Fortunately there were no casualties. In the words of the accident report, 'It was decided to abandon the aircraft on the ice. Airplane fate: written off (damaged beyond repair).' In that instance at least, it was not a case of the aircraft damaging the ice, but the ice breaking the aircraft.

Such speculation about what might happen is however pretty superfluous when you are two minutes away from landing. All that remains then is to buckle up and trust in fate and the skill set of the pilots. When the plumped up tyres of the Antonov plant a kiss on the ice it may be more like a hard snog, that is true, but it is rarely rough and tumble. In fact having touched down we sped remarkably smoothly down the runway, flashing past little figures on the periphery of the base who lined the strip before Barneo came into view. At one point I did wonder when we were going to stop but in the end we suddenly decelerated and rolled to a halt outside the entrance to the base in front of the fluttering welcome flags. It was pretty much a perfect delivery. In the time honoured tradition of passengers anywhere having survived an adventurous arrival, we all spontaneously broke into applause. That it had all looked remarkably easy, better in fact than many conventional landings, was entirely due to the expertise of the pilots, a fact that shouldn't be forgotten. This wasn't a routine landing, however much we might end up believing it was. Nevertheless we will probably keep that illusion until the day arrives when the nose wheel comes off.

Once we had landed, the rear of the aircraft yawned open and about twenty skiers and trekkers tumbled out with all their gear. The Doc, college teacher and me gingerly stepped down the stairs at the front and trudged through the snow, heading towards what looked like the largest tent in town, the equivalent we guessed of the village hall. When we went inside Doc's glasses immediately steamed up.

One of the remarkable things about Barneo is that like

its near namesake it is actually a bit of a tropical paradise. (In the official version of its history the base was initially given the radio call sign 'Borneo', but to prevent any possible confusion with the South China Sea tropical island this was later changed to 'Barneo'. Of course that may just be a Russian joke).

Anyway, the whole place is literally pumped full of hot air twenty four hours a day. Outdoors it might have been minus thirty degrees centigrade but once you had cracked open the porch like door of the premises and parted the dimpled quilt curtains of uncertain but magically insulating material, it felt more than warm, it was toasty even, courtesy of whatever fire breathing equipment was kept out back. The hope is of course that the generator that keeps the dragon going never packs up or runs out of fuel.

The mess tent at Barneo is the community hub, the place where the serious research scientists mingle with the expedition teams and have to contend with the pesky tourists passing through. It is part assembly area, part cafe with plastic table cloths, a tea urn and serving counter for those hearty, nutritious stews and breakfast bowls of porridge that keep you going when the chill outside may be enough to seal your anus should you attempt any al fresco toilet functions. In any event exposing yourself to the elements and in particular leaving any waste footprint is the ultimate taboo in the Arctic and Antarctic world: literally nothing is left behind in these places, including any traces of last night's curry. There are after all breezy facilities at the end of the camp for relieving yourself and these must be used on pain of death. The helpful Barneo leaflet for visitors made it clear: 'Please keep the snow and ice around the camp pristine white. Exercise self control. Remember that *we…* *will not tolerate your YELLOW PISS!*'

There were other rules as well, equally sensible. 'Never walk on the runway,' it counselled. 'Please keep in mind that besides the risk of being run over by a plane, there is always the risk of meeting with a polar bear.'

Also: 'Never leave the base on your own. Leaving the base means stepping outside the perimeter of the camp by more than 25 metres.' To do so you had to be,' Accompanied by a guide with a flare gun,' the implication being that if the bears didn't get you or a plane land on your head, there was always a chance that you would fall through the ice. The rules, we were told, must be strictly obeyed, the orders of the Camp Chief being mandatory, *'WITHOUT EXCEPTION.'* No one was about to quibble with that.

In the relative safety of the mess tent, the man himself, Victor Boyarsky, greeted the new arrivals, some of whom were old acquaintances on the expeditionary circuit. He looked remarkably unaffected by having his camp almost blown away and dumped in the ocean. Although a bear of a figure himself, he was a friendly and self-effacing bear, almost squeezing the life out of one veteran expeditionary he recognised, now in her advanced adventure travel years, who was crushed like a tweety bird in his hugging embrace. She was however, a tough old thing. Later when it was time to settle down in the sleeping tent she happily bedded down in the draughty spot at the flapping entrance. Needless to say, I went straight to the back to find the warmest spot.

It being a pleasant day, (or maybe night), in the locality of the North Pole, after a cup of coffee I decided to go for a walk in and around Barneo in the company of the college teacher. She was busy making notes about everything so that she could tell her class all about it when she got back. We were careful not to stray outside the twenty five metre perimeter of the camp and even more circumspect about stepping on any suspicious fissures underfoot. 'Step on a crack and a bear will get you,' I said knowingly, thinking that she might write it down. 'And that's if you don't just fall through,' I added, remembering the advice we had been given. Kids just love that sort of thing.

We were rather disconcerted however to find that just outside the entrance to the base a couple of guys were busy carving a large hole in the ice. The space was big enough for a person to climb through. At the bottom we could see the Arctic Ocean. The most worrying thing about it was that the hole wasn't that deep.

'Is that a good idea?' the College teacher asked, echoing the thoughts inside my head. But then this was just another day at Barneo. The fact was that the base was chiefly there for research and if you wanted to research the ice you had to get under it, and to do that you had to cut a hole in it. Despite the number of tourists passing through the camp, serious science was actually the main reason for Barneo's existence with its staff of scientists doing work on climate change, oceanography and of course everything to do with the frozen stuff. The great man himself, Dr Victor Boyarsky, besides being an explorer, was first and foremost a scientist: he had PhD in Radioglaciology, his particular field of study.

There was however something horribly fascinating about someone going for a dip at the North Pole. We watched as one of the guys, dressed in a dry suit, put on his scuba gear and flippers and dangled his legs in the mushy, frozen, congealing water at the bottom of the hole. Bit by bit he eased himself into the little hatch way and then he was gone, slipping under our feet and for all we knew eventually drifting seal like under the tents where people were working, sleeping or just gossiping over a cup of coffee.

When the bubbles finally disappeared, I found myself shivering a bit. 'My feet are getting cold,' I complained to the college teacher. 'Do you want to go back indoors?' 'Great idea,' she said.

Back in the mess tent it was almost time for bed. That's what we were told anyway. Outside it didn't look much like bedtime- the sky was white and the little canteen was flooded with daylight. I no longer knew what day it was and I didn't really care. On the wall of the tent was a superfluous analogue clock with its hands pointing to ten minutes past something, which it might well have been back in Svalbard. But the islands were some thousand kilometres south where the bulge of the earth's globe gives longitude a meaning when it comes to the hour of the day. Here near the North Pole where all the lines were converging it was like being in an eternal present, a limbo land without time, because strictly speaking there is no time at the North Pole other than that you may wish to make up. All in all when you reach this stage in the proceedings of your Arctic tour the whole concept of where you are and when begins to become confusing, if not meaningless. (In fact time is a bit of a thing at the Poles or rather it isn't. For practical purposes we divide the earth into 'Time Zones', based on a global 24 hour day. Here at the Poles we can skip around these time zones, *as tourists often do*, within seconds, making the whole thing rather redundant. Usually Greenwich Mean Time is adopted for use instead, or some local time that makes sense. For example at the South Pole the Amundsen Scott station often runs on New Zealand time since all flights to and from the station must pass through that country).

Inside the darkened sleeping tent, I stumbled between bodies already fast asleep on the bunk beds, some no doubt scientists and staff on shifts, others like myself passing through in a weird kind of time warp. Most of them were in tee shirts and shorts. Some were snoring their heads off. I picked a place at the back where the dragon's mouth would breathe fire on me, the silver tunnel of its throat bellowing out a summer's heat. By the time I had stripped down to my underwear I had decided that I was pretty tired after all and that it should be officially declared night time. Whatever dreams the far north brings, it is almost certain that they will be vivid, although I don't remember mine that night. That, together with the calories required for surviving and working in such a hostile environment tends to create a particular atmosphere in the sleeping tent. I lost consciousness listening to the guy next to me revolve and fart in his sleep. It would be a warm, sultry, noisy night in the high Arctic.

In the morning the sky was still white, the snow crisp and the day bright and freezing outside. In fact at first it didn't look as if anything had changed. One thing was different though: the choppers had arrived.

They squatted on the edge of the base near the runway, sturdy craft in red and blue livery, big and with chunky enough blades to haul twenty six passengers to their ultimate destination and back. These Mil MI8 type helicopters were built to be rugged. Originally developed by the Soviets and latterly the Russians as troop carriers, they have been used both in the military and as civilian transport. In 1986 a number of them were called into service during the Chernobyl nuclear plant disaster, to help smother the burning reactor with lead. Most of those that took part in that desperate enterprise ended up in the 'Machines Graveyard', near the abandoned plant where their irradiated shells will presumably continue to have a half life for a few thousand years. In the light of such a history, the idea of bussing a few tourists up to the Pole was undoubtedly a doddle.

THE NORTH POLE

Anyone who has been in a transport helicopter for the first time will know how strange the experience feels of being lifted bodily into the sky, or perhaps that is just me. As it happens, the inside of the Mil M18 was as functional as the Antonov but without the added comfort, a grey painted, riveted porthole peeping tube with benches, so that we passengers sat facing each other in full outdoor rig while the noisy rotors cranked up and craned us off the ground. It was however a smooth ride, so much so that I had trouble working out if at any time we were going up, down or forwards, my brain totally disorientated by the experience. We had to turn around in our seats to get an outside view and when we looked it was one of Barneo receding into the distance as a few blue specks, its fabulous ice runway dwarfing the frost covered tents, a big shiny lick on the surface of the snow.

We flew over much the same landscape as when we came in, a mostly flat terrain of sea ice with bumps and wrinkles on its surface where the stresses below showed through, but perhaps more solid and locked together than before, now that we were in the coldest spot in the ice box.

After a while there was a change in engine note and then we began to descend. At this point everyone with a GPS handset started getting very excited and looking intently at their screens. In the early days of Arctic exploration no one had such an aid and consequently mostly had no clue where they were. The problem is that at the North Pole there is never any indication you have arrived; it is not like reaching the source of the Nile or coming across the Grand Canyon: everything outside your window looks just the same. In the Twenty First Century it has come down to this: the numbers tell you everything. When they count down to zero you know, in the words of Sat Nav speak, that, 'You have reached your destination.'

In the meantime there was a lot of circling and shouting of numbers, the figures going up and down, sideways east and west. This went on for some time. Eventually everyone's GPS crashed and turned off, a good enough indication of success given that when your software is asked to calculate an infinite singularity on the earth's surface it has a right to give up. I took a photo of Doc's handset which had bravely done the figures just before it had a nervous breakdown. *'North 90deg.00.0000'* it said. Frankly, to this day, it is the only solid evidence I have that I made it to the North Pole.

We hovered just above the surface. One of the crew opened the door and let a blast of freezing air in. He leaned out and probed the ice with a long stick. Then he jumped to the ground and like some strange ritual of anointment, poked at the four corners of the patch on which the Mil would finally rest. Satisfied that everything was solid, he motioned for the helicopter to drop down the last two feet. We settled on the ice and the engines died, the rotors swishing a few revolutions more before coming to rest; absolute silence.

As befits its status as the most northerly spot on the planet, the North Pole is a place of epic desolation and emptiness. Nothing has a right to live here, although remarkably Polar bears sometimes pass through and the tracks of an Arctic fox are occasionally found in the snow. That apart, it might as well be the Moon and like a Moon landing, the Mil pilots had found a broad flat spot to set us safely down so that we could survey the scene.

They were lucky. Beyond the relatively smooth plain of compacted ice and snow that we had landed on, the frozen sea water was smashed and twisted, piled high in boulders or peaks where the slow violence of the shifting currents had squeezed the pack ice together or tried to tear it apart. The tourists gravitated towards its drama, unfurling their banners and flags and huddling in photo opportunity groups.

An orange glow at the horizon illuminated the jagged landscape of ice. Just above it the sun hung low in the sky, a milky ball of light devoid of much power at this latitude. It would remain there for a few more months before setting again and plunging the whole place into darkness. It wouldn't be seen again until half a year later.

Here we were at a spot so hostile and difficult to reach that no one had sight of it until the third decade of the twentieth century, let alone visited it, (all disputed claims aside). Nowadays things are somewhat different. We come here as tourists. At a pinch we could get from Svalbard to the North Pole and back in about six hours. The whole thing then becomes a day trip.

Of course by rights the North Pole should be one of the loneliest places on earth, but on days like these it can get quite crowded. We stayed for a couple of hours, exploring the natural ice sculptures and walking around bumping into each other. It was an unusually fine day at the top of the world, the temperature reaching a balmy minus fifteen degrees centigrade. After a while though, my feet began to tingle. Before we left I borrowed the candy striped stick with the words, 'North Pole' on it for a photograph, because there is nothing like a real pole for emphasising the point that the actual spot rather inconveniently cannot have a marker stuck in it. In fact by the time we were ready to depart, the North Pole had long drifted down the road. Visiting the top spot on the globe, centre of the earth's axis, the place where every line and even time converges was a fleeting experience after all, almost dreamlike.

In the distance, beyond the mash of snow and ice, stood the red and blue Mil helicopters, ready to take us home. The journey back to Barneo was uneventful, as was the flight back to Longyearbyen, although made fuzzy with the vodka generously supplied by the Doc. By the time we landed everything was a little blurred.

Back at the little house on the prairie, things had moved on. The friendly Russians with the hats and their own predilection for vodka had long gone and had been replaced by two stern looking individuals who spoke little English. They looked like they had taken the long way round to the Pole, possibly on skis. They looked battle hardened, hewn out of rock almost.

Indoors, I was glad to see that my little room with the one bar fire was free and that I could take occupation again, my little private space, so admired and seemingly commented upon by all those who passed through the log cabin. I decided to turn in.

As I hovered on the threshold, I noticed the two Russians staring. They looked at me, then at the room and then back at me. Then one of them went red in the face. He seemed to have difficulty breathing. I saw his mouth working but nothing came out of it. Eventually he managed to splutter the words out: 'This is the room of Mr Victor Boyarsky,' he told me and then his voice rising, '...What are your intentions please?'

I looked back into the little room. It was barely a cupboard, but then I supposed that when you spend a lot of your life sharing a tent in freezing conditions and with toilet options outside that are likely to seal up your backside, the idea of a private room with an outside lavatory is not only an unimaginable luxury but a coveted recognition of your status.

'I was told to stay here,' I said, thinking that to blame it on someone else was expedient when dealing with two six foot Russians with outraged expressions. Besides, I wasn't going to give up my quarters with the one bar fire. This might have been Victor Boyarsky's sleeping space but Victor wasn't here right now and in his absence, as far as I was concerned, he had loaned me his room.

Breakfast next day was a frosty affair, but I was saved by Alexi picking me up for a ride into town. The streets were still snowbound but the snow was beginning to lose its crisp compactness and before long would turn into shapeless slush. With the melting of the ice, the season at Barneo would also come to an end. 'Every year that happens earlier,' he told me.

Before I left we took it in turns to be photographed by

the famous Polar Bear sign just outside town. Alexi wore a joke hat that seemed to have reindeer horns poking out of it. 'So, was it worth it?' he asked me, 'All the waiting?' 'Of course,' I told him, 'It was an incredible place.'

Some two thousand kilometres south of Longyearbyen and the 'Cold Edge' of Svalbard lies Oslo, Norway's capital. It is a city surrounded by forests and full of green spaces, so much so that straight from the Arctic all this lushness can take some getting used to: at first it stings the eyes. Ten minutes boat ride from the central waterfront area is the even more verdant and generously wooded peninsula of Bygdøy which is home to a number of places of interest including the Viking ships museum and the Fram maritime centre. The Viking boats are finds from burial mounds which date back to 800 AD during an era of plunder and exploration that would see a Norseman as the first documented European to reach the Arctic and in subsequent centuries his people expanding their reach to places as far away as Greenland and the north coast of America.

The Fram centre houses the famous ship that the Norwegian explorer Nansen used in his 1893 expedition and which was subsequently Amundsen's vessel on his trip to Antarctica. On the wall of the museum is a map of the Arctic basin depicting various expeditions and attempts on the North Pole from the mid nineteenth century to the Second World War, all squiggly lines in different colours, some of which end up nowhere. At least two have question marks at their end, suggesting an intrepid march into the unknown. The allure of the Polar Regions has always caught the imagination of explorers. There is something compelling about standing on the top of the world. The Arctic was one of the last places in our maps to be filled in, a place so open to possibilities that even as late as the 1920's there was speculation that it harboured an unknown continent. In the event this turned out to be an 'Empire of Ice'. It is no less interesting for that.

I took a ferry back to the UK. London was loud, busy and crowded. It was all very confusing. For some reason the entire population seemed in a great hurry. When I got home everyone wanted to know where I had been. 'I got delayed,' I told them, 'The runway had a crack in it.' Apparently it happens all the time. So while they fixed it, I had to disentangle some huskies, pop down an ice cave and go and find bears that weren't there. Oh, and there was a lot of hanging around.

When you do go somewhere extreme, people always want to know what it's like. 'What's there?' They ask. At the North Pole this is tricky. 'Well nothing really,' is the honest answer.

But that is not the point. The North Pole and the whole of the Arctic is probably not so much a geographical location as a state of mind. It is a bizarre, frustrating and ultimately rewarding place. People look at me today and I can see that they still have no idea why I would go to a spot on the earth where there is nothing but ice and stand there for a couple of hours with frozen feet until it is time to go home.

They just don't get it. In the end it is all about getting there. The important thing is that you just had to wait for it.

A number of private operators take tourists on flights to the North Pole and arrange skiing expeditions, from the USA and Canada, Europe and Russia, through Longyearbyen, Svalbard and Barneo ice base. In 2016, following military exercises by Chechen paratroopers on Barneo, Norway enacted a flight embargo which it later lifted. Barneo was open in 2018 but with a shortened season as the result of a problem with sea ice. At the time of going to press, bookings were being taken for the 2019 season. The North Pole can also be reached by ice breaker.

Association of Arctic Expedition Cruise Operators, (AECO): www.aeco.no

Suggested reading

Lonely Planet. 1999. **The Arctic**. *Lonely Planet Publications Pty Ltd, Australia.*

Officer, Charles and Page, Jake. 2012, (second edition). **A Fabulous Kingdom, The Exploration of the Arctic.** *Oxford University Press, Oxford.*

Bomann-Larsen, Tor. 1995**. *Roald Amundsen***. History Press UK edition 2011, UK.

III

Toffs on Ice: The Cresta Run St Moritz

The Cresta is like a beautiful woman... to love her once is to love her always.
A Cresta rider

SIMPLY TERRIFIED

There can be few, if any, 'fun' activities that start with breakfast and a 'Death Talk'. But the Cresta Run is one of them.

Located in the exclusive resort of St Moritz, high up in the majestic Graubunden section of alpine Switzerland, it is probably the most famous, if not to say notorious ice toboggan track in the world, a place where bones are broken and blood spilt. It is not a spot for the faint hearted.

And yet here I am, all kitted up and about to enter the ice arena. And I am not alone. Today there are about twenty of us who have turned up just for the chance of joining this elite group of sportsmen who find comradeship in risking their necks. We wait with some trepidation for our turn in the snug clubhouse bar overlooking the track, all dressed up like modern day gladiators in rake riveted boots, knee and elbow pads, thick gloves with metal hand guards and a helmet of 'approved design' provided by the tobogganing club. While everyone else is sporting white functional head gear, for some reason my helmet is a striking red with a pretty pattern on it. I don't ask why and I never intend to; we have each been given a copy of a slim red book, (1991 edition), entitled *Hints to beginners on the Cresta*. I open mine with trembling fingers. One of the first things it tells me is not to read it.

The guardians of this hallowed place of sliding and authors of this piece of advice are the members of the St Moritz Tobogganing Club, or SMTC for short, a quintessentially British institution which takes daredevil eccentricity to a new level. This is after all the birthplace of the Skeleton, that seemingly suicidal winter sport which involves riders sliding down a frozen track headfirst, belly down, at speeds in excess of eighty miles per hour, all on a sled not much bigger than a large tea tray. Suffice to say, they invented it.

Surprisingly they let anyone have a go. In fact six hundred Swiss Francs is enough to buy you three bites of the ice to see how well you like it. If you find you have a certain talent you may well become a member of the club one day, but don't count on it. To become a Cresta rider requires a certain something, athleticism coupled with raw physical courage for sure, but you also need to be, 'Their sort of chap.' It helps if you are barking mad.

In terms of courage, on the day that I report at 7.30am sharp for my slide, (a particularly freezing and sombre January morning, at least inside my head), I have pretty much lost most of it already. It is one thing to contemplate

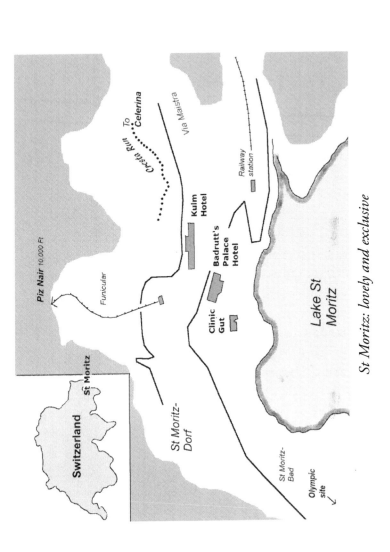

St Moritz: lovely and exclusive

the thrill and kudos of being an ice devil from the comfort of your home in England, quite another to be faced with the cold and hard reality. Up close the run is a horrifying lick of frictionless terror over a kilometre long, tumbling down a natural mountain ravine and dropping over five hundred feet in the process- the equivalent of a fifty storey building. Its ten banked twists and rolling turns are designed to whip the sled around and even spit the rider out if their technique is found wanting. Braking isn't much of an option: by the time you are halfway down you will be going faster than the local train service as it flashes above your head on an insanely suspended railway bridge that cuts across the scoop of the ice. In the final stretch you will probably be pulling the sort of G's that are usually the preserve of Formula One drivers or astronauts. One thing is certain: The Cresta is still the fastest method of transport between the town of St Moritz and the pretty village of Celerina down the valley. If you make it that far your one remaining problem is stopping; apparently there are some mats for that.

There is no getting away from it: it *is* dangerous. Oh, the stories!: a rider once flew so high off the run that he struck his head on a concrete bridge designed for spectators. There have been more than a couple of incidents involving finishing: in 1999 Anthony Freeland, a British Cresta veteran, was going so fast that he became the first rider to jump the snow banked buffers at the end of the course and ended up in a car park. A few years later another rider outdid him when he took out an entire vehicle together with a couple of bystanders in a similar show of exuberance. There is a famous manoeuvre that is named after the two competitors who performed it in successive years: the 'Shipton- Stoker'.

It involves misjudging a vital bend and crashing head first into the ice wall opposite. No doubt that sort of thing hurts.

There have been plenty of cases of broken skulls. In the early days of forgoing helmets it was even worse. There is a favourite tale by some of the club members about one chap who disappeared after a fall only to be found later that afternoon in a bar in some adjacent village, enquiring what time his ride was due. Concussion for Cresta riders is an occupational hazard.

Mercifully, deaths are rare on the track: five *(only!)*, since the Cresta began in 1885, but splintered bones are fairly common. So too are the pinched or detached fingers that can come as a result of their being trapped underneath the toboggan or between it and the walls of the run.

In particular, beginners are given tips about jewellery and its lack of place here: 'Gentlemen, please remove all watches and rings; in event of an accident these might have to be cut off, and a hand or finger with them.' These are the actual words we will hear in the course of our instruction.

Even worse than a pinched finger is the 'Cresta Kiss', a condition that results from the intimacy that being head down only a couple of inches away from the ice can bring. In those circumstances it is literally possible for you to lose said face.

But to veteran Cresta riders these are trifles. When things go seriously wrong, they do so horribly. The last incident of note involved captain Bernie Bambury, who in 2008 hit a marker post with his foot at eighty miles per hour. According to reports, still high on adrenalin at the finish, he asked a friend, 'Is my ankle broken?' before being told, 'No, it's gone.'

In the event the Captain's lower right leg was retrieved

further up the course and surgeons were able to re-attach it. Later when told he would never recover full mobility he requested an amputation.

Such stories only enhance the Cresta's reputation for danger and daring-do and no doubt makes some people even more eager to sign up. There is certainly no shortage of them wanting to give it a try. I wonder if the book of 'Helpful' hints can provide some comfort; in the event, possibly not.

The first thing it says is that, 'It is very important to clear your head of any information previously given to you,' and continues: 'It is also important that you stop reading this book at the end of this introduction. After two rides continue reading and learning.'

I take a sneak preview anyway. What it tells me next is that, 'Tobogganing is a dangerous sport,' which is not very encouraging. It then goes on to give fairly redundant advice on steering and breaking, (there are no steering and breaking mechanisms on a Cresta sled), what to do when you fall and a detached forty kilogram sled is coming after you, ('If it should overtake you it will in all likelihood injure you,'), and counsels that to ride well takes time and study. Any short cut, it says will lead to the hospital. Finally, it signs off cheerily, 'Above all we hope you are having fun.'

Fun! Outdoors it is another beautiful day in the Engadin valley, a lovely Swiss snowscape on which fresh beetling flakes are falling. Children are playing in the snow, adults enjoying the scene. I want to join them. Here inside the mood is more sombre. And it is about to get even more serious. Enter the Colonel.

In the early years of the new millennium, at the time of my visit, the job of welcoming the suicidal or just plain crazy to the run fell to Lieutenant Colonel Digby Willoughby, MC, MBE, veteran of the Gurkha rifles and secretary of the SMTC. According to Michael DiGiacomo, Cresta rider and author of *Apparently Unharmed*, (probably one of the most authoritative works on the institution to date), Digby's pep talk was the closest thing a civilian will ever get to a military briefing. That, I can verify.

Now sadly deceased, but for twenty four years a mainstay of the Club, the Lieutenant Colonel had a way of doing things that we might call anachronistic in our modern world, a charge that some may still lay at the door of the club that he nurtured and protected for so long. Eschewing anything as vulgar as electronic devices apart from a public address system through which he regularly barked out instructions to riders on the ice, Digby ruled the track from his lair on the top of a tall boxy building half way down the run known as the 'Tower' from which vantage point he could see all the goings on. He did it the old fashioned way, by dint of pencil and paper and force of personality.

The lieutenant Colonel was fiercely protective of his ice from the unwonted attentions of spectators, regularly admonishing the parents of wandering children to restrain their offspring, 'As I don't want your child to fall into the run where he may hurt one of my riders.' By today's standards he may have been guilty of a somewhat parochial attitude to women, telling those who perched too near the edge, 'Madam, please remove your bottom from the Cresta Run. We all like it very much, but not on the side of the track.'

The riders themselves had specific instructions on what to do if they came off the course. They were to stand up immediately so that he could see that neither of their legs were broken and wave their arms in the air to show that those limbs too were still attached and would be able to tug the toboggan out of the way. At this point Digby would likely start to lose interest and feel the rider was just, 'Wasting our time down there.' Anything short of death or critical injury would elicit a fairly languorous statement over the loudspeaker that so- and- so was, 'Up and apparently unharmed.'

But what Digby really became famous for was his initial chat to those ingénues who were waiting nervously for their very first experience of the run. A seasoned Cresta rider himself with numerous spills under his belt, at some point he would rather alarmingly tell his audience that the only reason his head stayed on was because of the two metal pins holding it in place and that he had the X-rays to prove it. Not for nothing did his introductory briefing become known as the 'Death Talk'.

When Digby comes into the room, our backs automatically stiffen to attention. The Colonel has an air of quiet authority, as befits a man who holds the Military Cross and whose exploits include once saving a former Sultan of Brunei from the mob surrounding his palace during an insurgency, all with a handful of Gurkha soldiers. He doesn't have to raise his voice but should he need to tick you off in front of the others, you get the feeling that it would not be a pleasant experience.

We sit in tense anticipation, in neat rows facing him like fighter pilots ready to learn our mission. The cosy little clubhouse with its bottom sinking easy chairs and slightly boozy conviviality now takes on a harder edge, almost like a military command post. The body language says it all: we are literally on the edge of our seats, hanging on his every word. There is a hush in the room, a deadly serious sense of concentration.

Except that is not entirely true. Rather shockingly one of us at least appears to find the whole thing amusing. A young chap in the front row slouches in his seat. He has a smile on his face and is happily chuckling to himself. Occasionally he takes a bite from a pastry and a sip of coffee. He looks totally unconcerned about the fact that he is about to take a toboggan ride into oblivion. Here is a man who in the face of possible injury or even death has found time for breakfast. Not only that but he is eating it with obvious enjoyment. Clearly, he has lost his mind.

Digby, who no doubt has seen all manner of men from the thoughtful coward to the idiotically brave, ignores him and starts his talk by laying down some ground rules: among other things he tells us that should we come out of the run we must throw away the toboggan. There is after all no point in hoping for a soft landing in the piled straw and snow on the banks of the run if the sled hits you on the head.

There are other procedures to follow: when you're name is called over the loudhailer you must raise one hand in the air so he knows you have heard him and are ready for your ride. When the run is clear you will hear a single bell being rung, (a ship's being kept for this purpose). Three bells mean that the previous rider has fallen. Should *you* fall you are to wave with both arms at the tower to show that you are in one piece.

After telling us about the chopping off of fingers and hands, he outlines what happens at the end of the run: 'When you finish you are to remain on your sled until it is retrieved by a meat hook,' (after all letting it slip back down the run is impolite; besides, it will likely kill the next rider coming up behind). Errant laces can be lethal, so we must tie them around the top of our boots. 'You will remember that from your days of rugby football.' (I have no idea what he is talking about).

If this wasn't bad enough, what follows is even worse. It is time for 'The Skeleton' to arrive.

The 'Skeleton' is actually a paste up job of genius, a montage in X-ray of every conceivable injury that has befallen a Cresta rider in the past, put back together in the form of a whole and life size but rather unwell human being.

The most worrying thing is the amount of metal involved. There are enormous pins holding together broken femurs and a profusion of smaller ones stabbing into shattered wrists, broken ankles and busted shoulders. For good measure a ruptured kidney makes its appearance together with the metal bracing that keeps Digby's neck intact. These are all actual X-rays of Cresta riders. Amazingly we are told that most are still at the club and walking around. You could even shake their hands, albeit carefully.

The doll is a gift from a local surgeon, possibly working at the appropriately named 'Clinic Gut', which is handily close to the run and where the staff are wearily expert at sewing and pinning together bits of Cresta riders. This is the place that you go to after a spill. Not only does the clinic provide an elite standard of medical care but it also fits in perfectly with the exclusive St Moritz lifestyle. It is said that when a patient buzzes a nurse for glasses the orderlies know it is not always water that will fill them; most of the time they return with champagne flutes.

Digby obviously has a soft spot for the skeleton and it is centre stage for much of the proceedings. The chap likes it too. 'Haw, haw, haw,' he goes with delight, its splintered cartilage and mushy insides burst like ripe fruit obviously tickling his own funny bones.

In fact throughout the Colonel's briefing he has met every new horrifying statement with increasing mirth. By the time the paste up of human wreckage arrives, he is positively honking away in a shower of pastry crumbs. He is, I tell myself, either genuinely one of the bravest men you are likely to meet or perhaps just a complete moron.

While it is unfair to say that the St Moritz Tobogganing Club attracts such individuals, it definitely embraces the eccentric and plain odd. It is also undeniably posh. Michael DiGiacomo, a veteran rider and someone with obvious affection for the institution admits that, 'While the Cresta is open to anyone, and farmers to hairdressers to grocers ride the run, the Cresta has a significant quotient of public school Englishmen, affluent Americans and preppy Swiss.'

That may be understating it. The list of presidents of the club, past and present, reads like an extract from *Who's Who* or *Debretts*. Of the twenty individual presidents since the club's inception in 1885, no less than six have been peers of the realm, (including a couple of Viscounts and more than one Baron), and three have had the rank of Knight. Stir in an Air Vice Marshall, a major and a captain and you have an institution with a uniquely British upper crust and military flavour.

Many of the incumbents of this position have been colourful characters. They have ranged from the hated autocrat, (one Hon. Francis Curzon who failed to be re-elected even though there was no other candidate), to the popular and legendary John Theodore Cuthbert Moore-Brabazon, First Baron Brabazon of Tara. By any standard he had an eventful life. During the Second World War he served in Churchill's cabinet. He was the first to hold a private pilot's licence in the UK, and also raced cars before taking up the Cresta, breaking many records along the way. He was still riding at the age of seventy nine, just one year before he died.

The preponderance of Lords and military brass should not be surprising. After all, the club was born in the late nineteenth century out of the boredom of the British aristocracy and its empire's army men, at a loose end between whatever colonial wars were happening at that time. Together they adopted St Moritz as their personal playground. Since no one had yet invented skiing, they had to look for other entertainment and soon hit upon the idea of hijacking the locals' wooden sleds or 'Schlitten' and adapting them for hair raising chases through the narrow winding roads of the old town. Alarmed at the mayhem that ensued, the local authorities forced the tourists to build a proper racing track and form their own club with actual rules. The rest as they say is history and no doubt as far as the SMTC is concerned you can like it or lump it. Exclusive it was then and that's how it has remained. It perpetuates its exclusivity as succeeding generations of schoolboys at Eton, Harrow and other public schools are encouraged to take up the sport and are initiated into the society that surrounds it courtesy of the old boys periodically revisiting their Alma mater with the objective of recruiting a fresh band of do or die volunteers.

The 'chap' may be a case in point, although perhaps the worst case you can think of. But there is an undoubted arrogance about him, born, unless it is just prejudice on my part, to be 'superior' to the rest of us. He certainly looks out with a supercilious expression at the fear in the room.

Still, the club itself would undoubtedly argue that any charges of elitism are unfair. After all it is open to anyone to join as long as they have the right stuff. One of the greatest Cresta riders of all time was a local man who ran a store in the town. Dubbed, 'The flying greengrocer', Nino Bibbia won more races on the run than anyone else and an Olympic gold medal to boot. And today, as the Club likes to point out, all sorts of people ride: accountants, lawyers, bus drivers and presumably hairdressers too.

There is however no getting away from the rarefied ethos of the place. There can be few clubs whose members have at times included a Liechtenstein Prince, a white Russian Cossack and a NATO general secretary. During the cold war between the west and the Soviet Union, American generals and their Warsaw Pact counterparts regularly raced each other on toboggans down the track, such competition at least being preferable to nuclear armageddon.

All of this is overseen by the British in their own idiosyncratic way. When I contacted the club about coming here for a slide, the lady who answered was in fact a bona fide real lady, Harriet Frances Hamilton, daughter of Mervyn Peter de Courcy Hamilton and wife of the Third Baron Brabazon of Tara. Harriet, (if I may be presumptuous and call her that, since that's how as membership secretary she signs off), has been lovely and both patient and diligent in answering all my queries. Back in the UK, I liked to think of her twirling her pearls with one hand and clacking at the keyboard with the other as she responded to whatever nonsense I whisked her way through cyber space. (Sometimes these weird fantasies get the better of me).

Oh the glamour of rubbing shoulders with the upper echelons of society! There is a certain frisson about it.

Undoubtedly the Cresta fits right in with St Moritz and its sporty jet-set image. Many luminaries have been down this run, from American presidents including John F Kennedy, to movie stars like the legendary heart-throb Errol Flynn who supposedly posted the slowest time ever because, the story goes, he stopped along the way to charm some pretty ladies.

Even James bond has been down the Cresta: In *On her Majesty's Secret Service* for example, Ian Fleming tells us that the normally unruffled 007 finds it a jittery experience:

> *"Bond had once gone down the Cresta from 'top' to prove he dared. Helmeted, masked against the blast of air, padded with leather and foam rubber, that had still been sixty seconds of naked fear. Even now he could remember how his limbs had shaken when he rose stiffly from the flimsy little skeleton bob at the end of the run-out."*

The fact is that the Cresta is quite unlike any other sporting institution, undoubtedly anachronistic in the modern world. For one thing it is fiercely protective of its amateur status. Although a number of riders have gone on to win medals in world Bobsleigh and Bob-Skeleton championships, no one rides on the Cresta for money. The Prize winning ceremonies for the annual races, which are held on the outdoor terrace of the opulent Kulm Hotel are not your usual affairs. What the winner usually gets apart from the trophy is a bottle of champagne and a kiss from a 'designated female', together with a bit of camped up theatre. One year, for example, the prize giver, a senior member of the club, came dressed as Count Dracula with a glamorous vampire 'assistant'. Since the trophies had not turned up he substituted them with Barbie dolls. When one of the riders was asked to pick his doll, he promptly put his arm around the 'assistant' and led her away. Another year the trophies were handed out by 'Her Majesty the Queen', a club member in drag with a toy corgi. There is a tradition that the last placed finisher for one cup has to treat the other competitors to as much bratwurst as they can eat. Why? Probably no one knows. They make up the rules. It is not for us to question them.

To be a member of such a club you do need to be the right sort. In the words of the second Lord Brabazon, being interviewed for a Sports magazine in 1975:

> 'If a man's technical qualifications as a rider are equal and no one says he's a bloody bore or another king of bounder, if he's a good drinker and a good bloke, then he'll be in, won't he? There is room for all kinds-we need occasional clowns, you know, to keep it all alive, all going, and one fellow who is not a very good rider but in a very loud way is good fun will be elected quite without trouble....' ('Every man has a mad streak' Sports Illustrated magazine).

Should you want to enter this colourful world of clowns, good blokes and seriously good riders, and are not a cad or bounder, you need to go through the proper procedures. You will find that apart from the paperwork and the mother of all disclaimers to fill in, there is a bridge to cross, quite literally.

This walkway, giddily slung over the track, connects the outside world, (if St Moritz can be called the 'outside world'), with the nerve centre of the Cresta operation, a squat two storey white box with picture windows and a grandstand view. In summer this stub of a building seems oddly stranded on a grassy hill speckled with wild flowers. But in winter it commands the slick of ice that races under its windows. Then it comes into its own. On its front face the words 'Cresta Run' are picked out in giant red letters.

The bridge itself is guarded at one end by swing gates sporting maroon and gold livery with SMTC picked out in white, the letters split in the middle. 'Private club, members only,' it says. To crack open the gates is to enter a unique place, one which is both thrilling and daft in equal measure with its own throwback sensibilities. Once you have passed through, you will find that you have crossed some kind of Rubicon. It is a bit like entering *Narnia*.

On the way over the novice may be lucky and catch a glimpse of a speeding bullet under his feet wrapped in a Lycra stretch suit and hugging a tea tray that in shape is not unlike the kind of toboggan used in the Olympics. It is called a 'Flattop'. Here we are already a third of the way down the run and those veterans who have earned the right to start from what is quaintly called 'Top', have already built up quite an acceleration. Beginners are only allowed to start their run from outside the clubhouse at 'Junction' and are handed a 'Traditional' toboggan to ride on which is of a wholly different type and much slower. It is one thing to like speed but you need to accumulate experience before you are allowed to be suicidal about it.

The journey of the novice starts very much like a first day at school, on the ground floor of the clubhouse where the Cresta changing room is found, at first sight a brutal place of wooden benches and steel mesh lockers with boots and helmets stowed in regimented rows, the battledress of racing suits hung at attention on wall pegs. It is the nightmare of school sports days all over again.

Large bulletin boards are hung up everywhere, offering information you would rather not have. One notice concerns the correct way to remove an injured rider's helmet without paralysing him. Another one deals with ambulances and the need to inform the driver of the clinic of your choice. Perhaps even worse is a schedule of Sunday services at the local Anglican Church.

The locker room walls themselves are adorned with Gods of the Cresta, men like Billy Fiske, who between the world wars dominated the run, posting a sub minute time that stood for almost twenty years. The son of a wealthy Chicago family, William Meade Lindsley Fiske III married an English woman and adopted Britain as his home. When not smashing all Cresta records he could be found competing with the US bobsled team and winning Olympic gold. In his spare time he raced cars. In the Second World War he got fellow Cresta rider Lord Blediscoe to pull strings at the Air Ministry so that he could take part in the Battle of Britain. Shortly after he was shot down and killed. All this happened before his twenty ninth birthday.

There are many others. They seem to look down on you with a critical eye as you fumble with the unfamiliar boots, helmet and knee pads. There is more than a whiff of testosterone about this place- it is in fact a thoroughly masculine preserve. One prominent sign on the wall, its words picked out in bright gold lettering on a plain chocolate background reads: 'SMTC: where women cease from troubling and the wicked are at rest.'

This pretty much sums up the atmosphere of the SMTC. This is a boy's own world without much concession to contemporary social ideas. Looking around at the novices who have turned up today while they listen to Digby and his *Death Talk*, it is impossible not to notice one startlingly obvious fact: I am in exclusively male company. Democratic and inclusive the club may claim to be, it just bans women from riding. (This was not always the case-see *The bare bones of it: a history of Skeleton riding).*

In fact the only female presence I have seen since entering the club house bar, (which has taken on increasingly the aspect of an all boys public school common room), is Harriet. The Lady Brabazon is here in her function not only as the membership secretary but also as a purveyor of ties, another quaint custom of the club that bestows upon those who fail to stay within the bounds of the run and live to tell the tale, a particular piece of neckwear in commemoration of that feat. (The tie features little gold coloured shuttlecocks in honour of the bend where a significant number of people part company with the track-[*more about that later]).*

I am in no hurry to claim a tie, nor am I impatient for the Colonel to wrap up his briefing. In fact I am grateful for anything that might delay the inevitable moment when I have to climb on to my toboggan and launch myself onto the ice. My heart is pounding and my mouth is dry. I have the distinct feeling that whatever illusions I may once have had about my bravery have now disappeared leaving only questions about why this was a good idea in the first place. I am pretty sure that I don't belong here, while the others do-the chap for example. With his obvious sense of arrogant superiority and admirable lack of nerves, I have no doubt that he fits right in. As the colonel's speech draws to a close it is clear that if last night was relatively sleepless and I arrived this morning in a state of anxiety, my fear has since stepped up a gear and now threatens to overwhelm me completely. I am to all intents and purposes, absolutely terrified.

And then amazingly, Digby seems to offer a chance of escape. Should it all get too much and you wish to bail out, he tells us, foregoing any runs remaining to you, there is a telephone outside the clubhouse, a direct line to him. It should be used once and only once for this purpose. To terminate the Cresta run experience you utter a single word: 'Scratch.'

Looking back, that was the one bit of information that really sunk in.

BATH

It is a well known fact that when people are frightened they just don't pay attention to what is going on around them. In fact in extreme cases the brain just freezes over like the surface of an icy pond that is sealing itself off from the rest of the world. They often start stressing on the smaller things while their awareness of the wider world diminishes. From airline pilots to ice skaters, this is not a happy state to be in. Sometimes it is downright dangerous. Psychologists have a term for when the periphery of our consciousness starts to be lost and all that is left is a centre of tumble down panic. People in that state are said to be experiencing 'Tunnel vision'.

My own version of 'Tunnel vision' presently involves being far more interested in my gloves than in anything Digby has to say. The room has receded and I find myself desperately involved with mastering the puzzle of the various straps and buckles I am presented with as if the conquest of my hand wear is the key to dominion over the whole Cresta run. Even worse, once I have triumphed over the technical challenge of fastening my gloves, I am presented with a fresh conundrum: there is no way I can get my helmet on, at least not with the thick sausages that my fingers have inevitably turned into. This is a well known school boy error for any novice attempting the run. There is a strict order of doing things here that no doubt I should have known from my extensive experience in 'Rugby football'. Some of us, I am sure will have no trouble at all.

It may be of dubious comfort to know that while the absolute beginner is undoubtedly prey to first day nerves and all that entails, even veterans of the run are not immune on occasion to feelings of terror, however reluctant they are to make a fuss about it. In *Apparently Unharmed* Michael DiGiacomo recites the story of one Cresta rider waiting to start from 'Top' who after a period of reflection calmly announces to the others that, 'I think I am not going to do this; I'm going back down.' There followed a polite but firm discussion during which his fellow riders were able to persuade him to continue. They no doubt convinced him that if he walked away from the run now he would never come back. And they were right: once you sign up for the Cresta there is no turning back. To do so would just be bad form. In a perverse way it probably takes more courage to remove your helmet, pad and gloves and head for the nearest exit than it does to face the ice.

And so I remain stuck in my chair while the *Death Talk* comes to an end, petrified at the idea of what is about to happen but unable to escape for fear of the shame that such an act of cowardice would bring. One thought does rattle through my addled head: 'I wish I'd thought this through.' That however is a fallacy. You really don't want to think it through. Going down an ice run, like sky diving or standing on the top of a ten metre swimming pool board, is an all or nothing activity. Nothing can quite prepare you for it. You just have to jump in and see what happens.

It is a worrying fact that however many books you read on the Cresta or videos you watch before you turn up, none of this preparation will help you much. The truth is that no one has any idea what it is going to be like until they crouch at the start with their toboggan and face the prospect of freefalling down almost a mile of ice without any brakes. Anything else is pretty academic.

That said, it might help if you actually take the time to get some sledding practice in before you attempt something like this. The question is where? It's fine if you live in a country that sits on a high latitude mountain chain and whose inhabitants are born on skis, but for the populations of places like Dubai and Jamaica it is not so easy. The British Isles are another case in point when it comes to snow based activities: they simply don't have 'proper' mountains or snow. As a result it is impossible to support the natural slides or ski runs that other countries develop on an industrial scale. True, there are now many warehouse sized indoor slopes in the UK that feed our growing skiing habit but they are no substitute for having a Matterhorn in your back yard. In fact until the start of the twenty first century the peak experience for Londoners anxious for home grown powder was the

Beckton Alps, a now defunct and over grown dry ski slope made out of toxic spoil from the local gasworks. Even fully functional and devoid of weeds, it was hardly Courchevel.

And yet there is one place in the British Isles with a facility that matches anything else in the world when it comes to winter sports and which cries out to be visited before you set foot in St Moritz. Forget Lillehammer up in the lofty peaks of Norway, or even the billion dollar run at Lake Placid, USA, where a mile of twists are carved out of the Whiteface Mountain area of New York. These and many other venues may be epic frozen wildernesses with majestic snow cover where the inhabitants are born to play in the stuff but perhaps if you live in the UK you want to stay closer to home. If so you are in luck, of course you are: because there is always Bath.

Bath, In England's West Country, is a lovely city, a historic treasure trove of eighteenth century Georgian squares and crescents dressed in honey coloured stone. These building materials were cut from nearby deposits of limestone laid down during the Jurassic period when the whole area was a shallow tropical sea. The stonework of its neo-classical buildings frequently contains the imprint of shells and the fossils of marine life over two hundred million years old.

The Romans came here in Sixty AD, saw the potential of its geo-thermal springs and covered them with Bath House architecture. In Regency times it became fashionable to take the waters and the town flourished. Jane Austen lived here for a while as the poor but talented relation of rich aristocratic cousins and several of her novels are centred on its social life. Today it is both a world heritage site and a vibrant modern Spa town. Genteel it may be, exclusive it's not.

It is not however the first place that comes to mind when thinking about winter games. Built on the flat floodplain of the River Avon in the rural county of Somerset, (the nearby Cotswold Hills can at maximum stretch only get up to a thousand feet), it is fair to say that it lacks elevation. Then there is the climate: generally it is mild and wet.

And yet the city has been at the centre of an extraordinary renaissance in British winter Olympic sport, an endeavour that has focussed particularly on the Bob Skeleton. From the early days of the twenty first century it would become *the* place to be for those with aspirations in the sliding world.

How did such an unlikely thing happen? The answer is bound up intimately with the history of the St Moritz Tobogganing Club and the way the modern world in some respects left it behind.

The early glory days of sledding were in the years between the first and Second World War, when St Moritz was in many ways its epicentre. The resort hosted both the 1928 and 1948 Winter Olympics and the Cresta track was used for the Skeleton event. On both occasions members of the St Moritz Tobogganing Club took part and won medals; In 1928 David Carnegie, (aka 11th Earl of Northesk), claimed bronze, and in 1948 at the other end of the social scale, 'The world's fastest greengrocer' Nino Bibbia rode to Olympic gold.

But by the 1950's the public were to fall out of love with Skeleton and ironically for those who participated in such a frightening activity that was because it didn't look exciting enough. In the 1950's and 1960's skeleton riders were still using the same 'Traditional' toboggan some eighty years after its invention, (it is the same toboggan that Cresta beginners use today). Revolutionary it may have been back before the turn of the nineteenth century, but Its design was limited by the fact that the rules of skeleton allow no braking mechanisms on the sled and the Cresta course was too narrow. Basically it was just a piece of wood on metal runners with a sliding pad so that the rider could move up and down in order to adjust his speed and try not to crash. In the turbo charged technological era of the late twentieth century it was undoubtedly a bit antiquated and slow.

In 1954 The International Olympic Committee dropped Skeleton entirely from their program and any funding for the sport dried up. It is one of the axioms of sport that success follows funding and funding follows a TV audience. What TV audiences tune in for is spectacle. What spectators really wanted was the thrill of the three people Bob Sleigh on its own broad and fast track: that's what filled the grandstands.

And that might have been it for the activity of tobogganing. It could have been left in relative obscurity for the enjoyment of enthusiasts such as those in the SMTC rather than becoming the worldwide phenomenon it is today with its massive television coverage. In the end the reason for its renewed success had nothing to do with a sudden change of heart by the viewing public or even the efforts of those charismatic sportsmen and women who risked their lives on the track. What finally saved it was quite simply a bunch of 'boffins'.

From the 1970's onwards the fate of a lot of winter sports would increasingly be in the hands of men and women in white coats who knew about such things as aerodynamics and tested stuff out in wind tunnels. What they gradually developed was a sled that could be used on the big bobsleigh runs, (hence the name Bob-Skeleton), where it was not necessary for a rider to come right back to reduce speed, thereby doing away with the sliding cushion. This allowed a design that was a sleek one piece ergonomically crafted piece of kit moulded to the rider's body. It was faster and more manoeuvrable. More importantly it looked sexy. Cresta riders adopted this and created their own version: the 'Flattop'. It smashed all previous records.

This design was further refined in the 1980's and 1990's. The economic advantages of being able to use the Bobsleigh runs for more than one sport became obvious. Improved tracks were built. More countries joined in, enough to start up a world cup competition. TV followed and it drew a following. With this higher profile came the 'big bucks'. The icing on the funding cake arrived in 1999 when Bob-Skeleton was included once again in the Olympic Games programme for Salt Lake City in 2002, (for the first time in over fifty years). Then the money really started rolling in. The whole business of sliding was back.

The promise of Olympic glory spurred on ever more intensive research. Academics in fields as diverse as fluid dynamics and computer modelling suddenly became interested in how they might apply their knowledge to someone essentially bowling down a hill for a lark, although that hardly describes it at a professional level. They started to write PhD's about it. One of the most influential push starts to the sport would come from Kristan Bromley, a British engineering graduate from Nottingham University who specialised in Mechanical Design. In 1999 after becoming involved in the sport he wrote a thesis titled *Factors Affecting the Performance of Skeleton Bobsleigh*. He then built a sled that was so successful that he rode on it himself and won the world cup twice. The press gave him the nickname *Dr Ice*.

All of which goes to prove that when it comes to achievement in winter sports in the modern world, it is not really mountains or snow that matter: what you really need is science. And for that you need a centre of research like a university. It also helps if a generous dollop of lottery funding comes your way to build a cutting edge sports complex. That's what happened at Bath.

At the start of the new millennium however, much of this development and with it Britain's Olympic success, still lay in the future. In those days anyone who had a passing interest in the sport or even the idea of sliding down the Cresta Run on a whim, inevitably found themselves struggling to find anything in the UK that would help them prepare for it. There was a British Bob- Skeleton Association, but it is quite possible that at that time their entire membership could have fitted on one toboggan. For some reason they all seemed to be located on the south coast. This was beautiful for sailing but for skeleton not so much. They hadn't yet begun to win many medals.

In the summer of 2002 it was fair to say that things had yet to get off the ground; it was still a question of seeking out any enthusiast you could find and pestering them for advice. I started by e-mailing a random group of tobogganists. 'I am considering trying the Cresta run as a novice next year,' I told them, 'Have you any recommendations as to clothing and more importantly any padding that will reduce the risk of injury? Is any training in this sport available for novices?' I added hopefully.

One reply I got seemed to indicate that there was an ice run up in the Welsh mountains but this turned out to be a chilly mirage or perhaps a case of shovelling a bit of snow and putting down jumpers. This country just didn't seem yet equipped with anything like a proper Skeleton run.

But that was not entirely true. There was a track and it was at Bath University, a brand new one hundred and forty metre long contraption that was not actually made of ice but of concrete. It had grooves in it on which a tray could run on wheels and a bungee system at the bottom to catch your sled and wind it back up elastically to the top. If that sounded a bit 'Heath Robinson' that was about as realistic as it got but it is after all what the British Olympic Bobsleigh and Skeleton team still train on today for their push starts and provides some semblance of the experience of riding on top of a sled as it whizzes along, at a not inconsiderable forty miles per hour, albeit down the slope of a grassy hill in an English rural idyll.

Amazingly they were prepared to let anyone on it. There was however a good reason for this. With all the science and funding in the world, what sport can't dispense with is the athletes themselves. Like formula 1 racing it is no good having all that kit without a driver at the wheel; Team GB needed an Olympic team, and in many ways they were starting from scratch. They needed to identify an unknown pool of talent somewhere out there in the UK, and so they cast their net wide. They invited everyone to have a go. They even invited me.

'Thank you for your interest in Skeleton,' they said, 'The BBSKA is hoping to run talent identification trial days in the middle of July, which would give novices an opportunity to see if they are suited to the sport. We will contact you with details of these dates when we know what they are.'

In July they wrote to me again: 'Thank you once again

for the interest you have shown in Skeleton. We will be holding a trial day on Friday 9th August at Bath University, when you will have the opportunity to come along and find out more about the sport and see how suited you are to it. There will be physical testing, followed by push start trials. At this stage we are trying to get an idea of the number of people who will attend so please reply to let us know if you are coming.'

Who could say no? Besides, a day out at Bath sounded a pleasant way to spend some time. There would be Roman Baths to visit along with the Jane Austen centre, perhaps even a Regency cream tea to enjoy. The bit about, 'physical testing,' and 'push start trials,' seemed to escape my mind. Consequently I turned up at what was probably the very first audition for the modern British Olympic bob skeleton team with a rather naive understanding of what was involved and its importance for the future of the sport. I certainly overlooked the bit about, 'talent identification.' No doubt about that.

That day in August an awful lot of people turned up for their chance at sledding superstardom, crowding out the centre of the complex of buildings that was Bath University. The university itself didn't look anything like the historic honey stoned town nearby, being born out of an explosion of higher education building in the 1960's that aimed to transform the opportunity of a significant number of young adults to access the kind of further learning which until then had been the preserve of an elite. Like many other establishments it was built in the contemporary style of sixties architecture out of concrete, glass and steel, giving it a utilitarian look. It was not so much 'Dreaming spires' or

'Red Brick' as quite simply, functional and down to earth 'Plate glass'.

At the centre of the campus at Bath was the 'Main Parade', a concrete piazza surrounded by high rise blocks which housed the library, administrative buildings and various cafes. It was here that we were invited to congregate at 9.50am sharp, outside 'Strollers', a sandwich bar next to the glass box of the 'Learning centre'. The path to world sporting domination has to commence somewhere and for all those who turned up that morning, it was outside a shop selling cheese 'toasties' and cut priced bacon lettuce and tomato baguettes.

What this diverse assembly from all corners of the United Kingdom appeared to have in common was a worryingly healthy vitality that came with regular attendance at the local municipal sports centre or playing fields. I was the possible exception. They arrived with gym bags and sweat pants: It looked like they were used to a serious work out. In addition they all seemed to be quite young, much younger than I was. About a half of those who had turned up were women. Unlike the SMTC, the British Olympic authorities did not seem to entertain the notion that your gender mattered when it came to riding a board on your stomach down an ice chute. This would undoubtedly prove to be a good thing once it became clear that the women were often better riders than the men.

After a while milling around 'Strollers' we were shepherded into one of the concrete boxes that ringed the parade. This proved to be a lecture theatre where we were given an introductory talk and then shown a film. This demonstrated what would happen if the most 'talent identified' amongst us spent the next few years practicing without respite. Such a future would involve a lot of spandex and possibly some broken bones. Eventually if we were good enough we would sweep round corners and shoot down straights at a hundred kilometres an hour like sleek stealth bombers in speed suits. (Or at least that is how it looked in the movie).

There were without doubt many interesting things to discover about the attributes of a successful Bob Skeleton rider: It helped for example if you had a thick neck. In fact the forces on the bodies of Skeleton riders are such that the maximum training runs they are usually able to endure in a day may be no more than three. This is because every time they go down the slide it can feel like the equivalent of being headlocked by some professional wrestler trying to tear your head off. A background in track or field sports was also helpful, (many Bob Skeleton riders are ex-sprinters), so that you have enough power at the start and the stamina to make it down to the bottom. You needed to be the sort of person who would be the last to leave the gym and loved doing those reps: muscle strength is all important. And it was a bonus if you liked cottage cheese. In matters of food, as for every athlete in training, there was a strict dietary regime to adhere to in order to get the right intake of those carbs and proteins. Apart from curds, this was likely to include a lot of stuff like egg whites, oatmeal, and smoothies made of such things as kale and blueberries. Burgers with extra fries and fat shakes were unlikely to feature in the daily diet of an Olympic hopeful, otherwise you just wouldn't be able to squeeze into that speed suit.

In fact to be a successful bob skeleton rider seemed to require an awful lot of will power, perseverance and dedication. There would be a long period of serious training.

You couldn't just turn up for a couple of slides and then go to the bar. Not if you wanted something more than a plastic Barbie doll to take home with you.

This after all was a full time job, not a hobby. For some Olympic wannabes it might prove to be all too much: there was a danger in all this professional seriousness. It could actually cease to be 'fun'.

And then the lights came on and we were invited outside. There it was announced that we would be split into smaller groups and required to run our little socks off.

To be a really good skeleton rider you do need leg power: the stronger the better. After all there is no point in being able to ride with sublime skill if you haven't got the strength to make an explosive start and gather enough speed to propel yourself down the track; otherwise the race is all over before it has even begun, (In fact it is estimated that for every mile per hour you make in the run up, you gain three times as much on the track.). Equally important is remembering to hold on to the sled before you climb aboard; It is no good watching it go down all by itself: that, by anyone's definition is missing the bus. And it is more difficult than it looks, involving as it does sprinting with the toboggan while holding on with one hand and then clambering on to it. Some of us would discover how tricky that was when we finally arrived at the concrete and bungee push start track. After all, that is what it was there for, to iron out those little problems.

And so we emerged blinking in the sunlight and trudged past 'Strollers' again, back along the 'Main Parade', and among the buildings housing the developing 'Sports Complex' and emergent 'Sports Science laboratories', until we finally arrived at the athletics track of Bath University.

There on its brick red oval some official looking people were hanging around with stopwatches, clipboards and some cutting edge timing paraphernalia that involved laser beams linked to digital clocks. They stood about fifty metres down the straight and exhorted us to, 'Let rip.'

Some people love running but for others, let's face it: it really sucks. That tedious pounding of some running circle or suburban pavement just to clock up the miles, just to get better at putting one foot in front of the other-is it worth it? Even running enthusiasts seem to acknowledge that this can be a bit of a grind. One particular motivational post online starts: 'Just because I do track doesn't mean I love to run. Running sucks!' But there are reasons why people put themselves through all this tedium. The same motivational message goes on: 'I love winning tho'. I love competing....I love medals.' That may give some clue as to the mentality of those who are successful in any sport. Some of them were undoubtedly there on that day at Bath. They included club runners who had been exploding out of the blocks since they were teenagers, while others were team sports players or army fitness personnel. They thundered between the crisp white markings of lane one, leaving behind a considerable pile of discarded kit bags and unzipped track suits behind them, hardly breaking sweat.

I probably hadn't been made to run that hard since I was at school and that had been a very long time ago. I did have a hazy recollection of a school sports field and a running track in my youth which I trod when no one else was around, but that had been a long time ago, in the era before digital clocks and laser beams. Those were the days in which PE teachers wore nylon tracksuits and had a whistle on a string around their necks and when the running circle was picked out in the grass of a school sports field in white paint, periodically refreshed by an ancient caretaker using a squeaky wheeled contraption that was topped up with what looked like half a pint of emulsion. There were no iPads or smart phones in that world. Everything was pretty low tech and not that well organised, amateurish even. But at least it gave me the chance to become acquainted with the running thing. Courtesy of a bout of childhood asthma I was let off team sports like football and rugby and to be honest that was a relief. When it came to physical education I was pretty much left to my own devices. Mostly I just went round in circles.

Strangely I did find a certain enjoyment in running. There is after all something liberating about going full pelt and not caring. The desire for speed was no doubt ingrained into us from primeval times when we found it particularly useful while we being chased by such things as sabre toothed tigers. Today there are no tigers chasing us but they have been replaced by a psychological equivalent: the fear of being overtaken and losing your place, of coming second, or even horror of horrors last.

There was no doubt that this was a serious competition. For those with aspirations towards a sporting career flying on their stomachs, the trials at Bath on that day would decide whether they would go to Lillehammer and a real ice track. There they would have the opportunity to join a novice training programme for the Bob-Skeleton and perhaps even the Olympic team. Those who didn't make the grade would just have to go home and get on with their lives.

I didn't want to disgrace myself. I bowled down lane one, fairly spanked the track. It seemed to take an awfully long time before I reached the officials in the distance, finally tearing past them with a lung busting finish. There was the scratching of pens on clipboards and the testing of equipment. They looked at me in a non committal fashion, but not I like to think with pity. Meanwhile the real runners flew past me. 'I love pushing myself to the limit...I love feeling fast...I love my team.' No doubt that was what they were telling themselves.

At the push start facility a track suited official was waiting for us. In a request that would later become familiar he asked us to, 'remove any change in your pockets and take off any watches or other jewellery you might be wearing,' presumably on the basis that a scattering of possessions along the way would not only hold up matters but quite likely gum up the works. It would also look rather unprofessional; that sort of thing did not happen at the Winter Olympics. At least there was no mention of cutting off fingers.

the push-start track was a black topped concrete strip carved out of a hill nearby, bordered by the kind of shrubbery that might or might not afford a soft landing if you happened to exit early by making your run too realistic. There we were divided into teams and awaited our turn to have a ride.

It was an odd contraption that faced us, a rollercoaster ride the length of a football pitch with parallel groves in its surface into which a flat board on wheels fitted and ran at a lick along its length. After the initial straight at the top it descended sharply then climbed again in the distance before ending in a crash barrier just before the tree belt beyond. I wondered if anyone had actually got that far to see if it worked.

'I want you to lay on the sled like this,' the official told us and proceeded to place his stomach on the tray with his arms by his sides gripping the hand holds, knees bent and feet up in the air with his head raised so that there was just a touch of the circus seal about his posture. 'I will give you a push and you can go down the run so that you can get used to it. Then we can try running with the sled.'

Going down the push start track at Bath for the first time was an undeniably strange experience, a bit like being a marble rolled down a hill. You have no say in the matter; your job is to hang on as the concrete surface slips beneath your nose and then accelerates as gravity takes a hold. At the top you can just see the flat checkerboard fields of the English countryside in the distance before you dive down to the bottom and then shoot back up the other side. Just as you think you are going too fast to stop, the invisible hand of a bungee cord seizes the sled and brings you abruptly to a halt. Even stranger, you then find yourself going backwards and defying gravity as you are wound all the way up to the top again. Once there, back where you started, you simply climb off the tray.

'Let's try that again,' the guy with the clipboard told us, 'But this time run with it.' The point of the track after all, which has since been upgraded and is probably the best facility of its kind in the world, is to practice the running starts that are vital to winning the skeleton, and to get the speed you need going down a real ice run. But it doesn't aim to provide anything more than that. Once you have climbed aboard the sled you are a passenger so just enjoy the ride. There is no experience of steering and slipping and sliding like on a real ice run. It is all over in the first few strides and if you are sloppy you will have a poor time and then have to wait while you are unceremoniously reeled back like a fish on a line.

One of the most difficult things in the start is using one

hand to push off with. At some point you have to get on the sled and that involves transferring that hand over to the grip on the other side. You need to be using the right technique for your hips and legs in order to pick up speed even as you are thinking about getting on board. It can be tricky and the sled can get away from you. 'If you feel it get in front of you just let it go,' is the usual advice. Being dragged along by a tray doing forty miles an hour on a hard surface is something best avoided.

All of this is made even more difficult by being watched and having your performance graded. At any one time there were a number of legs in the air, including mine, all attached to bodies which were loosely hanging on to the sled on wheels as it careered away into the distance. That is not to say that some of our group weren't good, in fact there was a lot of Lycra clad athleticism and quick limbed coordination on display. But for others like me it was more a case of our own version of aerial 'Twister.'

We repeated everything a number of times while we were marked on the speed of our runs and notes were made on our tangle of arms and legs. Occasionally when someone did something particularly spectacular with those parts of their anatomy, the pens of our examiners worked overtime.

About three O'clock in the afternoon it was all over. So ended the first trial day at Bath. We trouped back through the 'Training Village' which even then was pretty high tech. Today it includes facilities such as, "A high-performance gym, hydrotherapy pool and 'Sports science lab', where 'The Human Performance Centre' offers a full range of tests, including muscle mass and body fat tests, as well as VO2 max tests to identify the athlete's optimum heart rate training zones." *(I have no idea what this means).* There is more stuff: as part of the intensive coaching scheme, computer programs are on hand to monitor skeleton athletes' performance with a, 'Frame by frame video analysis of their runs,' overlaid with their competitors. A team of dedicated medical staff are on hand to ease the aches and attend to their sprains. At the end of a hard day's training there is a delicious purpose made 'ice bath' for them to plunge into.

All this science and resource is enough to make your head spin. What is certain is that this is no 'amateur' organisation in the broadest sense of the word: professional and top flight sport is in fact a big and costly multi faceted operation, with a whole army of white coated lab assistants, scientists and coaching staff all providing the back up to develop the potential of the elite athlete and train the absolute beginner.

A few weeks after my visit to the West Country I received an e-mail from the British Bob Skeleton Association: ' Thank you for coming along to the trials and I hope you had an enjoyable and worthwhile day. We have been going through the results of the testing and pushing, and have selected a group to go to the novice course in Lillehammer. As promised, we advise below those who have been selected...'

Suffice to say my name was not on the list. True to its egalitarian principles and belief in meritocracy, Team Bath and the university had truly selected those worthy of talent identification. Here it didn't matter how well connected you were or even if you were a good chap: what mattered was your raw ability. No one cared who you were; they were just interested in your times. Mine weren't quite up to scratch.

But if it was any consolation, I was up against some stiff competition. The little group I was in on that trial day in August 2002 which ran and pushed so hard included both Amy Williams and Shelley Rudman. Eight years later Amy

Williams would become the first British athlete to win a gold medal in an individual event in the Winter Games for thirty years when she came first in the bob skeleton. Shelley Rudman would go on to become a Skeleton world cup and European cup winner as well as a silver medallist in the 2006 Winter Olympics.

Today whenever the subject comes up I like to say that I once tried out for the UK Olympic Bob-Skeleton team and only failed to make the first stage because the future Olympic champion slid in front of me. Technically this is true. Strangely though, no one seems to believe me.

So what was there to learn from Bath? The truth was almost nothing that would be of practical use to me later. Unless you were a serious athlete it was simply a nice day out. The principle remains that concrete is not the same as ice and there is no bungee cord on the Cresta run.

Not a single thing can really prepare you for what might happen at the Cresta : that is a fact. And if you want to prove it read all the books you like and then chuck them in the bin. None of them will help you.

But oh the lure of the place! The call of the ice is so seductive. And so is its rich glitzy Mecca St Moritz, an adventure capital where the excitement of mingling with the wealthy elite never becomes tiresome. Bath is fine with its Royal Crescent, tea shops and shopping centre but what about St Moritz with its golden sunshine, crisp powder and head in the clouds sensibility. Who wouldn't want to go there? Who wouldn't love it? I couldn't wait.

ST MORITZ

God, St Moritz is an awful place. There, I have said it. Billed as, 'The top of the world,' by its tourist agency, (a place of, 'Style, elegance and class.'), it is to my mind just a ghetto for very wealthy people. It is so exclusive practically no one can stay here unless they can fund the kind of lifestyle that lets them park their private jet down the road at what is naturally the highest airport in Europe. Real estate can change hands for the equivalent of 30,000 Euros for the size of a telephone box. This is a place of caviar and champagne, of high level polo tournaments where the spectators chug up to 1,400 bottles of Perrier-Jouët. In summer you can sail your yacht on the crystal waters of Lake St Moritz while in winter it is solid enough to support several tons of horse flesh in the annual 'White Turf' social events. It is, 'Sporty, chic, luxurious.' It knows how to indulge itself. Those fans of fine dining can look forward to gourmet festivals with programmes that include such things as, 'Celestial wines,' and, 'Illustrious kitchen whispering,' all set to provide, 'An unexpected and intense delightment,' to make, 'Gourmet hearts...beat faster.' If lighting up is your thing there is even a 'Cigar Workshop' which is, '...An occasion for epicures to learn everything worth knowing about the enjoyment...,' of fine smokes. I have come to an extremely rarefied atmosphere.

In fact St Moritz is so exclusive that far from joining the Gourmet nights, I can't actually afford to eat at all. In Bath at least there was a sandwich to be had that didn't cost a fortune. Here I am reduced to 'slumming it' at the one admittedly upmarket Co-op in town, and sneaking cheese and crackers into my hotel room in the pretty but less opulent village of Celerina down the valley. There my wardrobe has been appropriated as a kind of down at heel larder.

The evenings are the worst. I wander around the streets where the warm glow of Michelin starred restaurants and black tie bars spill out onto the snow and I cannot go into any of them. There is literally nowhere to go and nothing to do. Each night, after a fruitless search for a drink and meal I can afford, I trudge back along the Via Serlas, ('The world's highest shopping street! The greatest density of top brands in the universe! Prada, Versace and Asprey!'), and then down the lonely mountain road that leads to my hotel. In the darkness the stars are like diamond necklaces in the sky. It is cold outside, very cold when you are not let in. Sometimes it is cold enough for the hairs in my nostrils to freeze. They sing a melancholy little tune with each breath as I make the journey back to another cheese biscuit supper.

Despite its opulence the actual town of St Moritz cannot be described as beautiful. The most striking bit of architecture is the luxurious and historic Badrutts Palace hotel which commands the slopes to the lake and which looks part chalet, part Disney castle on steroids, while behind it stand the imposing honey coloured cubes of the Kulm Hotel, (the original place to stay and intimately bound up with the history of the Cresta run). The more recent town however includes many drab non- descript concrete blocks, not out of place in a Moscow suburb. That is not to say that they aren't well appointed in the interior.

Nevertheless, the old village is there somewhere, buried under the brutal squat luxury apartments and hidden among the glittering multi star edifices of top flight hotels. On the western side of the blue jewel of the lake can be found the mineral springs which were the reason for St Moritz's existence in the first place, albeit they are now covered by a phalanx of five star palaces offering pampering facilities. St Moritz started off as a spa town. The waters bubbling out of its folded Jurassic rock were known and favoured as far back as the Bronze Age but became increasingly popular in the 18th and 19th centuries when their health giving properties made them fashionable to visit. Still, for the British who clearly had their own spas at home in Bath, it was a long way to go and chilly in the winter. Come September the few hotels and guest houses that clustered around the waters tended to shut up shop.

What happened next became the stuff of legend. In the autumn of 1864 local hotelier and businessman Johannes Badrutt bet a number of his departing British guests that if they came back to St Moritz in winter they would fall in love with it all over again; if not, he would pay all the costs of their stay. In the event they liked it so much they remained until the following spring, and where they led others followed, so kicking off St Moritz's first winter seasons and beginning its startling transition from sleepy rural spa town to the jet set paradise it is today.

Of course what St Moritz has going for it is not just its location high in the stupendous Alps. It also has the sort of glittering champagne ice bucket of a climate where the snow is always on tap and the days are golden, (322 days of sunshine a year! perfect powder to carve and break a leg on!) Nestling at the bottom of the valley, hugging the lake at its floor, it is surrounded by glittering peaks that soar into a (usually) cloudless blue vault, their upper flanks providing over 350 km of skiing fun while their lower slopes are thick with conifer forests freighted in winter with dollops of gorgeous white fluffiness.

Luckily for the upmarket clientele of this resort, 'At the top of the world,' all this stupendous loveliness has not always been easy to get to, which at least keeps the common people out, (that is unless they are really determined). Back in the Nineteenth century the only transport up the mountain was horse power and it was a long and expensive journey. Nowadays if you can't stretch to a private jet at the airstrip at Engadin airport, the most practical way of getting here is by train and what a train ride that is. In a country carved by impassable mountain ranges and cut by deep valleys, the Swiss have had to blast and bore their way through granite peaks and sling bridges and viaducts over countless sheer drops just to get from A to B, or in my case from Zurich in the north to St Moritz in the south east. In the process they have burrowed some 1,800 tunnels through the Alps rendering it something like a Swiss cheese. They have even been able to conquer gravity. The Swiss railway system is one of cable driven funiculars and cog railways that slide up impossible slopes while their little red trains chug up the sheer sides of mountains by zigzagging or by chasing their tails on gently escalating 'spiral bridges'. Such genius eccentricities of engineering have been made necessary by the geography that they are faced with. There is no doubt that even on a local commute, riding a Swiss train is an adventure in itself.

And of course the whole thing runs like clockwork, aside from the occasional avalanche and short of nuclear war, (the Swiss have enough nuclear shelters for the whole of their population so that possibility is taken care of anyway). In fact I have found that pretty much everything runs smoothly in Switzerland and have no doubt that a lot of this is down to the Swiss character. There is of course the old joke that in heaven the Swiss are the organisers and the French the lovers while in hell the Swiss are the lovers and the Italians organise everything. This doesn't take account of the fact that the country is actually an amalgamation of cultural and linguistic groups that include French and Italian speakers, (with the German group in the majority), but as with most stereotypes there can be a grain of truth in the fun we poke. Switzerland, land of mountains and cheese, cows and watches, is a place of gorgeously romantic vistas that just happens to be run by accountants.

The Swiss are punctual, strictly organised and clean, (my guesthouse room looks like they took the plastic wrapping off when I arrived). They are innately conservative and love rules, (guinea pigs must be kept in pairs, dogs are taxed and in some districts men are banned from urinating after ten pm so as not to create a commotion). The Swiss are very, very clever, being top at maths in the world and when they say they speak English, 'a little,' what they mean is that they speak it better than the English do. They don't get involved in wars and keep everyone else's money. After an exhausting day observing all the rules and regulations they go to bed, usually around ten pm after their last wee. They are probably a bit shy, reserved even, and keep themselves to themselves. There is a saying in Switzerland that best sums up the national character: 'Everybody takes care of his own business and the cows will be well guarded,' although something may have been lost in translation.

But in St Moritz no one goes to bed early: the British and Italians see to that. This place is in its own champagne bubble, rich and eccentric. And at the heart of this eccentricity lays the St Moritz Tobogganing Club and the Cresta run.

I have now spent a week in St Moritz and frankly I am bored. I have sampled all that the town has to offer, from numerous turns around the solid lake at its base to cable car rides in the powdery heaven of the nearby 10,000 foot Piz Nair. I have paid a visit to the old Olympic site and watched the ski jumpers practice off the ninety metre facility, hanging suspended in mid air, (and floating the length of a football pitch), before coming to earth in what is just another insane winter enterprise. I have even taken a 'Taxi ride' on the famous Bob Sleigh run that snakes close to the Cresta, as a passenger in a four person vehicle, a disorientating experience that I can only describe as like going for the full cycle inside a washing machine, (or at least I imagine that to be the case). The only thing I haven't tried is the Cresta run. I have thought about it constantly, admired it, trudged around it in thigh length snow and watched its proponents shoot beneath my feet-I just haven't been on it. The fact is that I am prevaricating like mad. The truth is I am actually scared.

The Cresta run starts its terrifying journey in the quiet and pleasant surroundings of the old town. There is a pretty stone church a little further down the run which the riders probably don't notice as they pick up speed, although it does have a bend named after it: 'Church Leap'. Here the descent is so sudden and sharp that going over it has been described as, 'Falling off a cliff.'

You can always tell a Cresta rider around 'Top'. Quite apart from sporting the full rig, he will be the one walking around as if in a trance, hands flapping and lips moving in an interior monologue while he rehearses every move he will make to propel himself quickly and safely to the bottom.

In my scouting around in the last few days I have managed to interrupt any number of these courageous men on the way to their possible doom with my inane questions, so breaking their dream of visualisation and probably sabotaging their run; all without exception have been exceedingly good about it. The main advice they have given me is, 'Just stay away from the edge, don't fall in!'

At the start of the run is an octagonal wooden hut where the riders congregate to await their turn. Here their concentration is so intense that one rider has confessed it to be the only place where he doesn't think about sex. To make it to the finish means negotiating some ten bends, each with their own distinct challenges and each bearing a different and imaginative name, ranging from 'Scylla' and 'Charybdis' which were sea monsters in Greek mythology, (and which being next to each other roughly translates as, 'Being between a rock and a hard place,') to the more whimsically titled 'Battledore', a forerunner of the generally non lethal game of Badminton.

But the most notorious turn of all is 'Shuttlecock', a low, declining radius, left-hand turn whose centrifugal force will spin you out like a marble shooting around the lip of a cup if you approach it too low.

The point of 'Shuttlecock' is not so much to be difficult as to act as a 'safety valve' that will literally throw you out of the run if your line is all wrong, thereby saving you from more serious trouble down the course.

There is a trick to this bend and that is to aim high as you go round, a manoeuvre that is screamingly counterintuitive when all you want to do is hug the safety of the bottom. To help you find the spot to reach for, the club have helpfully stuck a broom in the snow at the top as a guide.

As one of the first bends that beginners face, 'Shuttlecock' claims a fair number of novices, not to mention quite a few veterans. It is a favourite spot for spectators to congregate to witness the airborne trajectory of those who are slingshot over the top and they are rarely disappointed in the show. A wooden stand has been erected for their convenience. It has been christened, ' The Vultures' pit'.

For those who succumb to its physics there is at least the consolation of becoming a member of the 'Shuttlecock Club' which not only celebrates those who have flown off here but furnishes them with a swanky tie covered in little golden coloured shuttlecocks. There is also an annual 'Shuttlecock' dinner. One year a horse fell at the top of the bend and was invited. It actually turned up.

On the day I arrive to take a peek at this nemesis I find not only a sprinkling of women in fresh kill furs but a cameraman and stills photographer. The latter are officially there on behalf of the club to capture every thrill and spill and sell copies to the tourists as mementoes of their attempt at the run. Each evening after a day of skeleton action the results are shown on a big screen for all to relive, usually in one of the Cresta themed bars in town where the film showing is accompanied by plenty of alcohol. It can get lively and the laughter loud, particularly when epic pratfall spills are on offer.

One of the amazing things about 'Shuttlecock' and indeed the whole Cresta run is that it is built from scratch each year, and although the twists and turns may differ slightly each season, the same basic blueprint remains. The

Cresta is in fact the only natural ice run of its kind in the world, (see *The bare bones of it: a history of Skeleton riding.*)

The Cresta is only open for a couple of months from Christmas and then only in the morning, before the sun begins to tug it out of shape. Pretty soon it will melt away entirely for another year and the wild meadow flowers will appear again. Time is ticking and for me it is running out.

On the evening before my last day in St Moritz I decide that there will be no more equivocation: tomorrow I will definitely and absolutely take my ride. Consequently the night before is not a peaceful one, inhabited as it is by dreams of lost limbs, detached thumbs and me screaming, 'Noooooh!'

The next day I find myself on a patch of snow next to the track finally staring at the 'Traditional' toboggan that I am about to ride. It looks like a piece of junk. Essentially it is a flat board with looped runners attached to the underside and a sliding pad on top. That is what will take me down the run. Our novice group is gathered around it and a man called Arnold is talking to us. There is not a lot to say. Basically the idea is to slide the body back and forward on its pad for speed and some semblance of control, while gripping the side bars. Steering the thing is pretty much a question of using the hand holds and the distribution of your weight. The rakes on your boots and the knife like 'teeth' machined into the back portion of the runners are your only means of braking. Being preoccupied with my gloves I take none of this in. I am also convinced that the chap is sniggering at my helmet. I am in fact in a world of my own.

Arnold, or to give him his full name, Arnold Von Bohlen und Halbach, is one of three 'Gurus' or tutors whose job it is to provide the requisite instruction to traumatised beginners before sending them down the run. He is of course a volunteer and receives no remuneration for his efforts other than a bottle of champagne at the end of the Cresta season.

A softly spoken Austrian German, Arnold is a veteran rider himself and like everyone else has his own X rays to prove it. He seems a kindly man although according to some accounts not immune on occasion to messing with your head.

One of his charges has sworn for example that just before he was due to set off down the run Arnold whispered in his ear, 'At all costs, disregard all the instruction you have received, it will only confuse you.' The unfortunate ingénue flew off half way down the run, no doubt still debating in his mind precisely what it was that he should believe. At least that's the story.

But with me there are no mind games, Arnold seeing perhaps how petrified I am. In any case such kidding would be useless. However wise Arnold Von Bohlen's words are, and his expertise is not in doubt, I am in no state to take anything in. I simply haven't listened to a word he has said.

One by one Arnold sends us on our way and when it is my turn I lie on my stomach on the sled as directed, well back, my thighs resting on the rear of the sliding pad, feet dangling, toes pointed downwards, ready to rake like mad. I grasp the side bars of the sled in a death grip. Arnold asks if I am ready to go. Only his foot resting on the skeleton keeps me from falling into oblivion. Then he lets go.

GOING DOWN

At first nothing seems to happen and then slowly the ice beneath the runners begins to move and then gathers pace. My first thought is that I cannot see out of my helmet properly: I am sure that it has in fact fallen down over my head so that the outside world is shut off. All I can see through a small post box slot is a field of white, its surface rutted by the erratic ploughing of previous beginners. Thankfully there is no blood.

Even at a walking pace I am digging in with those rakes: I just don't want to let go. Like a climber clawing at a rock face as he slips, I am hanging on for dear life. The Cresta has been described as falling for a woman. If so, I am desperately fighting her advances. There is a sense of helplessness about it, the feeling that once you launch yourself into this relationship there is no way back, at least not under your control. It is not a good way to start a romance.

But then it is no use fighting the Cresta: gravity always wins. The ice under my nose slips by faster and faster until it becomes a blur; I can feel the acceleration of the sled through every bit of my body. There is no going back now.

Junction Straight where all novices start their ride is a long run up but not it seems long enough. I bounce off its snow packed walls, gently at first but enough to knock my helmet a bit further adrift. That doesn't help. And then the first bend looms. It is too early for me.

The number one turn, at least for beginners, is upliftingly called 'Rise'. In fact it announces itself as a ten foot tall ice wall, a smooth banked ninety degree curve that I can see winding off to the right. Going into it is like entering a tunnel. Its sides and top are protected by brown canvas material slung between poles, the better to protect it from the heat of the sun which could make it sloppy. To me it looks crisp and unyielding at this time in the morning but few accidents happen here. My toboggan manages to slip round it and then into the sunlight. A bit further down is 'Nani's Bridge', a short walkway slung over the track where sometimes spectators gather and cameramen take shots of the riders shooting underneath it. I don't notice any figures that may be up there. To be honest I don't think I even see the crossing.

This was the spot where one rider connected his head with the concrete side of the bridge and spent weeks in a coma. To be fair, he was going considerably faster than me at the time.

After 'Rise' there is a quick, sharp right hand turn, ('Battledore'), before I am whipped into 'Shuttlecock' where the truth lies for all Cresta riders. By this time I am totally disorientated- I am not sure which way is up or down. I suspect that I am dwelling deep in the well of this notorious bend, precisely where I shouldn't be. But then everything is white and all the surfaces merge. It is like trundling along the floor of an infinite white tiled room with no door, no windows and no idea where the sides might be. This of course is nonsense. Such an illusion cannot last. Nevertheless, I am still surprised when the slot of my helmet is suddenly filled with the green of trees and even the blue of the sky. The 'floor' was in fact a wall all this time and I have been climbing it remorselessly. Inevitably I have gone over the top. I have now officially exited the Cresta Run.

Time really does slow down when you find yourself in mid air clinging to a heavy toboggan. I seem to be suspended there for ages. Eventually though, I have the good sense to chuck away the sled and jump head first into the pile of snow and straw thoughtfully left by the side of the run. This I find is not unlike diving into water in that I literally disappear below the surface and have to claw my way back up again to take a breath. Once out I wave my arms, not at the 'Tower' where Digby might be watching but at the trees that line the run: totally the wrong direction.

For the rider that falls at Shuttlecock there is only one thing to do and that is take up their toboggan and get ready for a long walk. There is an icy path that runs parallel to the track and follows it down the valley in the direction of Celerina and the finish. It is chiefly a matter of man handling the sled or dragging it down this incline. It is so heavy I actually try to ride it but then the results are so erratic and dangerous that I have to give up that idea. On one occasion I even crash into the net fencing that protects the side of the run, so almost falling back into it and cutting out Shuttlecock altogether. I don't think anyone has ever done that before.

At the bottom of the path is a road bridge where the less triumphant are picked up and taken with their sleds back to the start. There, it is a matter of waiting for the 'Camion,' a twelve seater Mercedes van with 'Cresta Run' on its side which makes the continual journey of ferrying the riders and their toboggans from bottom back up to junction and top throughout the season, with a stop off to pick up those who like me fall at Shuttlecock. When it arrives, its back doors open to reveal eleven faces, their eyes all upon me. Among them is 'the chap', who is smirking and no doubt thinks the whole thing is a bit of a lark. When he sees me in my cherry red helmet puffing away and incapable of speech, he finds it terribly funny. 'Look,' he tells the others, 'its spod!' (At least I think that is what he said. Was this Public school slang for loser? Or the children's cartoon character, 'Bod,' with its oversized head? To this day I am unsure).

The ride back up to Junction is bumpy and crushed as we pick up other stragglers. Back at the start, Digby's voice is blaring over the loudspeaker, tearing a strip off one of our number. 'You're a bloody disgrace,' he tells him. His crime: the unfortunate man raked all the way to the bottom.

Arnold is waiting for me. 'You need to push down at Shuttlecock,' he tells me in his soft voice. In fact the racing line requires going up early towards the broom stuck in the snow, (what broom?), and then pushing hard left to manoeuvre the toboggan so that it slides properly into the next bend called 'Stream' and continues down the run. Experienced riders do it by gripping the top of the sled with the hand nearest the side of the run and using the other hand at the bottom, while shifting their weight and using differential raking. They look like Superman. I am not Superman. 'That's what I will do,' I tell him nevertheless.

I go down junction straight again, into the tunnel of Rise, under Nani's bridge and then get flipped around Battledore and hence into Shuttlecock. There is only one thing in my head, 'Push down-left!' I try summoning all my weight to nudge the toboggan away from the side. At which point it serenely and remorselessly climbs the banks of the run and flips me over the side for a second serving of snow and straw. At least this time I wave in the right direction.

I have one more ride. Better make it good. 'You really need to push down you know,' Arnold says. 'I totally will,' I tell him.

And so down 'Junction straight' for the third helping, the canvas awnings of Rise greeting me, darkness followed by light as Battledore whips my toboggan into Shuttlecock for the last time. There I try to go high, look for the brush of the broom, miss it and skid along the lip of the run with one leg dangling unceremoniously in the air. There is no doubt I am going to come off again, no doubt at all. But before I am launched into space one more time, something unbelievable happens: I start to feel the tug of gravity and find myself gradually being pulled back into the Cresta. The toboggan slips down the ice wall and then climbs the other side, wheeling around stream corner before I am deposited into the deep and rapidly descending groove of the 'Straight' which greets me promptly with a side swipe of epic proportions. That is not the right way to take shuttlecock by any means but what does that matter? Getting round, as many riders will tell you is the thing. It doesn't always have to be pretty.

Many beginners find the experience of 'Straight', at least in its initial stages is like being the pin ball in a giant machine operated by a vindictive giant: the sled ricochets off its sides until you can get some semblance of control. By this time everything is happening very quickly. Here you can stop raking and lift your feet from the ice, come forward if you dare for speed.

The ice walls that pen you in are by this time spinning past you very fast. There is the whistle of the wind and the rattle of the sled on the ice. Your blood is pumping in your ears and the breath is being sucked out of you. The 'Straight' is in a direct line down to the village of Celerina in the valley below. Lift your head, (if you are able to), and you can see it in and the mountains beyond in the distance, bathed in sunlight. It looks quite a long way away. In truth you will be there in seconds.

At the end of this long stretch is the stone arch road bridge where I was picked up by the camion. Its O mouth grows rapidly in size and then swallows me whole. In its shadow I am tipped at a hard angle by the sharp curve of 'Bulpetts', before the sled briefly rights itself and then there is another crossing looming, this time for the local train service. It sways at a drunken angle before I dive underneath, clinging to the high banked left bend of 'Scylla' before I am tipped the other way at 'Charybdis', riding its seemingly vertical wall into a steep descent, ('Cresta Leap') which accelerates the sled even more. At some point a just perceptible red line flashes under my runners. Although this is officially the end of the Cresta, there is the business of stopping to attend to. At this point the run goes up and switches back on itself in a steeply banked turn that it is hoped bleeds off most of the suicidal speed. This is always only partially successful. I enter what seems to be a tunnel roofed with canvas and timber before finally I see daylight. This really is the end. I can see some mats and a foam sausage and plough into them, folding them up like a concertina. Then I simply tumble off the sled. Thus ends seventy seconds of pure terror and adrenaline.

The 'Arbeiters' or run assistants take the toboggan nonchalantly. 'Danke,' I want to tell them but I don't have any breath or spit. They don't seem overly impressed since they have seen it all before. But to those who make it down the Cresta run as a beginner it is a very big deal indeed, a triumph of ballsy courage and self-belief over adversity and maybe even a chance to join the elite that make the Cresta the special institution it is.

The trouble is that none of that actually happened, at least not for me. I would have liked for it to happen, and I could have pretended it did but it is better to tell the truth. What actually happened is that after my second fall I came back to the start outside the Cresta bar and there I met Arnold.

'You really need to push down you know,' he tells me. I nod but I am not really listening. I know what I should do but theory and practice are two separate things. Besides, something else has intervened. At some point during the last rickety ride of shame in the Camion I came to a decision. I am tired, bruised and adrenaline fatigued. Whether it is a physical or mental thing or likely both, the simple fact is that I have had enough.

I go to the telephone at the base of the 'tower' and pick up the receiver. 'Yes?' booms Digby's voice at the other end. 'Scratch,' I tell him. 'Whaaaat?' he thunders. '...Scratch!' I squeak.

The relief is overwhelming, the euphoria at being alive and unharmed a palpable, delicious feeling. I rip off the ridiculous spikey gloves and knee pads, stow my cherry helmet in the brutal and austere space of the changing room and then climb the stairs back to the comforting embrace of the clubhouse bar with its soft chairs and warmth. There I find memorabilia for sale. 'I would like a tie,' I say to Harriet, pointing to one with lovely golden shuttlecocks on it. 'You know...,' I tell her proudly, 'I came off twice.'

Also, I decide I would like a drink-preferably more than one. The Cresta slug of choice for those who exit the run precipitously is usually a 'Bullshot', a warming stew of a cocktail with its generous measure of vodka bubbling with beef bouillon, lemon and pepper. The alcohol swims with the adrenaline coursing through my veins. It is a heady feeling. I decide to have several.

And that as they say is that, it is all over. Except of course it's not -there are questions to ask and reasons to be given.

The first is why I let myself down. The second though is the more pertinent: why did I do it at all? Why put yourself in jeopardy, just for a bit of 'fun?' Every year several hundred people go down the Cresta Run for the first time and while extremely few are ever injured or killed, none of them would pretend that it is an activity without danger. Putting ourselves in harm's way is it seems something we tend to like; some embrace it even to death.

This is more common than we would like to admit. We all tend to adjust our lives to the level of risk with which we are comfortable. When air bags were put in cars the overall death level did drop but not as much as expected: people simply drove faster. When the parachuting industry came up with an automatic device to eliminate 'low pull' accidents where the cord is operated too late, it undoubtedly saved lives but the overall mortality rate from parachuting accidents did not go down. Sky divers simply felt free to execute more tricky landing manoeuvres. In the blunt words of '*The Agile Lifestyle Blog*' which promotes an adventurous and healthy existence, 'Skydivers compensated by trying to get themselves killed in other ways.'

The clichéd response to all this lunacy is that the sort of person who indulges in these activities is an 'adrenaline junky', or is seeking some peer recognition or compensation for failings elsewhere. It is however much more complicated than that. Taking risks it seems is hard wired into the psyche of human beings. It is after all what got us out of the caves; according to one scientist studying reckless behaviour in adolescents: 'If human beings weren't wired to take risks, we wouldn't be here.' 'Someone had to leave the village to search for water ... to mate with other groups.' In other words it gives us an evolutionary edge.

Such thrill seekers or, 'T People', as they have been dubbed, may have been the ones who left the village in the past but now they like to skydive or go up mountains. They tend to be, 'Optimistic, energetic, innovative and highly self-confident, with a conviction that they can control their fate.' They tend to believe they will come back alive.

But we can't all be like that. And we all have our different attitudes to taking a chance. Some are happy to play recklessly with the stock market but would never dream of exceeding the speed limit let alone plummet to earth while debating at what point to pull that cord; and vice versa. And some of us simply do not have the courage we would like to think we have, the kind of bravery that the Cresta riders display and which comes naturally to men like Lieutenant Colonel Digby Willoughby whether under fire or on his stomach on a tea tray. When you scratch your last run because you have come to the end and cannot face another go, it tells you something about yourself, however uncomfortable that knowledge may be. It is undoubtedly a difficult lesson, humiliating even.

It was The late Lord Brabazon, veteran rider and for many years president of the SMTC, who once neatly summed up the human dilemma about adrenaline sports when talking about the Cresta : 'When the exhilaration is worth the fright, then you must do it....but when the exhilaration is not worth (it) then you must give it up. That is merely sensible, isn't it?'

When asked why in his later years he had stopped participating in the Cresta run, the Lord, whose Father had been the recipient of the military cross for valour and holder of the first private pilot's licence in the UK and who undoubtedly came from a family of risk takers, replied simply : 'Because it scares me.'

And so it should. Unlike 'the chap', the most successful at these terrifying pursuits know what it means to be afraid and to overcome that fear. Lizzy Yarnold, the greatest Olympic skeleton rider ever, winner of two gold medals and a world cup, has described the Bob-Skeleton as, '.... Petrifying and unnatural but I love it.' She has however avoided the Cresta Run even on the odd occasion when it does open up for women to have a go. It seems she prefers the ethos of Bath and the system which identified and nurtured her talent. 'I love the skeleton,' she is quoted as saying, 'That's the greatest thing about our sport ... it's equal funding, equal support. That's what I love about the Olympics ...' Besides', she goes on, 'The Cresta is different. I don't know if I'd have the balls to do the Cresta.'

And so the SMTC continues to go its own way. That evening it has its regular get together at one of the upmarket hotels to view the film montage of the day's action on the run. Everyone is invited, including the novices who turned up that day and paid for their chance for glory. Above all the SMTC is a social club whose members become a tightly knit group in the shared endeavour that is the Cresta. One veteran rider explains it by saying that, 'Everyone is afraid and therefore very close...it's like trench warfare.'

Less alarmingly Michael DiGiacomo has written that, 'The bond between Cresta riders....transcends language, educational background, nationality, age or station in life.'

That may be so but I don't think I am going to be asked to join them. Suddenly I am up on the screen in full view as each mishap is recorded for posterity. There is me waving my hands in the air and signalling in the wrong direction. There I am trying to lug the heavy sled down the icy path from Shuttlecock, attempting to ride it before crashing into the netting that protects the run from fools. I slip, stumble and fumble as I try to haul the sled into the camion at the bottom of the run before I am carted back up to Junction to start all over again. Best of all there are my startling attempts at Shuttlecock, which display all the grace and control of a loose cannon ball being shot put out of a pit, before I jettison the sled and swan dive into a thick pile of snow and straw. ('Impressive,' the cameraman says to me, 'I haven't seen anything like that in a long time.') Undoubtedly the St Moritz Tobogganing Club thrives not only on fear but also on humour. There is a lot of laughter, it fills the posh bar.

I can only reconcile myself to my fate. This, I say to myself, must be what it's like at your first day at boarding school where you are a nobody in awe of the big boys and afraid of the headmaster. I never went back.

The Cresta Run is usually open, (depending on snow conditions), between Christmas and the end of February/early March. Beginners can book a practice slot from the online calendar and pay a deposit with the balance payable on the day of riding.

www.cresta-run.com

British Bobsleigh and Skeleton Association: www.thebbsa.co.uk

Suggested reading

*DiGiacomo, Michael. 2000, **Apparently Unharmed, (Riders of The Cresta Run).** Texere, New York.*

*Lonely Planet. 2000, (third edition). **Switzerland**. Lonely Planet Publications Pty Ltd, Australia.*

High rise living: Ancient people's granaries at Nankoweap.
Photo: US National Park Service

The Canyonlands: a big baked brownie.
Photo: Daniel Mayer, use under Creative Commons licence

The Colorado...a lazy river. Photo: author

At Poop Rock-many river runners have shit themselves here.
Photo: author

*Longyearbyen:
A nice town with
bears and guns.*
Photo:author

The 'Monkey Ears Express'. Photo:author

The North Pole-a desolate place. Photo:author

Full of tourists...
Photo:author

The Cresta Run looking towards, 'The pretty village of Celerina,' in the valley below. Photo:author

Bath: gold medals are won on this track. Photo:author

*Exiting in style: the newest member of
the 'Shuttlecock Club'. Photo:author*

PEOPLE AND PLACES

1

River Runners of the Colorado

*Rivers know this: there is no hurry. We shall get there some day.- **A. A. Milne, Pooh's Little Instruction Book***

EARLY DAYS

Everything has to start somewhere and if you are looking for the source of the Colorado you will find it in a muddy spot high up in the Rockies next to a perfectly pleasant summer hiking trail, (there is supposed to be a lake there but depending on the season it may be more sodden meadow). The path nearby runs along the La Poudre Pass (elevation 10,184 ft) which itself follows the great 'Continental Divide' of the Americas. In theory you could spit on one side of the track and it would end up in the Gulf of California, try the other way and it might become a drop in the Atlantic Ocean.

From such humble beginnings the Colorado ends up a mighty river 1,450 miles long that drains an area of almost a quarter of a million square miles and sustains a population of over 40 million in America's Southwest. Starting life as a mountain stream before slipping down the western slopes of the Rocky Mountains, by the time it reaches the arid plateaux of Utah and Arizona it is a powerful force, capable over a period of several million years of carving canyons a mile deep and eighteen miles wide. Past the Hoover dam and the artificially created 'Lake Mead' the river runs south through Arizona and over the Mexican border. By rights it should then reach the Gulf of California and therefore the Pacific Ocean but the reality these days is that it never gets to the sea. By that time due to the demands of a thirsty population and an even thirstier agriculture and industry, it has literally been sucked dry.

But in the stretch of the river that flows through the Canyonlands, south of Moab and through the length of Cataract Canyon and the Grand Canyon beyond, the water is fast and wild, especially after the spring snow melt when on average 50,000 cubic feet per second can surge through the sometimes constricted pipe of the Colorado, (it has been known to top twice that on occasion). There are essentially three ingredients you need for rapids: a swift river current, an uneven river bed and an elevation drop. It is the rubble strewn river bed that is mostly responsible for the turbulence and in the desert climate of the Colorado Plateau there is no shortage of debris falling into the river, often washed from side canyons, particularly after a very occasional heavy downpour. The resulting slip of rubble and sediment can park boulders the size of cars on the river floor.

Consequently there are some 150 rapids to negotiate in the Grand Canyon alone and another twenty eight in cataract canyon. Nowadays this brings joy to the adrenaline seeking tourist in professional hands but in the early days of discovery in the Grand Canyon it just caused consternation as the first river runners were in perpetual fear of what might await them on the water. Their tale is one of courage and perseverance, as well as on occasion suicidal stupidity. It is remarkable that they came back alive. Some of them, of course, didn't.

The first peoples to inhabit the Grand Canyon on a permanent basis probably did so around 4,000 years ago. These 'Desert Culture' peoples were basically nomads and hunter gatherers and were followed by the Ancient Pueblo Peoples, (also known as the Anasazi). Whether they actually took to the water is unknown but they were expert climbers and knew the trails like the back of their hands, establishing a web of overland communication linking their settlements and providing access down into the canyon and back to the mesa top above. They left pictographs behind in the rock, some of which have symbols marking the route, ('this way is up!'). It is also said that they may have had had traditional songs to help them remember the tangle of paths that were vital to their survival.

After the Ancient Pueblo Peoples left the canyon, other Indian tribes moved in and continued the business of settlement and agriculture. They were still there when the Spanish arrived in 1540 and later still when the first boating expeditions ran through the canyon in the late 1800's. In 1882 their communities were uprooted when they were relocated to reservations by the American government and their land taken. Today there remains a small group of Havasupai Indians in one part of the Canyon who still tend their fields. To reach them requires permission and an eight mile trek on foot or the back of a mule.

A small party of Spanish Conquistadors were the first Europeans to see the Grand Canyon and view the Colorado River. From the start the sheer size of the Canyon bamboozled them. Their leader, García López de Cárdenas, sent three of his men to hike to the bottom only to find that within a few hours they came back and told him that, 'What seemed easy from above was not so.' To emphasise the point they claimed that boulders which from the rim looked the height of a man were actually on closer inspection as big as the tallest tower in the world. To be fair to them, the sheer vastness of the canyon often defeats perception and estimating scale is difficult. It was likely that to reach the bottom of the canyon from the rim would have involved a steep seven to ten mile trek and they were running out of water. Cárdenas went home without ever reaching the Colorado, stating that the chasm was impassable. The Spanish did not come back for another two hundred years.

When they did return, this time they had trouble not only with their sense of distance but also vertigo. In 1776 Father Francisco Tomas Garcés, a Franciscan missionary visited the Havasupai Indians in the same side Canyon where they tend their fields today. He wrote that in order to reach the Indian village at the bottom of the Canyon, he had to traverse a narrow straight on one side of which, '.... Is a very lofty cliff, and on the other a horrible abyss.' Once past this queasy ledge, 'There presented itself another and worse one.' Eventually he had to scramble, ' Down a ladder of wood,' to reach the bottom, knowing that he would have to climb back up the precipitous canyon wall on his return. That was his last visit.

In 1848 the whole of the Canyonlands area and most of the Colorado basin was acquired by the United States of America, following a war with Mexico. In order to protect its new territory and supply its army forts, the United States became interested in the Colorado and its potential for navigation. Following some early attempts to survey the river spurred on by the prospect of mineral wealth, ('Is it not probable that the walls of this mighty crevice will exhibit many rich deposits?' asked one commentator of the time), in 1857 the US War department sent Lt Joseph Ives up the Colorado in a steamboat to see how far he could go. In the end he made it to the present site of the Hoover dam before the boat hit a rock. He then proceeded overland by mule train to the Grand Canyon. Unlike some of his contemporaries who fantasised about the riches it would yield, Ives was less complementary about the, 'Mighty crevice', stating that, 'It is of course valueless,' and claiming that, 'Ours will doubtless be....the last party of whites to visit this profitless locality. It seems intended by nature that the Colorado River, along the greater portion of its lonely and majestic way, shall be forever unvisited and undisturbed.'

He couldn't have been more wrong. Within a few years any number of boat men had taken to the waters that ran through the Canyonlands. River running on the Colorado had only just got started.

JOHN WESLEY POWELL

The first man to run the Grand Canyon, all 277 miles of its length, is generally regarded to be Major John Wesley Powell in his 1869 expedition. This didn't stop others announcing they had got there before him. These include a certain James White, who two years before Powell's documented trip claimed that he had spent sixteen days in an unscheduled float after a disagreeable encounter with some local Indians.

White had been prospecting with two other men when they were attacked by what he guessed was a party of the southern Ute tribe. One of the men lost his life while the other two fled to the river where under cover of darkness they built a driftwood raft and launched themselves into the water.

A couple of rapids down the line White's companion got sucked into a whirlpool and he found himself alone with the mighty Colorado. There followed a tumultuous trip downstream in which his raft continually capsized and then sunk completely so that he had to build a new one. After a couple of weeks a starving White came across a group of Hualapais. A friendly squaw gave him a chunk of honey Mesquite loaf and he traded his pistol for the hind quarters of a dog. (He then promptly dropped one leg in the river and lost it). A day later the prospector, more dead than alive, was fished out of the Colorado at Callville, Nevada, after an epic journey of 500 miles in which he had survived Indian attack, starvation and above all the treacherous waters of the river. His was an amazing tale. It was just a pity that no one believed it.

The main problem seemed to be that his journey was too quick to be believable. At an average speed of 3-5 miles an hour and being detained by the numerous eddies and whirlpools along the way, the current could not have borne the raft the full distance in the time he says it took to get back to civilisation. Others disagree, citing differing water flows and the motivation of having Ute warriors armed with tomahawks on your tail. When all is said and done it is just conceivable that White's story was in fact true.

Nevertheless, the history books record that it was the Major who was the first to achieve the feat and his was a fully voluntary trip. By all accounts Wesley Powell was a remarkable figure. A 'Union' man on the side of abolishing slavery, he lost most of his right arm in the civil war battle of Shiloh but continued to fight in the conflict until invalided out in 1856. He was interested in any number of intellectual pursuits including the natural sciences and anthropology and on his discharge from the army was given the post of professor of geology at Illinois University.

Powell was fascinated by the desert Canyonlands and the Grand Canyon in particular. In 1867 he conceived the idea of an exploratory journey down the Colorado and its tributaries and began to research and plan accordingly, even at one stage interviewing James White.

By May 1869 he was ready and embarked with nine other men along the Green river, travelling down towards its confluence with the Colorado some 217 miles upstream from the mouth of the Grand Canyon. In keeping with the lack of knowledge at that time, the four boats he used, ('Whitehall' row boats some twenty feet long and four feet wide with a shallow draft), were probably more suited to a trip on the lake or for ferrying goods across a light New York harbour 'chop' than for negotiating the wild water of the Colorado, being too heavy and not manoeuvrable enough. The team he took with him were mostly hunters, trappers and soldiers from civil war days. Some of them had boating experience but none in whitewater. It would be an interesting trip.

It wasn't long before the first boat, the appropriately christened and dispensable *No Name*, was lost to the waters of the Green river together with a third of their provisions. Predictably enough, they called the feature at which it perished, 'Disaster Falls'. The first member of the party quit a few miles further downstream.

On 17th July, the expedition group reached the confluence of the Green river and the Colorado whereupon they found themselves having to run all of Cataract and Glen Canyon's swift and dangerous rapids. They finally entered The Grand Canyon on August 5th. Powell was apprehensive. 'We are now ready to start on our way down the great unknown. We have but a month's rations remaining. We have an unknown distance to run, an unknown river to explore. With some...anxiety and some misgiving we enter the canyon below...'

He was also concerned that the hard limestone rocks of the canyon walls, like those of Cataract were an indication of rapids to come. 'This bodes toil and danger,' he wrote. He was correct.

180 miles into the canyon is Lava Falls, which with its thirty eight foot drop is perhaps the fastest navigable river water in the northern hemisphere. Fearing for their lives, the group were forced to carry the boats and provisions around it, (it wouldn't actually be run until some years later and today it remains one of the high spots of excitement and terror for many of the tourists that take a trip down the Colorado.) But Lava falls was just one of many and for the Powell expedition, hungry and nearing exhaustion it was all becoming too much. When they hit the next inevitable patch of turbulent water, there were murmurs of dissent.

Three of the remaining party resolved to leave and could not be dissuaded. In the end Powell wrote a letter to his wife and entrusted it to the leader of the departing group, together with a copy of the expedition journals in case he never made it out. 'Some tears are shed,' wrote the Major,

'It is a rather solemn parting; each party thinks the other is taking the dangerous course.'

Two days later the remaining six members of the Powell expedition arrived safe and sound at the settlement of Callville, the same spot where James White had been dragged out of the Colorado a couple of years previously. The three men who had left Powell's expedition did not fare so well-they were never seen again. Having left the river for what they saw as the comparative safety of dry land, they were probably killed by Indians or perhaps the local Mormon community fearing they were spies.

Thus ended an epic river trip of 1,048 miles lasting ninety eight days with twenty four of them spent in the depths of the Grand Canyon. Later one of the boatmen in the party, John Colton Sumner, would write about the Colorado and the Canyon in particular:

'I never want to see it again...it probably will remain unvisited for many years....' He was equally uncomplimentary about the state of Arizona: 'What I have seen [of it] I do not consider worth settling. As a disgusted woodchopper put it: the whole damned territory is bilk.'

Of course, like Ives before him he was wrong, but had a point about the wisdom of trying to settle an essentially arid desert country. Later, Wesley Powell, an early proponent of land conservation, would argue for the sensible use and sharing of water together with low impact agriculture in the region. His views, which have particular relevance today, were largely ignored.

However hellish the trip might have been, Powell's expedition of 1869 was in fact a roaring success. Not only had he become the first to boat through the Grand Canyon but his group had extensively mapped and recorded the course of the river and the canyons it flowed through, as well as making detailed geological and other scientific observations. Where he led others were to follow, some even worse prepared for the rigours of the Colorado than he had been.

THE BROWN- STANTON EXPEDITION

In 1889 Frank Mason Brown, a real estate and mining magnate, proposed a survey expedition along the Green and Colorado rivers in preparation for his somewhat fantastical notion of laying a railroad track alongside the river on the canyon floor. To this end he had already established the ' Denver, Colorado Canyon and Pacific Railroad Company ', of which he was president, an enterprise that had the backing of hopeful investors to the tune of fifty million dollars.

By all accounts Brown was a 'genial and loveable gentleman, always happy and cheerful,' although in the words of the chief surveyor of the expedition, Robert Brewster Stanton, he could be, 'Optimistic to a fault.'

For one thing, despite confiding to Stanton that he could, 'not swim a stroke,' he would not hear of the idea of life preservers for him or indeed any of the party. The boats he ordered appear to have been somewhat unsturdy, being smaller than those used in the Wesley Powell expedition and made of thin planks of cedar. Also they were round bottomed, an invitation to capsize. Eschewing the need for experienced boat men, President Brown brought along two of his lawyer buddies instead whose experience of the river probably stretched as far as cocktails on a showboat.

Finally, although Stanton did organise an interview with Wesley Powell himself, he is said to have come away from the meeting with a somewhat innocent appreciation of what it would take to survive.

Nevertheless the Brown-Stanton river survey launched into the Green river on May 25th 1889, with two of its six boats already patched up where the wood had split. In a decision worthy of the saying, 'eggs in one basket' they put most of their food on a single raft which they towed behind them. On immediate contact with the waters of Cataract canyon this sunk to the bottom and two boats were badly damaged. The next day the cook's boat followed a large part of the remaining food when it was smashed to pieces on the rocks. With dwindling provisions and all the remaining craft leaking like sieves, the expedition by this time was not in good shape and this was no more than a couple of weeks since it had started out. Criticisms began to be voiced about the management style of President Brown and his lawyer friends and their competence to conduct matters in the wilderness. There followed a succession of boat flipping and loss of re-stocked provisions while another craft got sucked into and swallowed forever by the Colorado. By day seventeen it was mutiny. The expedition separated into two groups, one of which headed downstream while the other including Brown and Stanton continued their survey of Cataract and Grand Canyon.

On July 10th 1889 the boat carrying Brown capsized and finding himself in a whirlpool without a life preserver and the ability to swim, the president of the Denver, Colorado Canyon and Pacific Railroad Company vanished beneath the waves. Stanton did carry on the survey for a while but when he lost another two men he decided to call it a day, at least for a while. By that time the expedition had already clocked up the record for the number of deaths in a single trip.

Later he wrote: 'President Brown sacrificed his life, which could so easily have been saved if he had a life preserver to keep him afloat. A noble hearted man and a true friend, he won the love of everyone associated with him.'

Robert Brewster Stanton finally completed the survey on April 26th 1890 but not until five of his renewed expedition had left, (one evacuated with a broken leg), and a boat was lost. He probably got off lightly. The railroad was never built.

Following the disastrous Brown-Stanton survey, a number of other more successful expeditions ran the Grand Canyon before the turn of the century. Then In 1923 the US Geological society undertook a detailed survey of the Canyon by boat. They took among other things, a motion camera with them and the first radio on such a trip.

By this time, the 'heroic' and in some cases 'idiotic' age of private Canyonlands discovery was drawing to a close. But not before the tragic tale of Glen and Bessie Hyde and their mysterious end was done.

THE STRANGE DISAPPEARANCE OF
GLEN AND BESSIE HYDE

Bessie was a twenty two year old fine arts student at a San Francisco college, Glen the son of an Idaho rancher in his thirties when they met in the summer of 1927 on board a ship bound for Los Angeles. Romance blossomed and they got married in early 1928.

Glen had boated on a few rivers in Idaho but now he hatched an ambitious plan to run the Colorado canyons with Bessie, so achieving the notoriety and fame which would make them rich. He was intent on breaking the speed record on the river. That he thought, together with the romance of the daring honeymoon trip would make their story irresistible to the papers and to publishers looking for a book deal. And to make it more exciting still, they would not be wearing life jackets.

Bessie's enthusiasm for the project may have been more limited. She was a novice on the water, but clearly she was in love with Glen, some would say in thrall to him.

Glen sunk a full fifty dollars in wood and nails to build himself an Idaho drift boat. Green river local Harry T Howland was not impressed with the results. He remarked to a friend of his that it, 'Looks like a floating coffin.' But Hyde was, according to Harry's friend, 'Surly, conceited and stoopid,' and not about to take instruction on his boat building skills.

Later it emerged that during the course of their trip a number of experienced river people had tried to persuade Glen to take some life jackets but he was adamant in refusing to take them. One individual, who briefly rode with Hydes for a few miles said, '...It was the most inadequately equipped outfit I have ever seen. It was obvious that the whole object of the trip was to make money in show business.'

Nevertheless, on 20th October 1928 the honeymooners took to the water and successfully negotiated Cataract Canyon before moving on into the Grand Canyon itself. After twenty six days and 424 miles, (a record), they reached 'Phantom Ranch' about a third of the way down the canyon and hiked their way up to the Grand Canyon village on the rim. There they took on supplies and a passenger, a local businessman, who traded provisions for a brief ride. A little further down the river he got off. He would have been the last person to see Glen and Bessie Hyde alive. After that they simply vanished.

On December 19th a search plane spotted Glen's boat some three quarters of the way through the canyon. It still had all their possessions on it including Bessie's diary and a camera which revealed the final shot taken about 60 miles upstream. But Bessie's diary indicates that they had actually reached not far from where the empty boat had drifted.

There has of course been speculation ever since about what happened to Glen and Bessie Hyde. Part of it centres on their relationship: was Hyde a controlling husband who bullied Bessie to carry on with the trip when she didn't want to continue? One account has it that Glen was seen manhandling Bessie back into the boat when she was clearly reluctant to get back on board. Was Glen in fact an abusive man, a claim categorically denied by his family? The wilder shores of speculation have it that Bessie murdered Glen and hiked out of the Canyon-there is however no evidence to back this up.

In 1971 an elderly woman on a commercial boat trip claimed that she was Bessie and that she had stabbed her husband and walked up to the rim to a new life. She would not be the last to make such an assertion.

What happened to Bessie and Glen is probably more mundane. Mile 232 rapid on the Colorado was likely their nemesis, a narrow passage guarded by sharp teeth of rock that must surely have thrown them into the water. It is surprising though that Glen's badly put together boat was not another casualty-it actually survived, a little battered but most certainly in one piece.

What does seem clear is that towards the end Bessie did not want to go back to the river and there is at least one account of her face registering, 'stark terror,' at the prospect. Up on the rim of the Canyon pioneering river runner and photographer Emery Kolb had taken the couple into his studio for a publicity photograph just before they embarked on the final part of the odyssey which would kill them. Emery's twenty year old daughter Edith had accompanied them. Bessie had looked at Edith's feet and was no doubt thinking about the wilderness that she was about to go back to and the dangers that awaited her. 'I wonder if I will ever wear pretty shoes again,' she told them.

THE TOURIST ERA

Towards the end of the 1930's a new breed of river runner arrived: the commercial trip operator. The first trip purely for pleasure on the river had in fact taken place back in 1909 when Ohio millionaire Julius Stone engaged the services of one Nathaniel Galloway for a three month sightseeing expedition down the Green river and through the Canyon into California.

Galloway was a local trapper and prospector who found that guiding on the river could be as profitable as going after pelts and sifting for gold. He designed a new type of craft suited for river running which was flat bottomed and upturned so increasing its manoeuvrability and resistance to flipping. But his greatest innovation and contribution to river safety lay in the simple expedient of turning the boat around and rowing backwards: he found that facing the rapids with the stern of the craft made the whole thing much more stable. Soon everyone was doing it, although that was not to say that the whole enterprise of river running was now without danger. It was perhaps characteristic of the times that before Galloway and Stone set out on their expedition they were handed by a local Wyoming man not a flotation device in case they got into trouble but a bottle of rye whiskey to see them through an emergency. In the event, the trip passed without any major mishap and twenty five years later Stone still had the bottle, unopened.

Galloway's boats and technique undoubtedly helped make the Colorado safe enough to attract the pleasure seeker and establish an early tourist industry. The brothers Ellsworth and Emery Kolb sought his advice in their own trip down river in 1911-1912 which they captured with a motion camera for the first time, bringing the romance and excitement of the Colorado to a wider audience. Ellsworth and Emery's photographic studio is now a museum on the edge of the south rim, in the Grand Canyon village. In their time they photographed more than three million tourists who came to the canyon. The film of their 1912 exploits continued to be run daily until Emery's death in 1976.

In 1938 Norman D Nevills took a paying party down the Colorado that included the first two women to run the grand canyon, Miss Elzada Clover, a botanist from the University of Michigan, and Miss Lois Jotter, a student at the college, whose academic field trip to study the flora just so happened to involve negotiating some of the wildest water in North America. Nevills himself was an ardent river runner, having spent his honeymoon on the water in a boat of somewhat eccentric design, being built from a horse trough and with 'borrowed' Utah highway signs as oar blades. Rather disconcertingly for a river man, his fiancée was a Doris Drown.

That however had been in the early days and by the time he took Miss Clover and Miss Jotter down the Colorado, Nevills had built sturdier boats on the Galloway principle. He would run a number of trips in the late thirties and early 1940's, all of them successful. Importantly, he never lost a customer.

By 1950 the number of people that had followed John Wesley Powell in floating through the canyon still numbered no more than 345. All that would change, but first it would be the end of a geo-political fight thousands of miles away that in many ways would help provide a major impetus to the growing river trade. On 27th July 1953 The Korean War ended with an armistice between North and South that added to the huge mountain of surplus army equipment left over since the Second World War. Going begging were thousands of rubber boats and inflatable bridge pontoons at $10 to $20 a piece. They were so cheap that commercial river runners could buy up a whole fleet of them.

And they were ideal for river running, being tough, compartmentalised, (being so designed as to take a bullet and still not deflate,) as well as manoeuvrable, (turning like 'water bugs' and bouncing off the rocks like billiard balls according to one commentator). One of the commercial operators at that time was Jack Curry who did much to advance the use of rubber boats when a consignment of surplus bridge pontoons was delivered to him in the early 1960's. On arrival he found they were not quite what he expected, consisting of tubes or 'snouts' some twenty two foot long and three foot wide. While not useful on their own, Jack and his partner, Jake Luck, tried gluing them side by side and stretching a frame across to hold them, and came up with the J rig, the precursor to the boats that take tourists down the river today.

One of the first to recognise the potential of inflatable craft was Georgie White Clark, the first woman tour operator on the Colorado. She came up with the idea of lashing three large rubber boats together and sticking a ten horse power outboard motor on the back. The whole thing was thirty seven feet long and twenty seven feet wide and could carry as many as twenty people. Now passengers were no longer limited to small and relatively expensive expeditions in wooden boats and their numbers soared. In 1955, about seventy tourists were guided down the Colorado River. Within a couple of decades that figure would jump to over 16,000 a year.

Georgie would become a legend among river runners. She was tough, hard headed and fearless. In June 1945 she had decided to test the waters of the Colorado while dispensing with a boat altogether. She had simply jumped in clad in a windbreaker and a life jacket, with tennis shoes on her feet, and swum sixty miles through the Canyon and into Lake Mead. Later she rowed the full length of the Grand Canyon, entirely on her own.

By 1961 she had taken more people down the river than any other tour operator. She was however a controversial figure with her 'pile 'em in', no frills approach to business, not to mention her gung ho way of charging full tilt at the rapids. Riding on Georgie's raft, (an inflatable so huge that it was dubbed the *Queen Mary*), was a wild affair. According to Ghiglieri and Myers, White would whip her passengers up into a frenzy of expectation before letting loose at the most dangerous of the rapids, Lava Falls, causing them to, 'Scream like maniacs.' Unlike many of the other operators she did not balk at running the centre of this treacherous rapid with its particularly radical water. It paid to hold on tight on Georgie's boat which was apt to spin in such a 'Hole', while the souls on board, seated and facing out towards the river would end up, 'Wildly kicking their feet in the air.'

This was all very entertaining but not without risk. Georgie ran Lava falls 150 times before running into trouble. But on August 25th 1984 a misjudged entry made her boat tip at a forty five degree angle into the centre of the rapid and a number of passengers were thrown overboard. Among them was fifty eight year old Norine Abrams who slipped under the craft and later could not be revived.

White's reaction to the death would cause even more controversy. It seemed that when it came to mishaps Georgie would often go into denial, regarding the customers who expired on her as no more than a nuisance. When a ranger in a helicopter arrived the next day to pick up Abram's body, Georgie told him to hurry up before any new customers saw the body bag. 'Georgie,' the park ranger told her, 'You just killed this woman, now you want me to hurry up and hide the body?' White replied, 'You're damned right I do. Now get her out of sight before you scare these new people.' Some twelve years previously another of Georgie's customers, sixty four year old Mae Hansen, had drowned when the boat had flipped, making her the first commercial passenger to die on the Colorado, and two years before that a man had suffered a fatal heart attack on one of White's trips. Georgie's reaction on that occasion was to cover the unfortunate man with a tarpaulin and announce to the other passengers that he had gone home after feeling ill.

Right up to the end Georgie was active on the river. In her seventies she could still be seen at the tiller of her rig, beer in hand, sporting a leopard patterned leotard. She last ran the river when she was eighty. The following year she succumbed to cancer. But even after her death White was full of surprises. Those who went through her personal effects found the marriage licence of the same Bessie Hyde who had disappeared with Glen over sixty years earlier. In addition they found a pistol which appeared to match one seen in a photograph taken of the couple on their doomed trip. Moreover Georgie's birth certificate showed that her real name was actually Bessie DeRoss. This sparked a rumour that Georgie was actually Bessie Hyde and that far from expiring on the ill fated trip with Glen, she had actually shot her abusive husband and then climbed out of the canyon to start a new life. However, there is little to corroborate such a fanciful tale and few today believe it. It was probably a case of Georgie, (or should it be Bessie), wanting to keep us guessing. In the words of one commentator, even in death Georgie White was still capable of, 'Taking us for a ride.'

MODERN TIMES: THE GATEWAY TO TRANSCENDENCE.

About the time that Georgie White started her operation, no more than 570 people had run the river in the Grand Canyon. Today over 25,000 take to its waters annually, the vast majority on organised commercial trips with other paying customers. Since 1972 more than half a million people have floated through the Grand Canyon in one way or another and many more on the other stretches of the river, like Cataract Canyon. They spend big bucks. It is estimated that recreation on the Colorado River employs over a quarter of a million people and contributes $26 billion a year to the economy of the American Southwest.

How did such an explosion of water based activity, particularly rafting, come about? One simple answer is neoprene. This synthetic rubber like substance which is used in a variety of products ranging from wet suits to mouse mats, is tough, water resistant and good at keeping the air in. Together with other modern materials such as Kevlar and PVC, it forms a vital part of the inflatable rafts that have superseded the early army surplus rubber boats. Although the army surplus kit was revolutionary at the time, it did have problems of abrasion and was prone to rip and sudden decompression. According to one contemporary account it was not unusual to see the beached craft cook in the mid day sun and then promptly blow up.

Nevertheless, even from the start, inflatables had obvious advantages over the old wooden boats of the early runners. They did not get smashed to pieces for one thing but bounced around happily and stayed afloat, and they could get in close to the rocks whatever the river level. The most important consequence of their use however was that the river no longer became the preserve of the expert or just plain mad: the man and woman in the street with no special boating skill or experience could now join in the fun. Before long they became hooked.

That is often the way with many adventure activities: technological developments ensure that sooner or later what was once an elite activity becomes accessible to everyone. Bungee jumping for example was invented in the south pacific island nation of Vanuatu as part of a ritual in which the men would jump from high timber towers with vines tied to their feet to test their courage and to act as a rite of passage. Unsurprisingly this was a niche activity. Then it was appropriated in the west using factory-produced braided shock cord with latex strands and an appropriate harness. Once vines were dispensed with the whole thing took off globally; after all, we do not expect the latest man made materials to break. The people of Vanuatu, understandingly irritated at having their invention pinched, are seeking compensation: they want a cut of what is now a multi-million pound industry.

Another reason why whitewater rafting has become so popular is that the whole business of adventure activities has grown exponentially in the last few decades. The lives we are living are now too humdrum. We work cooped up in offices and beset by health and safety legislation. No wonder we want to escape to the wilderness and seek new challenges. Because in the developed world we are generally far richer than we were in the 1950's more of us can indulge in such pastimes and travel to the far flung places where the action can be found. There we can reward ourselves by being scared.

And all this has been put in the spotlight by the media, whether it is a magazine article on base jumping or a TV documentary on climbing Everest. What were once niche sports like snowboarding and windsurfing are now Olympic televised events. Skateboarding, surfing and climbing will undoubtedly follow. Such exposure is carried over into fiction. At a time when rafting was becoming ever more a tourist pastime, one of the most watched films of 1994 was, *The River Wild*, a potboiler drama starring multi academy award winner Meryl Streep as a whitewater guide who takes her family for a river trip and encounters fugitives who keep them hostage. To her credit Streep did some of the stunts herself and almost drowned during one shoot in which she was asked to repeat an action scene on particularly turbulent water. "Everybody on shore began screaming, 'Meryl's gone under,' " remembered the director Curtis Hanson later. 'One of the kayakers we had rushed over and hauled her up like a big fish. She was conscious. She was banged up. And she was mad. But she was also pumped up with adrenaline.' The film opened to mixed reviews but the real star, apart from Meryl, was the location: the Kootenai River in Montana and the rollicking ride it offered. Streep ended up with a golden globe nomination but the actual winner in the end was the whitewater tourist industry.

Today, the average river runner on the Colorado is likely to be someone out of town on a leisure break, who may be back at their desk on Monday morning. Long gone are the days of the early explorers like Wesley Powell, Stanton and Brown and even Glen and Bessie Hyde who were rafting into the unknown. Everyone wears a life preserver now. And there are regulations to follow, rules to keep.

Nevertheless, our reasons for coming to the canyon are probably much the same as those of the early river runners. We are curious, we want to explore. We love the beauty of the place. There is something fundamental for us in connecting with the river and immersing ourselves in the surrounding landscape. Most of all, we simply want the adrenaline ride it offers.

Those who indulge in the more extreme pursuits like base jumping will tell you that overcoming fear is a major motivation for them in doing what they do. One participant has described it as, 'A gateway to transcendence,' calling her sport, 'the ultimate metaphor for jumping into life rather than standing on the edge quivering.'

On some level whitewater rafting provides the same seductive feeling of danger. Up in the Poudre Pass on the knife edge that divides America, spit to the east and that is the land of the Mississippi, a beautiful broad river but one that mostly slips by at a gentle and secure walking pace. Spit to the west and that is the Colorado, a tumbling rushing ride through deep canyons that provides all the seat of the pants thrills you could want. A lot of people turn to the west. Who can blame them?

//

Running Dry: The Water Problem in America's Southwest

For those river runners who experience everything the mighty Colorado throws at them with its 'Big Drop' waves and billion gallon gush that propels them on a soaking and often chilly ride, the idea that there is a water shortage is something that does not immediately come to mind. In fact it sometimes feels like there is too much of the stuff.

Nevertheless, the river carves through parched country. The desert states of the Southwest USA, like Ohio and Arizona, experience temperatures in excess of 100 degrees Fahrenheit in summer and can receive less than nine inches of rain a year. It stands to reason that few people should live here, let alone try to farm the thin soils. But the Colorado changes everything. It helps sustain a population of over 40 million people and water five and a half million acres of farmland while its big dam hydroelectric plants keep the lights on. Without it this would be a barren and pretty empty quarter. Instead it is a place of big cities with sprawling suburbs where folks have swimming pools and sprinkle their lawns, munch on lettuce and lemons and make local grapes into wine. Slap bang In the middle of the

Mojave Desert is a metropolis of 2.3 million people which owes its existence to nothing more than having a good time. Once there, its visitors can take gondola rides on a scaled down version of the canals of Venice at the billion dollar Venetian Resort or relax by the eight acre lake in front of the nearby Bellagio hotel with its dancing fountains that spout almost five hundred feet in the air before landing with a choreographed splash. Some thirty miles south east of the Las Vegas strip is the Hoover dam, its transmission lines humming with the power that the river provides as it spins some seventeen turbines, each as big as a house. The hydro electric plant pumps out some four billion kilowatts of electricity a year. About a fifth of that is earmarked just to keep the casino's running.

The Colorado makes all this possible because in the course of the last century it has been plugged, diverted, and bored into so often that it is now one big water delivery and power generating system. It is in the nature of a long pipe feeding two large cisterns along its length, Lake Powell and Lake Mead, both huge artificial bodies of water created when the Glen Canyon and Hoover dams were built. These act as storage tanks and regulate the flow through the pipe. Each year the annual snowmelt in the Rockies replenishes that flow while the forty million inhabitants in states like Arizona, New Mexico, Utah and California together with their farms and industry tap it. They suck on the Colorado greedily-it is not for nothing that the huge concrete tubes that siphon the water from Powell and Mead for irrigation or drinking and which are big enough to drive a bus through, are called, 'Straws'.

On the face of it there is a lot of water in the Colorado. The official way of measuring liquid on this scale is to use foot acres which provide a useful way of trying to visualise such a large quantity. The Colorado historically gets about 15 million foot acres a year from the snow melt and other sources to keep it going. It can probably store up to four times that: sixty million foot acres. Put another way this is enough to drown the whole state of Utah in one foot of water.

The annual snow melt is however variable and so therefore are the annual flows of the river. On average for the first eighteen years of the twenty first century these have dropped dramatically; we have been in a period of relative drought for the whole of this time, (the driest period for a century), and it doesn't look like improving any time soon. Add to this the fact that the temperature has been creeping up over the same timescale due to global warming, (the first decade of the Twenty first century was two degrees Fahrenheit hotter than historic averages), and this is undoubtedly a cause for concern. And while the water supply has been dropping, the opposite is true of demand. Some estimates of population growth put the number of inhabitants in the Southwest as increasing by 70% in the next thirty years. By that time we are well on our way to needing two Colorados.

In fact it is possible that we are already taking out more water from the river than is going in. Certainly, the two cisterns of Lake Mead and Lake Powell are looking a bit like they need a top up. Lake Mead is now only 40% full and looks in the words of some locals, 'Like someone pulled the plug out.' There has even been a necessity to bore a new deeper 'straw' into the side of the lake because the old ones were in danger of being exposed by the drop in water levels. If that was the case, all they could suck would be air.

How did such an alarming state of affairs arise? The answer may lie partly in the history of the Southwest itself, a tale that involves epic courageous homestead settlement, conniving lawyerly scraps over water rights and a drop or two of unremittingly bare faced corporate greed.

Following the acquisition of much of the South West from Mexico in 1848, the Federal government of the USA wanted to attract settlers to these and other new territories and in 1862 brought in the 'Homestead Act' whereby it gave 160 acres of public land to any citizen who agreed to settle there for five years and make a go of cultivating his or her free holding. This proved popular and would eventually result in some 270 million acres of federal land passing to private ownership or some 10% of all the land in the United States.

Not everyone was convinced however that settling the dry lands of the west was a sustainable idea. John Wesley Powell, who had been the first to run Cataract and the Grand Canyon and who was not only an adventurer but also a serious academic, put his thoughts on the subject in writing when he published in 1879 his *Report on the Lands of the Arid Regions of the United States with a more detailed account of the lands of Utah'.* In it he addressed the need for land conservation and water management, stating that apart from the small proportion of the area close to water sources generally it should be held for grazing cattle. It seemed that no one was mentioning lettuce or fountains at that time. Instead he put forward irrigation schemes and proposals to avoid confrontation between the competing claims of different states to the waters that flowed through them, so that this scarce resource would not be wasted.

The Federal government was not however listening.

By that time it had been successfully lobbied by the railroad companies which had recently completed the first transcontinental railroad across the US and needed to see a quick return. As part of the financing deal with the government they had been given large tracts of land next to the route and these they sold at a handsome profit to speculators and settlers who were willing to pay the inflated prices they demanded. Leaving the land empty was not an option- they needed the homesteaders to pile in.

In 1883 Powell told an irrigation conference, 'Gentlemen, you are piling up a heritage of conflict and litigation over water rights, for there is not sufficient water to supply the land.' This turned out to be especially prescient in the light of future events, particularly the 'dust bowl' era of the 1930's in the American prairies where as a result of drought and over farming the soil of that region simply blew away.

With agricultural settlement in the Southwest there inevitably came the issue of water rights and with that came an army of lawyers. Water rights are tricky. Whose property is the river that flows nearby and how much can you draw from it? How much do you leave for everyone else downstream? Generally the idea prevailed that you had a right to extract water even if it wasn't on your property as long as you allowed the source on down the line for others to draw on. This seemed to make sense in a dry environment with few sources, unlike in a wet country like England where possession was ten tenths of the law. There was however inevitably scope for disagreement and litigation was never far away. In addition the seven states of the Colorado basin had to decide how to apportion the waters between them. It took until 1922 for them to reach agreement on this in the form of the 'Colorado River Compact' which allocated a quota of the flow to each. The only problem was that they probably divided up more water than was actually in the river.

Aside from the difficulties in sorting out how to share the Colorado, there was the problem by the 1920's of getting the most from it in the light of a burgeoning population that had put down its roots in the region. In 1860 there were probably just over half a million souls in the whole of the Southwest. By 1920 ten times as many people lived there. That population would increase by a half as much again in the following ten years. California in particular saw a rapid development. In 1860 some 4,385 people lived in Los Angeles. By 1920 it was 576,000 and by 1930 it was well over a million. Today it is the second largest city in the United States.

All these people together with the agriculture and industry that supported them were thirsty for water and so began the era of large infrastructure projects that included numerous irrigation canals and almost thirty dams along the river. The centrepiece of all this plumbing was the Hoover Dam, an epic feat of engineering that involved over 20,000 labourers and 6.6 million tons of concrete, enough it is said to lay a two lane highway right across the United States. Construction started in 1931 and took five years. By the time it was finished it was the largest structure of its kind on the planet, a sixty storey high arched shaped monolith, slung between the canyon walls at the bend of the river where it turns south and heads for the Gulf of California. While undoubtedly one of the wonders of the modern world, it cost 112 lives to build. For the men who broke the rock with 44 lb jackhammers while suspended 800 feet above the canyon floor, or those who poured the concrete, it was dangerous work. Death on the Hoover dam was even a family affair. The first official fatality was that of J. G. Tierney, a surveyor who drowned on December 20th, 1921, while looking for the ideal site. Some fourteen years later on exactly the same day, his son Patrick, an electrician, fell from an intake tower and was killed. The younger Tierney's death was the last recorded in the project's fatality list.

While the Hoover Dam succeeded in its objectives of providing water for irrigation, flood control and the generation of enough electricity to power an extra 1.3 million homes, its construction did have other consequences. For one, the Colorado never did get to the sea again. Prior to its damming the river had naturally flowed all the way out into the Gulf of California where it had built a wide freshwater delta capable of sustaining a rich ecosystem and providing a complex wildlife habitat. The Hoover dam backed up the waters of the Colorado, creating Lake Mead, a body of water over a hundred miles long and the largest reservoir in the United States. The penned up waters together with irrigation schemes near the mouth of the river had a devastating effect on the delta. In the next few decades it would become a place of brackish mudflats, cracked earth and poisonous salinity.

In March 2014, in an agreement between the United States and Mexico to provide water to rejuvenate the delta area, the last dam downstream temporarily opened its gates to release a 'Pulse Flow' that two months later reached the mouth of the river. This was the first time in sixteen years that a single drop of the Colorado had actually made it all the way down to the end.

The Hoover Dam opened the way to any number of dam and irrigation projects but it would be another thirty years before something on the same scale would be built. By that time society had changed somewhat and a growing environmental movement was determined to have its say. The proposals were therefore much more controversial.

To meet the increasing needs of the Southwest in the decades following the construction of the Hoover Dam, the United States Bureau of Reclamation (USBR), (the federal agency that was set up to oversee water resources and power generation), initially put forward the idea of building a number of dams, including one at Glen Canyon, some 400 miles upstream from Hoover and at Echo Park on the Green river before it joined the Colorado just below Cataract Canyon.

The environmentalists headed by David Brower and the 'Sierra Club', an early campaigning group, had a particular objection to the Echo Park proposal since it would involve submerging 100 miles of scenic canyon and strayed on the Dinosaur National Monument, an area of particular paleontological interest containing many fossil sites.

Brower faced some powerful interests and in particular the intransigence of the head of the Bureau of Reclamation, one Floyd Elgin Dominy, who proclaimed in a speech around that time that, '[The Colorado river without dams] is useless to anyone....I've seen all the wild rivers I ever want to see.'

Nevertheless in the face of public pressure the USBR finally backed down on the Echo Park project. The quid pro quo was however that a scaled up version of the Glen Dam would go ahead. David Brower and the Sierra Group were not that worried about Glen Dam, seeking to protect national monuments as a priority. Had they read John Wesley Powell they might have changed their minds. In

1869 he had written that the area was, 'A curious ensemble of wonderful features....carved walls, royal arches, glens.... mounds and monuments ...we decide to call it Glen Canyon.' By the time that Brower went to see for himself it was too late: the first concrete was about to be poured and a paradise drowned under the 500ft deep waters of Lake Powell which the dam would create. A half of Cataract Canyon's rapids would disappear and with it many petroglyphs carved by the ancient peoples together with the more recent signs left by the modern river runners who came to grief in the lost turbulent water. Today these live on at the bottom of the lake and can only be seen in some digital archive.

David Brower never forgave himself, calling his failure to prevent the dam being built as, 'The greatest sin I have ever committed.' In 1969 he left the Sierra club and went on to found, ' Friends of the Earth.'

Nevertheless, the successful opposition to the Echo Park dam is regarded as a watershed moment for the environmentalist cause. No longer could big government and vested interests have it all their own way. They were henceforth obliged to listen to public opinion when it came to trespassing on the wilderness. Some sort of line had been drawn.

The Glen Canyon Dam was not destined to be the last project along the Colorado and big schemes as well as smaller improvements will undoubtedly continue into the future, but it could be argued that they all suffer from a fatal flaw- there is simply not enough water and there never has been. It could even be argued that they just attract an expanding population with the promise of lettuce and hot tubs.

In the face of reducing supplies and ever increasing demand, what can be done so as not to disappoint them?

A few years ago the American Bureau of Reclamation published a study titled the, 'Colorado River Basin supply and demand summary: Managing water in the west'. In it were summarised the options it thought available to reduce the present imbalance between supply and demand. These broke down into four main areas: increasing supply, reducing demand, operating the system more effectively and better governance of the water system including closer co-operation between states and governments, (ie Mexico and the US).

Water conservation and more efficient energy use, including looking for alternative sources of power, will be vital to bridging the gap. Nevadans for example have become used to not splashing the stuff around: they are not allowed to just wash their car when they wish; they have to follow watering schedules. The water authority pays homeowners to replace thirsty lawns with rocks and drought-resistant vegetation. Golf courses are subject to water restrictions. Almost all wastewater is recycled or returned to the River itself.

It is certain that yet more expensive infrastructure and storage capacity will have to be built. Every year it is estimated that Lake Powell alone loses some 350,000 acre feet through evaporation even before the water is delivered through the pipelines. It goes without saying that the plumbing should not leak.

When it comes to the future even the mighty Colorado will not be enough to satisfy the thirst. The same Floyd Dominy who fought the environmentalists over the Glen Canyon dam understood this back in the 1960's when he addressed Congress on the problem. 'Sooner or later,' he told members of the House Subcommittee on Irrigation and Reclamation, 'and mostly sooner, the natural flows of the Colorado River will not be sufficient to meet the water demands, either in the lower basin or the upper basin, if these great regions of the nation are to maintain their established economies and realize their growth potential.' The desert states will undoubtedly have to look for additional supplies. Ideas on this range from rainfall harvesting to desalination of sea water and importation from wetter parts of the US or tapping other rivers like the Mississippi. The wilder options include piping in the Pacific, carrying water on tankers and even towing icebergs to the western seaboard.

All this may be possible in the long run with ingenuity, planning and co-operation. In the meantime states in the Southwest draw up drought contingency plans and get ready to impose ever greater restrictions on their citizens. But If, as some estimate, the population of the Southwest is going to top a hundred million in the latter part of this century, you can't help wondering where all the water is going to come from.

In 1922 when the basin states allocated the Colorado flow between them they did it on the assumption that something like 17.5 million foot acres of water would come down the river each year. In fact the real amount is something like 15 million foot acres, a shortfall that leaves about 12 million inhabitants dry. One commentator likens it to going on a rafting trip with a reasonable amount of beer promised to the party only to find that there is not enough to go around. How should it then be shared, who gives up what and who has prior rights to the beer? It is a tricky situation. It could get nasty. As the old saying goes, 'Whiskey's for drinking, water is for fighting over'. Let's hope it doesn't come to that.

A History of Arctic Exploration

You know how they say, 'What happens in Vegas, stays in Vegas?' What happens in the Arctic doesn't stay in the Arctic.
Kumi Naidoo, environmental campaigner

EARLY TIMES

The north Polar Regions have always been a place of mystery and wonder, a blank speculative space in our understanding and knowledge of the world that only really surrendered its secrets in the age of airships and nuclear submarines. Nowadays satellites record in detail its shrinking ice sheets from space while down on the surface we buzz around on snow cats or carve our way north on ice breakers in almost routine fashion, but it took centuries of failure to get there.

The first non native to visit the arctic was probably Pytheas, an ancient Greek explorer looking for trade routes in tin and amber. He not only visited the British Isles but pressed further north until he probably reached Iceland. There, he reported, the sea congealed and the sun never dipped below the horizon in mid-summer. Remarkably his voyage around 325 BC was contemporary with Alexander

243

the Great sweeping through northern India. Subsequent classical geographers thought he had just made it all up.

After all, it was well known that the far north was a dangerous place, guarded by huge mountains and fierce winds, and populated by dog headed people who wandered around like ferocious bears. Beyond such terrors lay a land of milk and honey but reaching it was fraught with difficulty.

Almost a thousand years later, no one still knew much different. Around seven hundred AD however, Irish monks began a number of voyages to the northwest to spread the word and seek the establishment of monasteries in new lands. Making the hazardous journey in open top boats of wickerwork and hides, they undoubtedly got as far as the Faeroes and Iceland from which tales of the 'Midnight Sun" again reached Celtic shores, one voyager priest noting that : 'Whatever task a man wishes to perform, even picking lice from his shirt, he can manage as well as in clear daylight.'

However it is doubtful they got much further and later folk narratives such as the 'Voyage of Saint Brendan,' (which some have interpreted as proof they landed in America), are more fantastical epics than fact based accounts. This is particularly true of the bit where the monks are greeted on the shore of the new world by a gnarled old man naked apart from a flowing white beard. That didn't happen.

When the Vikings arrived it was conquest, plunder and land they were after rather than quiet contemplation. Driven also by the need to flee tyranny and overpopulation back home they did not announce themselves quietly, embarking on a pillaging spree through Europe before raiding northern waters to find new places to conquer. By around 860 AD they had reached Iceland and thrown out the monks at prayer in their monasteries. In the early years of the tenth century they 'discovered' an even larger landmass to the west when a Norwegian, Gunnbjorn Ulfsson, found himself blown off course in a storm. It would be another Viking, Eric the Red, who would pull off the biggest PR stunt the world had known to date when he persuaded some five hundred settlers to come with him to the icy barren shore of this unappealing new land in 986 AD. He simply sold the idea to them by giving it an attractive name: he called it Greenland.

The Vikings eventually reached the coast of America in about a thousand AD, almost five hundred years before Christopher Columbus even set out on his voyage. At L'Anse aux Meadows at the northern tip of Newfoundland, Canada, there is evidence of one of their settlements, the remains of which were discovered by archaeologists in 1960. These show that they lived in timber frame buildings covered with sod to protect them against exposure to the elements. A number of everyday domestic items have been found in the earth, including a bronze fastening pin, an oil lamp and a bone knitting needle. It seems that it was a regular little community of over a hundred people. Other discoveries are being made that suggest to a surprising degree just how far the peoples of Scandinavia penetrated the continent, perhaps moving even further inland than we might expect.

Although the attempts at settlement on the American coast turned out to be short lived, the Norse colonies on the south western tip of Greenland did actually thrive for several centuries and at their height numbered several thousand inhabitants who subsisted by raising livestock and fishing in the nearby waters. In fact the Norse may still have had a presence there right up to the time when Columbus embarked on his own epic trip.

The Viking settlement was also remarkable in that the settlers must have been some of the first Europeans to encounter the native peoples who lived in those regions, so kicking off a history of contact between the white man and the 'Eskimo' that would become a perennial theme in the tale of exploring the north Polar regions. Such meetings would not always be happy ones, particularly for the indigenous peoples whose culture and very existence would become under threat, a state of affairs that continues in many respects today.

Some four million people currently live within the arctic circle and around 10% of them are indigenous to the area, people like the Inuit of northern Canada and Greenland, (population over 170,000), and the Saami who live in Finland, Norway and Sweden. In the Russian Federation there are over forty different groups alone. They face a number of challenges including climate change and economic pressures. The Reindeer herding Nenets in northern Siberia for example are sitting on what may well be the world's largest gas reserves, enough to keep Europe going for several decades. It is unlikely that they will benefit from such wealth. Presently they each receive a two thousand rouble (£40) subsidy every month. That is enough to buy a single barrel of heating oil in winter.

Nevertheless, in the days of the Norsemen, there does appear to have been a mostly peaceful co-existence, at least in Greenland, although it was not without periodic conflict. It may be that tensions between the local population and the settlers were one reason for the disappearance of the fleeting American colony.

In the end though what did for these Viking outposts was probably climate change. These places were settled during one of the warm 'blips' in the recent history of the earth's climate, (itself just a small episode in the longer running saga of an 'interglacial' period now considered subject to human influence.) During this so called, 'Medieval warm period', which lasted until about thirteen hundred AD, temperatures were the highest they had been for a thousand years and would only be subsequently matched by those we experience today. What would follow would be a cooling of the northern hemisphere that in Northern Europe would give rise to Christmas Frost Fairs on an iron hard Thames and which would be immortalised by Bruegel paintings of winter ice skaters on frozen lakes. This 'Little Ice Age' would continue until the middle of the nineteenth century. In such conditions no non native settlement at high latitudes was ever going to survive.

In fact for the next five hundred years until the age of Columbus, Europe had little to do with the Arctic, being preoccupied with such matters at home as bubonic plague, war and famine, not to mention the devotion of its energies towards the spiritual welfare of its population by means of the crusade or the stake. The Viking discoveries in Greenland and America were all but forgotten. Even as Europe left its so called 'Dark Ages' behind and embarked on a renaissance age of discovery with the ships of Spain and Portugal charting the Atlantic and Indian Oceans at the end of the fifteenth century, our knowledge of what lay very far north remained, to put not too fine a point on it, almost complete fantasy.

Even the foremost map maker of his era, Gerardus Mercator, had to resort to fairly wild speculation when he confidently announced in his 1595 world atlas that the

North Pole was bounded by four islands or countries and that:

> *'In the midst of the four countries is a whirl-pool . . . into which there empty these four indrawing Seas which divide the North. And the water rushes round and descends into the earth just as if one were pouring it through a filter funnel. It is four degrees wide on every side of the Pole, that is to say eight degrees altogether. Except that right under the Pole there lies a bare rock in the midst of the Sea. Its circumference is almost thirty three French miles, and it is all of magnetic stone.'*

And this over a hundred years since the new world had been re-discovered and some seventy since the entire globe had been circumnavigated by the ships of the era.

But then Mercator really had little to go on and in keeping with his time was duty bound to fill in the blanks by recording what the best authorities had to say on the matter. His 'Atlas', the first of its kind, was actually a tremendous achievement when it came to representing what we knew about the world at that time.

And besides, the notion of landmasses close to the Pole was not entirely fanciful. It would actually take until the age of aircraft for that myth to be dispelled.

In addition, the idea of a lodestone, or magnetic stone at the farthest north had a kind of logic. The magnetic compass had been around for centuries and was part of the essential navigational equipment of any sea voyage. Nowadays we know that the 'Magnetic Pole' is different to the Geographical Pole and wanders over the earth's surface, (presently it is in the Arctic Ocean between Canada and Russia), but in the sixteenth century all that was known was that the compass pointed due north and whatever it was that was tugging the needle was strong. Get close enough and no doubt it could pluck all the nails out of the ship's timbers. Why not a magnetic mountain?

In common with all other mapmakers on a large scale, Mercator faced the problem of representing a globe on a flat piece of paper. In the event he solved it by projecting points on the earth's surface and representing them on a cylinder which could be unfurled onto a flat plane. This of course meant a degree of distortion but it had the advantage that large areas could be shown on a single map and it expressly aided navigation by allowing seafarers to plot an accurate course by reference to its meridians or lines of longitude.

Unfortunately the whole thing broke down at the Poles. The earth is not a tin can with a lid and consequently the ends of the earth simply disappeared on a flat sheet of paper, or alternatively became infinitely big. So in his Atlas, Mercator included a map of the North Pole region that had us look directly down at it as we would if standing over a globe. It was revelatory. The big magnetic mountain and the four spurious landmasses at the centre aside, it is recognisable even to our twenty first century eyes. The northern coasts of Europe, Asia and America encircle and crowd the central Polar region and a significant part of them lie within the Arctic Circle. Northern Scotland, Scandinavia and Iceland are all recognisable and at the farthest tip of Asia the ring is broken by a sea passage between it and the shores of America that gives access to China and the Pacific. The map must have concentrated the minds of all the navigators of that era who looked at it. Not only is it an iconic representation of what we expect to see when we think about the Arctic but it also highlights an essential truth of which the early northern European sea voyagers were only too aware: the quickest way to the riches of the east meant sailing over the frigid polar sea.

THE NORTHWEST AND NORTHEAST PASSAGES

If Mercator's Arctic map was light on substance at the centre of the Polar world, it did include many of the more recent real world discoveries that had been made along the northern coasts of the land masses that fringed it. In the hundred years since Columbus sailed to America, sea voyagers like the Venetians John and Sebastian Cabot, the Englishman Sir Hugh Willoughby, and the Dutchman Willem Barentsz, had been busy sailing along the rim of the Arctic basin and gradually mapping more and more of the seas off northern Russia and Canada. Essentially this was a consequence of their attempts to reach China.

In the late fifteenth century world, access by Europe to the silks, spices and opium of the far east foretold fabulous wealth but necessitated a prolonged and perilous sea voyage round the southern tip of Africa or South America to reach the Indian or Pacific oceans, a round trip of potentially more than twenty eight thousand nautical miles that lasted many months. Shanghai to Rotterdam via the Cape of Good Hope for example is a 27,592 nautical mile round trip but only 16,092 miles using the Northeast Passage; how much more convenient then to go over the top of the world. And for countries like England or the Dutch republic, emerging from a recent war of independence from Spain, there was an added impetus to finding a northern sea route to the fabled 'Cathay', one which resulted from an agreement between the two most powerful nations of the day, Spain and Portugal, which purported to carve up the world and with it the sea lanes between them.

The 1494 Treaty of Tordesillas between Spain and Portugal was an attempt to settle any bickering between the two countries as to how to divide the spoils of the recently discovered new world. Considering that this was just two years since Columbus had set foot in the Bahamas and nothing much had yet been discovered, it was an audacious if not to say arrogant piece of treaty making in which everything east of a line running from Greenland through eastern Brazil was Portuguese and everything to the west was Spanish.

Unsurprisingly the other countries of Europe ignored this completely but it didn't stop the Spanish and Portuguese trying to lock them out of the Atlantic trade routes. Moreover by the time of Mercator's atlas, Spain had built a huge empire in central and southern America awash with gold and silver, while Portugal had claimed Brazil and had territories along the African and Indian coasts. To all intents and purposes it was the Spanish galleon and Portuguese caravel that ruled the waves of the Atlantic at that time.

The only alternative was to go north and seek a route there. A passage either northeast along the coast of Siberia or north west threading among the Canadian high arctic islands and out through what would become the Bering strait would break the strangle hold of Spain and cut voyage times immensely, possibly by up to a half. Finding such a route would be an immeasurable prize, and the search for it became a grand obsession.

The first to look for a north west passage was John Cabot, sent by King Henry VII of England in 1494 with the power to investigate, claim and possess lands, *'Which before this time were unknown to all Christians.'* Rather cannily, the King was set to receive one fifth of all the goods he came back with, although he invested no money of his own in the venture. In the event, goods were few and far between as Cabot did not get to Cathay but landed probably at Newfoundland or on the coast of Labrador and only stayed to take on fresh water and observe a human trail and the remains of a fire. His reward for re-discovering the continent found by the Vikings was the princely sum of ten pounds given to him by the King.

Following his father's failure to find the Northwest passage, Sebastian Cabot decided to head in the opposite direction and in 1553 organised an expedition to find a northeast route to China under the auspices of the The 'Company of Merchant Adventurers', an early joint stock business formed with the purpose of the, *'Discovery of Lands, Territories, Iles, Dominions and Seigniories Unknowen.'* Sebastian chose Sir Hugh Willoughby, a distinguished soldier, to lead the expedition together with Richard Chancellor, a mariner and native of Bristol as his second in command. They soon ran into trouble. In a storm off northern Norway, Willoughby and Chancellor were separated and Sir Hugh's ships drifted off the icy coasts of Russia before making landfall in northern Lapland, where seeing that the weather had turned, *'Evile'* he judiciously decided to spend the winter.

Chancellor had better luck, sailing unknowingly

past Willoughby's position and into Russia's White Sea, eventually reaching the port of Archangel. From there it was a six hundred mile sleigh ride to Moscow and the court of the fearsome Tsar Ivan the Terrible who nevertheless received his visitor warmly and conducted trade negotiations which ended with the Company of Merchant Adventurers claiming the monopoly on business with Muscovy.

Fate was less kind to Sir Hugh Willoughby. The following spring some Russian hunters and fishermen found his body and those of his crew still on board the ships that had taken refuge on the Lapland coast, ostensibly starved or frozen to death. There was however something strange about the manner of their passing, contemporary accounts noting that some of the figures were, *'Seated in the act of writing, pen still in hand,'* while others were, *'At table, platters in hand and spoon in mouth,'* or, *'In various postures, like statues, as if they had been adjusted and placed in these attitudes.'* Moreover, the supplies on board were still plentiful.

It seemed that Sir Hugh and his men had succumbed not to the cold or starvation but an even more insidious killer not properly understood at the time. In an effort to keep out the bitter chill, the crew had stuffed up every porthole and other outlet until the ship was sealed and then kept the coal fires burning inside. What had done away with the expedition were not the rigours of the climate but the no less deadly affect of carbon monoxide poisoning.

Willem Barentsz's expedition of 1596 faced a similar nemesis when they built a shelter on the ice and to keep the heat in agreed, *'To stop all the doores and the chimney.'* Barentsz had sailed due north from Amsterdam and on the way had discovered Svalbard before moving east and ending up on the northern tip of Novaya Zemlya, a six hundred mile long archipelago off the coast of Siberia. (This is a place so wild and remote that it would become in the twentieth century the Soviets' favourite spot for nuclear testing, including the detonation of the largest hydrogen bomb in human history, the so called, 'Tsar Bomba').

Inevitably Barentsz's ship got stuck in the pack ice and he decided to use some washed up timbers to construct a building to house the crew while they wintered there. While this offered shelter, it was understandably a cold place-so chilly that even with a fire burning the men would be covered in a layer of frost as they slept. Attempts to keep their feet warm resulted in setting fire to their socks and accordingly they took to going to bed with heated cannon balls. Eventually on the 7th of December, in the words of one of the ship's officers, *'It was still foule weather....which brought an extreame cold with it; at which time we knew not what to do....one of our companions gave us counseill to burn some of the sea-coles that we had brought out of the ship which would cast a great heat.'*

Sealing up the hut was not however a good idea. The men were soon, *'Taken with a great swounding and daseling in our heads,'* and it was only when the chimney and doors were opened that they, *'Recovered our healthes again by reason of the cold aire.'*

Barentsz's men had been fortunate in having a lucky escape. It was however not the only threat they faced. In a previous expedition they had been the first to encounter a Polar bear which rather unwisely they tried to take home. In the present trip east of Svalbard they found themselves actually caught in the claws of another of the beasts; one of the crew was attacked and had his head, according to contemporary accounts, *'Bit..in sunder,'* and his blood,

'*Suckt out.*' When the men tried to come to his aid the bear grabbed another, '*Out from the companie, which she tare in peeces, wherewith all the rest ran away.*'

After all the privations and horrors Barentsz and his men were still stuck in the ice the following summer, whereupon it was decided to launch some small boats and head off home. After seven weeks at sea they were rescued by a Russian merchant vessel and it was not until the first of November the following year that they arrived back in Amsterdam. Only twelve of the original members of the expedition survived. Barentsz himself died a few days after the boats left his abandoned ship behind.

Despite the travails and failures of these early expeditions the enthusiasm for being the first to find a Northwest or Northeast Passage remained undiminished. Men like Martin Frobisher, John Davis and Henry Hudson continued to explore the coasts of Greenland and Canada, reaching as far as what is now Hudson Bay.

Martin Frobisher, who would distinguish himself later in naval battle against the Spanish Armada, first made a fool of himself over the prospect of gold in the Arctic. Arriving on the south coast of what is now Baffin Island in his first expedition of 1576, he didn't stay long, being forced to beat a hasty retreat after the local Inuit had captured some of his men and he had taken a hostage in return. He arrived back in England with the sole Inuit he had taken prisoner and a lump of rock he had picked up. The Inuit promptly died of a bad cold but the rock was proclaimed on good authority to have the golden touch and there followed a number of further expeditions all blessed by Queen Bess in the hope that everyone's fortune would be made. In the process the search for the Northwest Passage was forgotten. Within the next two years over a thousand tons of Arctic dirt had been dug up and shipped back to Britain where it proved to be just that, or at best Iron Pirates, also known as 'Fools Gold'. Frobisher never went back. Later he redeemed himself by dying while fighting the Spanish.

John Davis, a contemporary of Frobisher, was a very different man, less impetuous and more interested in quiet contemplation and scholarly pursuits. With sterling British eccentricity he took with him a four piece orchestra on his trip and on encountering some threatening Inuit, ordered it to strike up and his men to dance. The locals were enchanted and quickly backed down. The next day they returned for another concert.

Davis covered much the same waters as Frobisher but unlike him was not slapdash and mapped and charted the territory assiduously, which was of immense assistance to the explorers who came after him.

He also had a somewhat enlightened approach to the indigenous population, writing that they were, *'People of good stature...with whom I have converced and not found them rudly barbarous,' unlike the,' Caniballs.....in the Southerne parts of America.'*

Henry Hudson is best known for his discovery of the bay that is named after him, a huge bite out of the top of the American continent whose waters cover an area equivalent to the Baltic Sea. Prior to his 1610 expedition north, Hudson had sailed up the river that would also bear his name, visiting New York Harbour on the way and claiming it for the Dutch who were his pay masters at the time. Back in England and put under house arrest for working for a foreign government, Hudson was eventually given backing for his expedition to find the Northwest Passage. His explorations raised hope that the route to China could be found. For some time there had been a belief that a huge water way would cut right through the American continent and link the Atlantic with the Pacific, speculation that was fuelled by the exploration of the wide rolling St Lawrence river by the Frenchman Jacques Cartier whose expeditions in the mid sixteenth century convinced him that he was not far from finding an outlet to the east. In the event this turned out to be a forlorn hope but the discovery of such a body of water as Hudson Bay was tantalising in that it could very well be the open sea that led to the riches of Cathay. It didn't take long to disprove this notion: five years later William Baffin was the pilot on an expedition that circumnavigated the area and proved conclusively that it was a bay and not the entrance to the China Sea.

At that point everyone pretty much lost interest in the Northwest Passage, at least for a time. Not only was the route to the east proving elusive but the original impetus to discover it was no longer there. The world of the seventeenth century was one of declining Spanish influence hastened by the economic dislocation caused by the very riches of its empire in the new world. By this time so much gold and silver was pouring in from the mines in central and south America that it was causing the sort of inflationary pressures that would give rise to a popular saying of the time: 'Everything is dear in Spain except silver.'

Besides, countries like England, France and Holland were now building their own empires over which they would fight each other during the next two centuries. They were more interested in protecting the riches of furs and sugar in their own territories than finding a frigid sea route. In fact for almost two hundred and fifty years no European would go farther north than John Davis did in 1586. When interest resumed in western arctic exploration it would be for reasons of protecting spheres of influence and imperial prestige rather than finding a way to China, which by that time was itself just part of the huge cake being carved up by the European colonial powers.

Following the defeat of Napoleon in 1815, one of the problems the British faced was that they had too many ships and not enough wars. It was Britain by that time that ruled the waves but what to do with the huge redundant fleet and all the captains and admirals going spare? The answer perhaps was to send them north.

THE BRITISH NAVY

One of the first British naval expeditions to be sent back to the Arctic was commanded by Admiral Sir John Ross with Lieutenant William Edward Parry as second in command.

Setting out in April 1818, The expedition is noted for re-discovering the entrance to the Northwest passage that had been forgotten since Davis's time, (or perhaps more likely kept quiet by the merchant company that sought to protect the knowledge from its competitors), and also for its encounters with the local population.

These people had lived in the Arctic for thousands of years and never having had the urge, like the white man, to explore much further north, regarded the admiralty expeditions sent their way with bemusement. There is no doubt they found these visitors strange. When John Ross met a party of Inuit on the ice during his voyage he greeted them in the full naval dress uniform of the time, stiff with rich brocade and gold lacings, his head adorned with a bicorn hat. 'Where are you from?' they politely asked, adding, 'Is it the sun or the moon?'

While the indigenous population were wary of the intruders who gate crashed their lands, sometimes assisting them, other times fighting them or more often than not simply ignoring them, for their part the Europeans, especially in the early days remained aloof. They often had a parochial attitude towards the natives, refusing to believe that such primitive peoples had anything to teach a more 'civilised' and 'superior' race, even about basic survival in such a harsh and alien place. Later that would change but in the nineteenth century days of British Empire its navy preferred its blue woollens to the Inuit furs that would have kept them warm and dry and often passed over the opportunity to use dogs for hauling supplies, a mistake that would cost many of them their lives.

This lack of understanding extended to the differing social conventions of these peoples which sometimes outraged the sensibilities of the delicate intruders. The good lieutenant Parry noted in the journal of his own 1819 expedition that as far as the local women were concerned, 'I fear we cannot give a very favourable account of [their] chastity, nor of the delicacy of their husbands in this respect.' His second in command George Lyon went on, 'It is considered extremely friendly for two men to exchange wives for a day or two [particularly when one was off on a hunting expedition], and the request is sometimes made by the women themselves.'

However shocking that sort of thing appeared to be, it did not stop both Parry and Lyon becoming quite friendly themselves with the natives. Some years later the explorer Charles Francis Hall would come across an Eskimo woman who claimed to be the lover of both men and was told that additionally Lyon had impregnated two others, both sisters. Such a tradition of close relations would continue into modern times. In 1900 the wife of American explorer Robert Peary was surprised to meet an Inuit woman who claimed to be married to her husband and had a baby by him. If that was true some of his descendents probably still live on in the Arctic today.

In terms of discovery, Ross's expedition effectively did no more than retrace the steps of Davis and Baffin some years previously. Sailing up the west coast of Greenland he then rounded the tip of Baffin Island at seventy four degrees latitude north before turning into Lancaster Sound, a stretch of water between it and Devon Island to the north. There Ross made a great blunder. He had found the real entrance to the Northwest Passage but he didn't pursue it, having had a 'Fata Morgana' moment where he believed he saw a range of mountains cutting across the sound and blocking his way.

A year later Parry, in his own expedition, would simply sail through these imaginary mountains and keep going, much to the consternation of Admiral Ross and the embarrassment of the British naval establishment. Later John Ross would redeem his reputation by surviving four winters in the arctic during 1829-1833 in the company of his nephew James Clark Ross and return to England a hero. During that time he mapped a significant part of the north Canadian coast, discovered a peninsula which he named Boothia after the Gin magnate Felix Booth, (who in an early example of commercial sponsorship, financed the whole expedition), and was basically kept alive by the local

Inuit whose diet of fresh seal blubber protected him from scurvy and whose furs kept him from freezing. In such an environment the steam engine he brought with him to help power his boat, (the first such engine in the Arctic) proved to be a somewhat unreliable and inappropriate encumbrance. It was unceremoniously dumped on an icy shore.

Parry's own expedition was the most successful to date. He sailed six hundred miles past the mirage in Lancaster Sound, threading his way through the high Arctic islands off Canada and travelling half the distance to the extreme tip of Alaska and the entrance to the Pacific Ocean beyond. He also managed to get to eighty two degrees latitude, further north than anyone else to date, a record that would stand for the next fifty years. For his efforts the British government granted him five thousand pounds, a reward of twenty thousand pounds remaining in the offering for anyone who would complete the whole passage, (a huge sum for those days).

Ross and Parry's expeditions undoubtedly advanced science and geographical knowledge but they also probably had another affect, in that they helped bring the notion of Arctic exploration to the attention of the public. The tales of such a desolate and beautiful landscape and the privations of the men who suffered its hardships captured the imagination of the time.

In 1823, inspired by Parry's voyage, the German romantic artist Caspar David Friedrich painted, *Das Eismeer*, (' The Sea of Ice'), a depiction of a stark, ethereal Polar sea of white brutally swallowing a crushed sailing ship. In the picture sharp splinters of Ice pierce the lowering sky like knives while in the foreground the brown timbers of the ship gradually merge into slabs of frozen sea. There is no sign of human presence, only the bleak loneliness of a scene in which nature re-asserts itself.

This was a compelling if somewhat pessimistic image, summoning up a mysterious and fantastically alien world set to overwhelm those who had been sent there to conquer it. Such a struggle between man and nature would provide any number of heroes for the Victorian public to swoon over, none more so than Sir John Franklin whose 1845 expedition simply vanished into the Polar vastness never to be seen again.

THE DISAPPEARANCE OF JOHN FRANKLIN, THE MAN WHO ATE HIS BOOTS

On the face of it such a loss was surprising. Franklin's voyage was no hare brained scheme, in fact it was the most lavish and well equipped expedition to date, involving as it did two sturdy ships manned by a hundred and twenty eight sailors and powered by steam engines, all provisioned for three years in the Arctic. It took with it the latest technology ranging from the central heating on board using the steam run from the engines to the foodstuffs preserved by the then novel process of canning, (although the can opener would have to follow. In those days access was by chisel and hammer). It even had room for a fully stocked library of almost three thousand books and a range of musical instruments, the better to while away the long Polar winter.

And Franklin was no fool, no matter how various commentators have tried to paint him since. His had been a long career with the navy; he had seen plenty of action, including at the battle of Trafalgar and had risen to the rank of Rear Admiral. Nor was he new to the Arctic exploration game, having been there twice before, including an 1819 expedition to the north Canadian wilderness in which he had been reduced to eating shoe leather to avoid starvation. Back in England he became famous as, 'The man who ate his boots.'

When after a year no one had heard anything from John Franklin, the British Admiralty was not unduly worried. As far as they were concerned he was in it for the long haul. His orders were specific: find the Northwest Passage and have done with it. By now they fully expected him to be in Alaska.

As time went by the navy continued to prevaricate but they had not counted on the redoubtable Lady Jane Franklin who in the next few years would hector, cajole and conduct a brilliant PR campaign in an effort to get the establishment to find out where her husband had gone. It would be a mission of love and later desperation in which she would spend her fortune and pull every string of social connection, right up to enlisting the help of British Royalty and even the American president who assisted in sending two United States parties to search for the lost British admiral.

But it was all to no avail. During the next decade there were launched some forty search and rescue missions at huge cost and still the mystery of what had happened to Sir Franklin remained unsolved. Then in the autumn of 1854 came word that a number of artefacts from his expedition had been recovered including an order of merit given to Franklin and a small silver plate with his name engraved on it.

The items were in the possession of a group of Inuit encountered by the Scottish surgeon and explorer John Rae on an expedition to map the Boothia Peninsula for the Hudson Bay Company. Moreover the Inuit told him that they had heard of another group of their fellow natives who four years earlier had spotted a number of white men dragging a boat and sledges on the barren ice of King William Island considerably further north. One of them fitted the description of John Franklin.

The Inuit could see that the men were starving but could do little to help them from their own meagre provisions. When they next returned all they had found were corpses.

This appeared to conclude the matter but it was not enough for the grieving Lady Jane. She sponsored one final expedition which headed for King William Island where the tragedy took place. There the written record of Franklin's voyage was found in a tin can buried in a cairn, consisting of two notes. The first dated 24th May 1847 stated happily that, 'All was well.' The second, almost a year later told the story of the abandonment of the ships that had been stuck in the ice for over twenty months and the decision to go south. It also recorded that Sir John had died on 11th June 1847, just a few days after the first optimistic entry.

The reasons for the fate of the Franklin expedition have remained a subject of debate ever since. Clearly they faced starvation and exposure but certain questions remain. They were actually dying in large numbers before they even abandoned ship. Then they set off with inadequate provisions for a journey through a landscape devoid of game that was a thousand miles from any civilisation. Included in the detritus strung along their march to death was a small boat they had hauled loaded with items that could not possibly have helped them survive, including any number of heavy books, among them a copy of *The Vicar of Wakefield*.

Something had got into the systems of these men, if not their heads.

In June 1981, Owen Beattie, a professor of anthropology at the University of Alberta undertook a study of the remains of some of the expedition members using modern forensic techniques to investigate their cause of death. As well as finding the physical effects of scurvy, bone analysis showed levels of lead concentration some ten times higher than normal. Suspicion fell on the lead soldering on the tin cans the expedition carried with them and also the water system and piping associated with the steam engines that helped drive the ships, although this has never been proven. If lead poisoning had been a factor in the demise of Franklin and his men, it would have accumulated from the day they set sail from England. In that case their fate would have been sealed from the start.

There was one final twist to the tragic story of the Franklin expedition, a matter that the Inuit had alluded to in their conversation with John Rae, but which would have so horrified the Victorian public that the British naval establishment tried to suppress news of it for years. Nevertheless Beattie saw evidence of it in the bones he uncovered, some of which were scarred by knife cuts or broken in an apparent attempt to get at the marrow.

For John Rae the Inuit description of what they had found made it clear: *'From the mutilated state of many of the bodies, and the contents of the kettles, it was evident that our wretched countrymen had been driven to the last dread alternative as a means of sustaining life.'*

The Admiralty of course suppressed his account. Having your boots for dinner is one thing, eating your own ship mates though-that was strictly bad form.

THE FINAL RITES OF PASSAGE: COSSACKS, A HERRING BOAT AND THE 'CRYSTAL SERENITY'

Following the failure of the Franklin expedition, the British naval establishment pretty much gave up on the Northwest Passage. While Franklin had been sent there and failed, ironically it was the numerous attempts at his rescue that finally resolved the question and brought about the mapping and charting of the Polar basin from Greenland to Nome, Alaska. In the process they proved that a mostly ice blocked northern shipping route was just not commercially viable.

Much the same would prove true of the eastern end of the Polar rim, at least until the faster boats and sturdier ice breakers of the twentieth century could cope with the vast distances along the Siberian coast and not have to winter in some frozen harbour.

After the early efforts of men like Willoughby and Barentsz, the seventeenth century in the east was the era of the Cossacks, those fearsome free ranging frontier peoples that the Tsars unleashed on the huge territory beyond the Urals which they conquered in the name of the Russian empire. The Indigenous peoples who met them, often armed with nothing more than bows and arrows were quickly swept away with prodigious cruelty and by 1640 the Cossacks were on the Pacific coast, just north of Japan, having added hugely to the Tsar's domains.

The Cossacks also took to the sea, hopping along the coast between river mouths in Kochs, small flat bottomed ships that with their strengthened timbers and rounded lines were perfectly designed to sail in the ice chocked waters. In many respects the design characteristics of a Koch were those taken up by modern ice breakers which ride up on the ice and then break it with their weight.

Bit by bit they inched along the coast until much of it was known to them. In 1648 one Semyon Ivanovich Dezhnev went further and in a perilous voyage almost certainly became the first to sail round the eastern tip of Russia in the sea between it and the western point of Alaska. Today this is known as the Bering Strait after the Danish sea captain Vitus Bering who some eighty years later repeated Dezhnev's feat. By that time however, the Cossack's torrid tale of shipwreck and attack by the local natives had all but been forgotten.

Bering's expedition was part of an ambitious project launched by the Tsar, Peter the Great, with the intention of achieving nothing less than the mapping of the entire northern Russian coast. It was supposed to take two years to complete this task. In the event it took ten. While it conclusively proved that America and Asia were separated by water and that a Northeast Passage was theoretically possible, the ice locked waters off Siberia did not make it a practical proposition for the sailing ships of the time. Many of those who took part in the expedition succumbed to the cold or disease. Baring himself died in 1741 off the coast of Russia's fiery and bear ridden Kamchatka peninsula. He had been driven there by the perennial storms that blow in the strait that took his name.

As far as the Northwest Passage was concerned it would not be a flotilla of mighty admiralty ships that would first sail its entire length, but a herring boat with a crew of six. In 1906, Roald Amundsen who would go on to become the conqueror of the South Pole, (and possibly the North Pole too), reached Nome, Alaska, after a three year voyage hugging the north Canadian coast in the *Gjoa*, a forty five tonne shallow draft fishing vessel. It was a remarkable feat of navigation but served to emphasise that the Northwest Passage was just not economic-the really big ships would get wedged in the ice and would never get through.

That is, until today. In recent years the Northwest Passage has been opening up, a trend that with global warming looks set to continue. In the summer of 2007 the sea route became totally ice free for the first time in centuries. In 2012 the forty three thousand tonne passenger ship, *The World*, re-traced Amundsen's herring boat route but this time with almost five hundred passengers on board, enjoying facilities that included six restaurants, a fitness centre, a spa and several cocktail lounges. The following year the commercial bulk carrier *MS Nordic Orion* made a transit of the passage when it carried a cargo of over sixty six thousand tons of coal between Vancouver and the Finnish port of Pori, reducing the same trip through the Panama Canal by over a thousand miles. There followed the *Crystal Serenity*, a cruise ship with a thousand passengers and six hundred crew which left Vancouver, Canada in August 2016, used Amundsen's route and reached New York on September 17th. A single ticket for the thirty two day trip started at $22,000, undoubtedly many times the cost of Amundsen's whole expedition. They quickly sold out.

The last time these waters were navigable in this way may well have been in the age of Eric the Red and his Greenland PR stunt. The dreams of a millennium may be about to be finally realised courtesy of climate change abetted by the stuff we are pouring into the atmosphere. It is an odd sort of triumph.

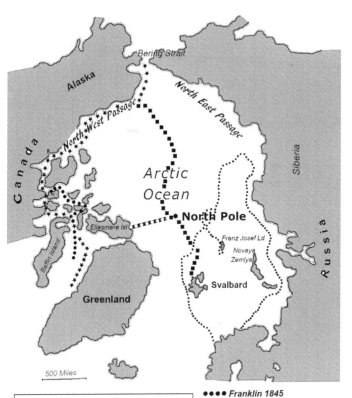

Alaska

Bering Strait

North East Passage

North West Passage

Canada

Arctic
Ocean

Ellesmere Isl

Baffin Island

Russia

Siberia

Franz Josef Ld

Novaya
Zemlya

North Pole

Svalbard

Greenland

500 Miles

Arctic exploration: the 'race'
around the Polar basin.

● ● ● Franklin 1845
· · · · · Nansen 1893
* * * Amundsen 1903
⊂□□□⊃ Peary 1909
■ ■ ■ ■ Wally Herbert 1968

THE NORTH POLE

While, by the final decades of nineteenth century, the Arctic lands of the Polar rim had been almost entirely discovered together with the sea routes that hugged their coasts, no one had still ventured much beyond latitude eighty degrees North. That most glittering prize of Arctic exploration, attaining the North Pole, seemed ever more far away.

This was not for lack of trying. In 1827 William Parry, with British admiralty backing, had set off north of Svalbard with the specific intention of reaching the pole. In the event after a month on the ice he gave up, but not before reaching eighty two degrees, a record for that time and one that would stand for another fifty years.

Parry's expedition and others of the time suffered from their encounter with the impenetrable mass of ice they found once they sailed north, but also laboured under a fatally flawed appreciation of what the Polar region was about, being still in thrall to the seductive myths set out in Mercator's maps almost three hundred years ago.

While no one believed any longer in a whirlpool, or magic magnetic mountain at the top of the world, the notion of an inner Polar sea did persist and with it the belief that once you had got past the plug of pack ice it would be pretty much plain sailing all the way to the pole.

Today of course, we know that the idea is absurd, but even in the age of the steam locomotive and the electric light bulb it remained adhered to, perpetuated by such luminaries as August Petermann, the Queen of England's geographer who pronounced with equal confidence that, 'It is a well known fact that there exists to the north of the Siberian coast ....a sea open at all seasons..[and that]...a similar open sea exists on the American side.'

As late as 1856 the first American to make a bid for the North Pole, Elisha Kane, believed he had found this open sea when an advanced party came back from the northwest coast of Greenland with the report that they had seen, *'Not a speck of ice.'* The reality was somewhat different. The expedition remained frozen in and had to start burning the ship's timbers for warmth and rely on the local Inuit to keep them from starvation. Eventually they were reduced to consuming a frozen bear's head which they had collected as a specimen.

Parry himself had hedged his bets by cleverly taking with him a number of small boats on runners, so possibly inventing the world's first amphibious vehicle. But even his ingenuity could not defeat the rough ice piled into pressure ridges. Moreover, the ice was moving south under his feet, propelled by the sea currents and winds, so that after a slog of almost seven hundred miles he had to give up, realising to his disappointment that he was getting nowhere.

By the 1880's it began to be appreciated that the upper Polar region was in fact one big frozen sea drifting around the place and that the only way to get to the North Pole would be to march there on foot. It was simply not possible to sail there, at least in the conventional sense.

An understanding of Polar currents and the circulation of the ice masses improved towards the end of the century, spurred on by the discovery that artefacts which started life on the coast of Siberia were often washed up on the shores of Greenland on the other side of the Polar basin. This sweeping motion around the clock face was used by the Norwegian Fridtjof Nansen in his expedition of 1893 to

1896 on board the *Fram* in which he had the startling and somewhat brilliant notion of letting the ice take him to his destination rather than battling against it.

The *Fram* was a specially constructed ship for Polar exploration, (Later, Roald Amundsen would take it to the Antarctic on his successful expedition to conquer the South Pole.) In a nod to the Cossack Koch from earlier times, Its rounded shallow hull allowed it to rise up over the ice rather than be crushed by it. It was also tremendously strong, built with layers of oak, pine and South American Greenheart timber so that it could withstand the kind of pressure waves that would smash other vessels to pieces.

On the 20th July 1893 the *Fram* left northern Norway and skirted the Russian coast before Nansen let it become stuck in the frozen sea off eastern Siberia. From there, he expected the ice to take him northwards but after a year of drift the ship's meandering course had still not taken them much further towards their objective. Nansen calculated that at their present rate of progress of about a mile a day, it would take them five years to get to the North Pole. On 14th March 1895 he duly abandoned the *Fram* to the rest of the crew and set off over the ice with another member of the expedition, Hjalmar Johansen, in a dash on skis, towing sledges behind them. By April they had travelled to within 226 miles of the Pole and eighty six degrees north, (a record), before having to turn back, the movement of the ice preventing any further progress.

Nansen and his comrade had truly jumped ship. Hundreds of miles from any possible rescue, they faced a hazardous fourteen month journey on their own back to Norway. Meanwhile the *Fram* drifted on, spending another year and a half in the ice. Nansen finally reached home in the summer of 1896, arriving shortly before the ship that he had originally sailed on. In the end the crew had managed to free the vessel from the ice, but only after they had resorted to dynamite to blast it out of the frozen embrace.

Nansen did not get to the North Pole but his expedition was responsible for much scientific work on the ocean currents and furthered our understanding of the geography of the Polar basin. It also confirmed the suspected difficulties in reaching farthest north. His reputation remains as one of the greatest Polar adventurers, a man whose expertise would be vital to those explorers who came next.

By the turn of the century no one had yet stood on the North Pole, but in 1908 Frederick Cook, an American surgeon and adventurer claimed the prize, followed by the Philadelphian born US navy lieutenant Robert Peary in 1909. Both had a number of expeditions under their belts but were adamant that they would not be denied what would be the greatest pinnacle of their Polar careers. Pretty soon they were at each other's throats as claim and counter claim flew between them. It would be a long if ultimately futile fight. Nowadays most people doubt that either of them really got there.

COOK AND PEARY: THE BITTER FEUD.

On 1st September 1909 the world woke up to the announcement that the Pole had been conquered. *'The North Pole reached,'* ran the headlines in the press.

'Dr Cook reached the North Pole on 21st April 1908,' the report went on, *'Arrived in May 1909 from Cape York at Upernavik', (Greenland.)*

A few days later there was more startling news. The 3rd September edition of the New York Times reported:

'Peary discovers the North Pole after eight trials in 23 years.' Apparently he had got there on 6th April 1909. The newspaper mentioned that when he got back to civilisation he had cabled his wife to tell her that, 'He had the D.O.P.' 'That meant Damned old pole,' the happy explorer's wife had told the press men.

By the time that Peary had managed to get his own good news out, Cook was already being feted as the true first to stand at the top of the world. Having spent over a year on the ice battling to get back to Greenland after reaching the pole, Cook was only a few months ahead of his rival in reconnecting with the world, even though Peary had started out a year later. But those months had mattered in the PR business of ensuring your name is the one in the history books. Peary had some catching up to do.

Robert Edwin Peary, who one day would become a Rear-Admiral, was nothing if not ambitious. He was not a man who liked to come second. 'I must have fame,' he wrote to his Mother after one of his earlier expeditions to Greenland, carrying on somewhat dramatically, 'I cannot reconcile myself to years of commonplace drudgery....when I see an opportunity to gain it now and sip the delicious draught.' He was sure that his exploits would lead to, 'Enduring honour....social advancement [and] powerful friends.' And so they did. Peary was well connected with a circle of admirers that included wealthy businessmen who helped finance his expeditions and patrons of the National Geographic Society who shared in his glory. They all had a vested interest in his advancement. With such back up he went to war with Cook and proceeded to trash his claims, telling everyone that his rival was a fraud.

Not that Cook actually helped his own cause that much. The dispute between the two adventurers does raise a tricky problem in connection with Arctic exploration: how do you prove you have been to the North Pole? Unlike Antarctica which is a continent, the north Polar Regions are under water. You can't plant a flag in the ice at ninety degrees north and expect it to stay there-the drift of the pack ice means that a couple of minutes later it is somewhere else and eventually it will end up around Greenland or Northern Canada thousands of miles away. In the absence of any possible physical evidence that you have reached the spot, the only way to verify your claim, at least in the years before satellite tracking and GPS, lay in keeping meticulous navigation logs and offering them as proof. These together with your speed of passage cross checked with the few known land marks might be enough to get you a gold Polar medal. Suffice to say that in the heroic age of Arctic exploration many of the logs kept were not that meticulous. In the case of some, they were downright fraudulent. Cook though, didn't seem to have any at all.

And then there was the story offered by his two Inuit companions about their fourteen month perambulation around the ice sheet and the frozen north Canadian islands before getting home. The trouble was that parts of it did closely resemble the plot of an actual work of fiction: Jules Verne's 1861 adventure novel, *The English at the North Pole*.

There were other problems with Cook's claim. His sketch map of the route included a number of features which didn't actually exist, including 'Crockers Land', a huge island on the charts of the time that was later found not to be there after all. (Ironically this was originally 'discovered' by Peary. A local Inuit hunter explained later that it was all just an illusion. He called it 'Poo-jok', which means mist).

Finally there were the speeds of his supposed progress in the final dash to the Pole: seventeen miles a day, or three times what was considered possible. None of this seemed to really add up.

In 1910 Cook was embroiled in another controversy when doubts began to be cast on an earlier feat of his when in September 1906 he claimed to have climbed the twenty thousand foot Mt Mckinley, the highest mountain in North America. In the event it appeared that he had got only six thousand feet up its slopes and then took a photograph looking up towards the 'summit' on one of the lower promontories. It became known as 'Fake Peak'.

Cook's failure to produce any navigational records of his Arctic odyssey did for him. A reporting commission found that there was no evidence he had got to the North Pole. Peary was crowned as the real Arctic hero. He had won. But then the question remains as to how far the victor's own claim actually stands up to scrutiny.

For one thing he would never reveal his own logs which remained jealously guarded by his friends at the National Geographic Society who vouched for him. Those records that are in the public domain are strangely silent on his final dash to the Pole, in which he would have had to achieve thirty eight miles a day to fit in with the dates, a speed faster than the snowmobiles used over fifty years later.

There is no doubt he played hardball in the war with the doctor: Cook maintained that three boxes of his records were left behind in Greenland which Peary refused to take on his own homeward bound ship and that subsequently they were lost. His backers also gave a financial inducement to Cook's climbing partner to swear that neither of them got to the summit of Mt Mckinley, so undermining Cook further in the public's perception.

Today, both explorers have their supporters and detractors but Peary got the glory and Cook's reputation was ruined. He turned to other means of gaining fame and fortune and in 1923 was indicted for fraud in relation to oil company stocks he was promoting. Cook pleaded ignorance but the judge was not on his side: he was sentenced to fourteen years in Fort Leavenworth.

There he was visited by the greatest Polar explorer of all: Roald Amundsen. Both men had first met on an expedition to the Antarctic in 1898 in which Cook as the ship's doctor had been instrumental in alleviating an outbreak of scurvy among the crew by hunting and supplying them with fresh meat. As far as Amundsen was concerned, the good doctor had been responsible for saving his life.

Cook's announcement that he had reached the North Pole back in 1909 had one immeasurable affect on history. Amundsen had been preparing his own attempt when the news came through. He had simply turned around and conquered the South Pole instead. There he showed he had learned the lessons of the Cook and Peary feud. His meticulously recorded celestial observations were checked and cross checked and the whole of the Pole area staked out with flags to ensure that he stood right on Ninety degrees south and not anywhere else-all this just to make sure that no one would ever, in any circumstances, dispute what he had achieved. Better to be safe than sorry.

AMUNDSEN, THE 'MAUD' AND THE 'BIG WHALE'

Following his conquest of Antarctica Amundsen returned to the Arctic for his own attempt at the North Pole. He had a new ship built, the *Maud*, with the intention of carrying on where Nansen on the *Fram* had left off some twenty five years previously.

Amundsen left northern Norway on 16th July 1918 and sailed east along the Russian coast, leaving behind a Europe still in the grip of war and in the throes of tumultuous revolutions. Further south the Bolsheviks were murdering the Tsar and the rest of the imperial family while Amundsen sailed serenely on through his icy kingdom. Somewhere past Cape Chelyuskin, the most northerly point of the Asian landmass, it hugged the vessel and held her fast.

It wouldn't let go for another two years, during which time the *Maud* drifted along the entire Northeast Passage but nowhere near the North Pole. While the meticulous Amundsen could dictate matters as far as possible on dry land and even in a clear water passage above northern Canada, here he was at the mercy of the capriciousness of the ice like everyone else. In August 1920 the *Maud* turned into the Bering Strait and anchored off the small gold mining settlement of Nome, Alaska for repairs. Some of the crew never came back. The four remaining members of the expedition didn't stay long, wanting to beat the winter lock in. It duly arrived the day after they left Alaska and another winter trapped in the ice ensued.

It was all rather different from the South Pole. The *Maud* expedition had become an odd outing, existing as it did on the margins of the known world but never quite leaving it, remaining in touch with the scattered groups of local peoples on the Siberian coast and using a telegraph station there to announce to the world the progress, (or lack of it), of his trip around the Arctic basin.

This raises an important characteristic of the North Polar Region that has been mentioned before: people actually live there. Unlike Antarctica which is isolated by an enormous southern ocean and has no indigenous population, significant parts of inhabited Europe, America and Asia lie within the Arctic Circle and ring the Polar basin.

From time to time Amundsen dropped in on civilisation. In the summer of 1921 the great explorer decided that the *Maud* should sail to the bustling city of Seattle for a refit. He was not on it, arriving in the port on a passenger liner, the *SS Victoria*. At this point it seemed that for all intents and purposes Amundsen had now lost interest, not only mentally but now physically absent from what he had started. In the end he was doing little more than commuting back and forth to his own expedition. Instead he began to formulate another plan: if he could not sail to the North Pole he would fly to it.

Meanwhile, after a year's hiatus the *Maud* set off again and Amundsen joined it briefly before finally jumping ship. The crew drifted on for another three years in the ice before finally being released. When the vessel did re-appear from the barren wastes, it was promptly seized by his creditors.

The world had undoubtedly changed since the days of Antarctic glory just over a decade ago. Technology was moving apace. Amundsen had been astonished when in 1925 he had been invited on to the bridge of a passenger ship by the captain and saw no one at the helm. The course he was told was set with electricity. And there were now powerful flying machines that could gobble up the distances that men with sledges and dogs once had to haul across. The explorer himself had earned a private Pilots licence. In his test the national hero had only crashed once and was duly passed.

On the evening of 21st May 1925 Amundsen set out from the small settlement of Ny-Ålesund on Svalbard's northwest coast in a Dornier Do J flying boat. Behind him were the steep mountain bluffs of Spitzbergen, in front of him nothing but hundreds of miles of frozen Arctic Ocean and then the North Pole.

A duplicate flying boat accompanied him. Amundsen had obtained the aircraft from Germany and they had been financed by an American, Lincoln Ellsworth who was heir to a coal fortune. Ellsworth senior also supported the trip but begged his only son not to go.

At the controls of the craft that carried the great explorer, (designated N25), was Hjalmar Riiser-Larsen, a navy office and keen pilot who later would found the Norwegian air force. The duplicate N24 carried, apart from its pilot, the coal magnate's son as navigator. Two mechanics completed the complement of six men.

The flying boats were just that, capable of landing on the leads of water that opened up or on the ice itself. They were loaded with skis and sledges for a more conventional crossing should anything go wrong. The cockpits were open to the air. At a cruising height of ten thousand feet it would be a breezy and somewhat chilly flight north.

After about eight hours Amundsen commanded the N25 to land to calculate their latitude. This proved that they had not reached the Pole but were some one hundred and twenty miles off. Worst still they had touched down on a stretch of water which then proceeded to freeze over, trapping them on uneven pack ice from which they could not take off. N24 had landed nearby but was a write off. N25 had been damaged on landing.

The situation of the six men was now precarious. The nearest depot was a seven hundred and fifty mile march away over unknown territory. With the supplies available to them, they would never make it. Deliverance depended on getting airborne again. But first they had to build a runway.

There followed a full twenty six days on the ice shovelling snow and carving out a level path over the surface, testing the engines and waiting for the right wind and temperature conditions. Much longer and the ice would melt; if that happened they would be doomed.

On 15th June Riiser-Larsen opened the throttle on a thoroughly overloaded N25, now carrying five passengers but minus the sledges and provisions that they would need for their survival if anything went wrong. It was a desperate final throw of the dice but it worked. The Dornier's engines continued to thrum all the way back to Svalbard, a journey that took another eight and a half hours.

Amundsen may not have got to the Pole but his flight proved one thing. Back in 1911 it had taken him and his men over three months to cover the 2,600 km trek to and back from the South Pole. Now, in the age of the aeroplane the equivalent of such a journey was less than a day's work.

Undaunted by the failure of his latest Polar venture, Amundsen next decided to change the type of aircraft he would fly in. He began to make plans to procure an airship which he thought would be more manoeuvrable and reliable in the hazardous world of Arctic exploration.

In August 1925 he paid a visit to Rome to meet Umberto

Nobile, an Italian aeronautical engineer and aviator who would design and pilot his airship, the *Norge*, a hundred and six metre long sausage shaped craft filled with hydrogen. The local Inuit would later dub it the *Flying Whale*.

The two men never really got on. Even as Nobile took the great explorer for a spin in his Fiat car around the sights of the eternal city, the explorer was already criticising his driving skills, and this was not even navigation in the air. 'His entire behaviour,' he wrote later, 'on this trip exposed his tremendous nervousness, eccentric behaviour and lack of quiet judgement.' It was not an auspicious start.

But this was unfair. Nobile was a talented designer and aviator. He would steer the *Norge* to the spot that Amundsen desired and fulfil all that was required of him. Besides, the expedition had powerful if dubious endorsement in the shape of the fascist dictator Mussolini who facilitated the building of the airship. Nobile was no fascist but he knew what Mussolini wanted and that was to bring home a triumph for the greater glory of the Italian state. Woe Betide him if he failed.

On 11th May 1926 the *Flying Whale* was let loose from its moorings in northern Svalbard and floated the six hundred and fifty miles to the Pole. On board were Amundsen, Nobile, Ellsworth and Riiser-Larsen. At 2.20 pm the next day they hovered over the North Pole. The Norwegian, American and Italian flags were dropped on the spot, as befitted such an international expedition. Amundsen would later complain that the Italian flag was flamboyantly large. The ship then sailed on in the unresisting air until it reached Alaska on the 14th. Amundsen and his companions had not only crossed the Arctic basin, more importantly they had been the first to see the Pole.

Or had they? Just three days earlier the American naval officer and pilot Richard E Byrd had also taken off from Svalbard, in his case in a Tri-motor monoplane named *Josephine Ford*, after the daughter of the president of the Ford Motor Company who had sponsored his flight. He claimed a sixteen hour return trip of over one thousand five hundred miles and a sighting of the Pole. But such a claim was dubious. Later his co-pilot would admit that they never did make it there. Byrd would go on to have an illustrious career in Polar exploration and in the US navy but on this occasion it seems that he was outflanked by an airship.

On 23rd May 1928, Nobile set off on his own expedition in a similar craft, *The Italia,* to explore the north Polar Regions. It crashed north east of Svalbard and an international search and rescue mission ensued. On 23rd June he was found and taken off the ice first because of his injuries, it being another three weeks before the other survivors were picked up. Mussolini never forgave Nobile for coming back alive, or at least being the last to leave his 'ship', taking it as a loss of face for the Italian state. Nobile left in 1931 to work in the Soviet Union. He returned after the war and had his rank and reputation re-instated.

Among the searchers for Nobile was one Roald Amundsen. It says something of the complexity of his character that he spent considerable effort on obtaining a new flying boat and going after a man he so obviously disliked in order to rescue him. He set off on 18th June and when a few days later no one had heard from him, the rescue mission began to turn towards saving the would be the rescuer.

Thus did the greatest of Polar explorers finally fall off the end of the Earth. The man who had conquered the South

Pole and most likely the North as well, the first to navigate the Northwest Passage by ship and take to the air across the Polar wastes, simply disappeared. He was never seen again.

THE COLD WAR: NUCLEAR SUBS, THE 'TSAR BOMBA' AND THE PILLSBURY DOUGHBOY

The disappearance of Amundsen and the end of Nobile's aerial perambulations around the Polar basin ended the heroic era of Polar exploration. The North Pole had now been identified together with the icy wastes that surrounded it, and it could be positively and conclusively reported that there was nothing there. Why go back?

But priorities change and whereas the seductive idea of discovering a lost continent was finally laid to rest, other reasons emerged for wanting to keep a presence in the north Polar regions and around the North Pole itself. These would increasingly have to do with strategic and military considerations. After the Second World War a new cold war emerged between the superpowers. The Arctic was one of the frontiers of this conflict, a place where east and west were within touching distance. They literally eyeballed each other across the roof of the world.

In 1932 a Russian icebreaker, the *Sibiryakov* had made the first transit of the Northeast Passage in a single summer, doing away with the need for a winter break lying frozen in some port. For the Soviets the passage and the northern sea route out through the Bering Strait was more than a matter of interest. In the Second World War with its convoys of food and military material, it would become a matter of national survival. By extension they wanted control over what lay even further north.

Stalin was a big fan of the Arctic. From the 1930's he set up any number of little outposts of Soviet communism on the ice, ostensibly for scientific research but probably for other reasons as well.

In May 1937 the entire contents of such a facility including its four personnel were airlifted and then dumped some twenty km from the North Pole. From there the frozen sea carried it all the way to the east coast of Greenland before they were evacuated some nine months later. For their carousel ride around the Polar basin the inhabitants of this base were awarded the title of 'Heroes of the Soviet Union'.

In April 1948 the Russians were back, landing three planes on the ice on the 23rd of that month. If the accounts of this expedition are correct, the twenty four scientists and flight crew ferried there would most likely have been the first human beings to stand on the North Pole.

But then by this time no one was that bothered. The symbolic value of attaining the Pole had strangely worn off-no one seemed to be in a rush to claim that prize any more.

Besides there were easier and more comfortable ways to get there like hitching a ride on a nuclear submarine. In 1954 the USA launched the world's first nuclear sub: *USS Nautilus*. The advantages of such craft were obvious. They could submerge for long periods of time and slip under the ice cap, so avoiding the challenges of surface travel. *Nautilus* could stay under for two weeks at a time, a huge advance on conventional submarines, (nowadays it is more like three months), and had a supply of power at its disposal that seemed unlimited, (the current generation of nuclear craft never need refuelling).

On 17th March 1959 another nuclear submarine, *USS Skate*, became the first to surface at the North Pole. The previous year *Nautilus* had become the first watercraft to reach ninety degrees north and slip under the globe's most northern point, a feat that boosted American morale at a time when 'Sputnik' was sowing paranoia and the USA appeared to be losing the race up in space.

Naturally the Soviets followed suit and soon a game of cat and mouse developed between them and the Americans as they chased each other under the pack ice. More seriously, the Arctic was the scene of the explosion in October 1961 of the most powerful nuclear weapon ever devised when Russia tested a fifty megaton bomb on the Novaya Zemlya archipelago off its northern Siberian coast. Nicknamed the 'Tsar Bomba' in the west, the blast was equivalent to ten times all the explosives used in World War Two and created a mushroom cloud about sixty four km high and ninety five km broad. In Helsinki and Oslo, over three and a half thousand miles away, doors rattled and windows broke.

It is to be hoped that such cold war madness is never repeated. However with renewed tensions between the powers bordering the Arctic and the intensifying competition for resources in recent years, it may be a forlorn wish. History has a habit of repeating itself.

But life still has to go on. Even though by the time of Russia's big bang, the North Pole had been sighted, dived under and flown to, people were suddenly reminded that the ultimate goal of walking there, (Peary, Cook and other claims aside), had not yet been achieved.

This was to be partially rectified by an insurance salesman who in the spring of 1966 walked into a bar in Duluth Minnesota and over a few beers came up with a plan. Ralph Plaisted was a college drop-out and amateur back woodsman who was nothing if not persuasive. Before long he had got together a team of adventurers who had one thing in common: they had never been on the Arctic ice before. Remarkably, despite being turned down by Campbell soup among others, Ralph was able to get enough corporate sponsorship to feed the expedition and help with the equipment. Not a man to be easily dissuaded when it came to liquid sustenance he had simply gone round the corner and sweet talked Knorr into providing him with what he needed.

Plaisted's team got as far as eighty four degrees north before they had to be rescued. Amateur probably does not begin to describe it. Nevertheless he had learnt a lot and one thing was definite: he would be making the next attempt on 'Ski- Doos', powerful snow mobiles which were tried and tested in harsh conditions.

Next year he was back, sponsored by the foot giant Pillsbury, whose most recognisable brand icon is the 'Doughboy', a jolly figure in a chef's hat who in numerous commercials does a trademark chuckle when poked in his soft stomach.

On the morning of April 20th 1968 Ralph and his party reached the North Pole, abandoned the Ski- Doos and were then flown out. No one seemed very impressed or even interested and there was little press coverage. But Ralph Plaisted had achieved what no one else had in several hundred years of Polar endeavour: he had reached the North Pole by surface route. He just hadn't walked there.

The next year British explorer Wally Herbert did just that by foot and sledge as part of an epic trek from Alaska to Svalbard. He reached the North Pole on 6th April 1969, sixty years to the day since Robert Peary claimed he had stood there. Some twenty year later Herbert was commissioned by the Royal Geographic Society to look over the records of Peary's attempt and came to the conclusion that he had not reached the North Pole. The matter however remains contentious to this day.

Herbert had been re-supplied by air so that for the total purist when it came to Polar expeditions there was still the challenge to get to the Pole unassisted. American adventurer Will Steger reached the Pole in May 1986 with dogsleds and nothing else but it was a one way trip.

The first persons to undoubtedly reach the North Pole on foot (or skis) and return with no outside help, no dogs, air planes, no re-supplies, nothing but sheer grit were Richard Weber (Canada) and Misha Malakhov (Russia) in 1995. No one has done it since. This surely must complete the history of such journeys. The North Pole has now been thoroughly conquered. Anything else begins to look like sheer masochism.

MODERN TIMES

With the success of expeditions like those of Wally Herbert and Richard Weber, one chapter in the exploration of the Arctic closed, only for another to open. In the future no longer would the North Pole be the preserve of such adventurers suffering the extreme privations of cold and hunger in their quest to achieve their goal. From the 1990's onwards it would increasingly become a tourist destination in which visitors would pay for champagne flights and luxury ship passages to the end of the earth. Possibly one of the first Arctic tourists was an American, David Fisher, who in 1991, just as the Soviet Union was collapsing, paid $30,000 in welcome hard currency for a trip on the Russian nuclear ice breaker *Sovetskiy Soyuz*. Where Fisher led, others followed, and an industry flourished. Nowadays huge vessels such as the '*Yamal*' and the twenty six thousand tonne '*Fifty Years of Victory*', make up to five visits each summer to the Pole carrying hundreds of visitors. The '*Fifty Years of Victory*', boasts a gym, two saunas and a heated swimming pool. In the evening you can enjoy fine dining in its restaurant and have a drink in its bar while watching the Polar bears. There is probably a honeymoon suite for newlyweds. Amundsen and others like him who spent their lives trying to penetrate this wilderness would be astonished.

We shouldn't get too blasé about it though. This is still an extreme destination with its dangers and uncertainties. And no one can quite predict what the impact of rising international tensions will be on the one hand and climate change on the other.

In theory the Arctic does not belong to anyone. By agreement the countries that fringe it have rights to a zone two hundred miles off their coast and no more but this is open to dispute and there are always attempts to grab a bigger slice of the ice. Russia made its play in 2007 when it sent a submersible to the sea bed two and a half miles under the Pole to plant a rust proof national flag. The message was clear: 'The Arctic is Russian.'

The Canadian foreign minister was not impressed at this stunt. 'This isn't the 15th century,' he told CTV television, "You can't go around the world and just plant flags and say: 'We're claiming this territory.'"

Nevertheless, since that time countries like Canada,

The US and Norway have been busy jockeying for position and making their own claims. A new cold war beckons and there is a lot at stake: military and political influence, not to mention an estimated $35 trillion in oil and gas reserves, all being uncovered by a melting ice cap.

Climate change is the other big issue presently facing the Polar region, (see *'The big melt: the disappearance of the ice cap'*.) Temperatures are rising and the already erratic weather is becoming crazier. The ice is getting thinner and its cover shrinking. Expeditions on foot like those of Wally Herbert and Richard Weber may be a thing of the past: there simply won't be anything firm enough to push your sled on.

Not that this has deterred anyone from visiting- the tourist numbers just keep going up. Perhaps they want to come here before the whole thing disappears. Before the 1990's only a handful of people had ever stood on the North Pole. Now that figure, while still relatively small, may be as much as 20,000 and no doubt it will continue to go up. It is estimated that about a thousand tourists visit the Pole each year and that there are over a million visitors to the Arctic region as a whole each season.

They come because the region still exerts an odd fascination. Speculated upon for thousands of years, it took centuries to break through the ice and find that there was no inland sea, no hidden continent and no mythical whirlpool at its centre, just a lot of nothingness. And yet for all that it is still a beguiling and beautiful place, strange and maddening even. That's why many of us yearn to go there.

John Wesley Powell
The original river runner

Photo: US archives, Geological
Survey. In the public domain.

Glen and Bessie
Hyde: a tragic couple

Photo courtesy of the
Huntingdon Library, San
Marino, California. Bessie
& Glen Hyde; Hermit Camp
1928, image VO67/0167.
Otis Marston collection.

*The seventeenth
century view of
the Polar world:
Mercator's atlas*

Photo: Faithful reproduction
of original. Used under
Creative Commons licence.

*Modern times:
the honeymoon
is literally on ice*

Photo: Tatiana
Posepelova

*Tobogganing
1910 Style*

*Photo: by unknown
resident of Davos.
Used under Creative
Commons licence*

Lizzy Yarnold shows how it's done
*Photo: copyright 2017 Garrett A Wollman. Used
under Creative Commons licence*

IV

The Big Melt: The Disappearance of the Ice Cap

Shifting seasons, thin ice, permafrost roads exploding in Alaska, the tree line marching north: there is plenty of anecdotal evidence that things are changing within the Arctic Circle and changing fast, much more so in fact than the rest of the planet.

We have now got used to stories of tankers and cruise ships slipping through the Northwest Passage, while documentaries have detailed for a number of years the impact on the indigenous population, such as the Inuit of northern Canada, of the 'mad' weather they now have to face. Such changes in climate have a profound effect on their lives: it skews their hunting grounds and makes navigation difficult. Most importantly it removes the old certainties and makes them question their elders. It is not a recipe for social cohesion.

What is rather startling is that the Inuit elders themselves not only blame the Southerners for messing up the planet but believe the whole globe has toppled over. They do have a point. The sun does not set in the same place anymore and the stars are not in their proper positions in the sky. This is not some mass hallucination, they are actually seeing this. The reason is that the warming Arctic air is refracting the rays of the sun in a different way, displacing it in the eye of the perceiver who is used to the optical effect of a colder climate.

Even seasoned research scientists who have studied the region for decades can be caught off guard. One remembers as a graduate student in the early 1980's surveying an ice cap in the far north of America that was over a mile long. He went back in 2016 to locate it only to discover that it had simply melted away.

As it happens 1980 is something of a nostalgic date for Polar climatologists. That was the last time the Arctic was, 'normal'. Since then it has behaved extremely badly, running amok with a temperature rise year on year that is twice as fast as the rest of the world. 2017 was the warmest winter on record, a fact that prompted the Director of the National Snow and Ice Data Center in Boulder, Colorado, who has been studying the Arctic since 1982 to exclaim, 'These heat waves – I've never seen anything like this. It's just crazy, crazy stuff.'

The small settlement of Umiujaq on the northern shores of Hudson Bay, Canada knows all about heat waves in summer. 'We try not to be out when it's too hot,' one resident told reporters, describing herself as a 'winter person'. 'Last year we had a heat wave for two to three days, I almost got heat stroke. It was around 29-30 degrees Celsius, or 84.2-86.0 degrees Fahrenheit—that's too much for me!'

Such quirks however are still rare even if they are becoming more common. The Arctic, for the moment at least, is still an epic frozen wilderness that astonishes visitors, even if it is creaking a bit.

In winter its sea ice covers an area equivalent to Europe one and a half times over, (in the summer it retreats to a third of that size as the sun comes up and melts everything before slipping below the horizon in September). In addition there are all the glaciers found in the landmasses that ring the region and the immense cap that covers the island of Greenland, all 1.8 million square kilometres of it. In places it is two miles deep and so heavy that it has pushed the ground beneath it into a great bowl, up to 360 metres below sea level.

Surely all this ice cannot just melt? But that is precisely what seems to be happening. The best way to view the shrinking fortunes of the Polar ice cap is in fact from space where satellites have been tracking its extent and thickness for several decades. According to the National Snow and Ice Data Center, (a body linked to NASA which regularly publishes data on the subject), the maximum extent of sea ice in 2017 was 14.42 million Sq km, making it the smallest cover for 38 years. When compared to the average for the previous 30 years that represents a loss equivalent to something like twice the size of Texas. While the extent of the sea ice varies from year to year there is no doubt that the long term trend is shrinkage. Scientists believe that we are losing as much as 4% of the ice sheet every decade.

Why is all this happening? Clearly the Arctic is warming up, be it as a result of human practices or the cyclical fluctuations of climate that occur naturally or both, but what appears to mark out the present upward trend is the astonishingly small time frame in which it is happening. The first decade of the new millennium saw temperatures some two degrees centigrade higher than in the last half of the twentieth century and were the warmest since the 17th century. It is said that current temperatures are the highest they have been for 40,000 or more years. This rather puts the warm and mild era of Viking exploration and settlement of Greenland into context.

One of the reasons why the Arctic outpaces the rest of the planet in temperature change is the so called 'amplification effect'. This happens in Polar Regions where the solar reflecting snow and ice, when it melts, uncovers the dark rock underneath. This absorbs the Sun's rays and raises the temperature even more, contributing to yet more melt which uncovers yet more heat absorbing surface. This 'feedback loop' accelerates the warming process in an ever increasing spiral. If this continues eventually the entire Siberian tundra will start to thaw and the vast lakes of methane gas under its surface will gradually be released into the atmosphere. Methane is a greenhouse gas and contributes to global warming so thawing the tundra even more. If the science is correct, that is a feedback loop of epic proportions.

At some stage in this process climatologists believe there is a 'tipping point' where climate change becomes uncontrollable, a train ride without a brake that is irreversible and leads to a wreck. That is one theory anyway. Some scientists believe that the loss of the sea ice could trigger this tipping point with disastrous consequences for the rest of the planet.

One of the effects of all this melt is its contribution to a rise in sea levels. While the sea ice floats on the surface and presumably like the ice in a drink will not contribute that much to the level in the 'glass', there is still some four million cubic km of ice in the Greenland sheet alone, which amounts to about a billion litres of water for each inhabitant of earth. Should this melt there is enough there to raise the oceans of the planet by twenty-three feet. If that did happen many coastal cities would be under water. Most of the island nations of the Pacific would simply disappear.

This however is not an immediate prospect. While the Greenland ice sheet is shrinking, even with a runaway melt it could take over a thousand years to disappear entirely into the sea. In the short and medium term the loss of sea ice is likely to have other effects. For one thing it offers a cooling surface for the winds that circulate around the region and drive the ocean currents. The Arctic is one big heat exchanger with the rest of the planet. Upset that and you change weather patterns around the globe from the monsoon in India to tropical storms in the Pacific. What happens in the Arctic doesn't stay in the Arctic. It does have wide reaching consequences for us all.

What can we do about this? Apart from responding to the usual exhortation to reduce green house emissions, probably adapt the best we can. Human beings are nothing if not ingenious. Wildlife may be less lucky. There is likely to be a profound impact on the species that live here, from the Polar Bears that breed and hunt on the ice to the algae at the bottom of the ice flows which form the basis of the food chain for many animals.

While the various doomsday scenarios espoused by a number of climate change experts are a matter of debate, there is no doubt that the Polar environment is undergoing rapid change. To the future visitor the Arctic may look somewhat different to the place it is today. Some scientists believe that by the middle of this century it will be ice free in the summer and the North Pole will be in the open sea. Rather than making the journey on sledges and on foot, Expeditions are now planning to use sailing boats. Back in the nineteenth century there was a belief in an inner Polar sea, one that ships could sail on right to the end of the earth. In the twentieth century we scoffed at the idea as quaint, unscientific and totally absurd. Now it appears, such a dream may become a reality. Time, it seems, together with global warming can make fools of us all.

V

The Bare Bones of It: A History of Skeleton Riding

Courage is being scared to death... and saddling up anyway. **John Wayne**

The frictionless world has served us for a long time. In an age before the motor car and high speed travel it was our ticket to fast trade and communication between isolated settlements. Over a thousand years ago the peoples of Scandinavia and northern Europe invented speed skating as a means of visiting their neighbours along the frozen canals and rivers of their Viking homeland. In the early days they did it by strapping bones to their feet.

The sled had already been around for millennia when the first skaters arrived. The ancient Egyptians probably used them to build the pyramids, hauling two ton blocks of stone on primitive wooden runners with upturned edges. Sand can be a frictionless medium but it helps if it is wet. The physics of it is complicated but it has to do with capillary action and gluing the grains together. A wall painting found in the tomb of a local official in Middle Egypt depicts the transport of a statue seven metres high in this way. At the front of the sledge there is a figure pouring water from a vessel. It is estimated that simply by dampening the sand in front, the force needed to move this 'colossus' was halved. The ability to slide is a powerful thing.

It was also necessary in the afterlife. About three thousand years before Christ, a noblewoman, 'Queen' Puabi of Ur in ancient Sumeria, (now southern Iraq), was buried with a wooden sled pulled by oxen. Her chariot was adorned with gold and silver lion and bulls heads and accompanied by four 'grooms' to attend her and the transport which would take her to a new existence. Theirs was not exactly a voluntary ride, being the result of either poisoning or head trauma with a blunt instrument.

On a more practical level, the Inuit and Cree peoples of the Arctic have throughout their history used stretched sleds or toboggans to carry food and people in the frozen wastes. They made them from birch or sometimes whalebone curved at the front, rugged and flexible enough to deal with the difficult terrain they had to cross.

As a pastime it took a while for slithering about to catch on, but by the fifteenth century the imperial courts of Europe were having sledding races, using richly decorated sleds for their own decadent amusement. The local priesthood condemned it as the work of the devil.

By the early 1700's, sledging trips had become a popular spare time activity with the wealthy bourgeoisie in the Austrian Tyrol. The earliest preserved sledges in this region of the Alps, (including the Engadin valley in which St Moritz lies), date back to the first half of the 18th century. They have skids or runners made of beef bone (shinbone) and intricately carved wooden seats.

But despite the potential for fun, until recent times

the function of the sled remained above all a practical one. For the people of the Engadin valley it was the quickest and sometimes only way to move goods and people in the surrounding mountainous terrain in winter. It represented a means of communication between snowbound villages like Davos, St Moritz and Celerina together with the nearby hamlet of Cresta. It maintained a lifeline between them.

St Moritz at the end of the nineteenth century was not the winter playground it is today. In fact it was just another pretty backwater with seemingly not much more to offer than the next picture postcard spot down the valley. What it did have however was sunshine in abundance, over three hundred sun filled days a year which made it a popular summer destination but little else.

The local hoteliers and businessmen, increasingly fed up with closing for half the year and seeing all that tourist money disappear, decided that they needed to attract the crowds to remain in winter. In the autumn of 1864, one of them, Johannes Badrutt, made a wager with four of his British guests that should they return in winter and like what St Moritz had to offer they could stay as long as they wished. If they didn't like the town in the off season he would reimburse all their expenses.

'Come back and spend Christmas in St Moritz. It's sunnier and less rainy than London,' he told them and that was undeniably true. On the day that they returned Johannes greeted them in his shirtsleeves. They had such a good time they stayed until Easter.

At first the visitor numbers were a trickle. After all, it did take up to two days to get there from Britain, including a twelve hour trek up a winding and slippery alpine road in a horse-drawn carriage. Such a journey was still very much the preserve of the adventurous and well heeled. But gradually the idea caught on, helped in part by the curative properties of the clear mountain air and bubbling mineral springs which attracted those suffering from tuberculosis and other respiratory ailments.

Before long it was clear that Badrutt's bet was working. In the same season as his wager the first tourist office in Switzerland was established in the town. A few years later his expanding Kulm Hotel switched on the only electric lights in the whole of the country. St Moritz was on the up.

There was only one hitch for the more adventurous visitors who were starting to flock to the town: what to do in winter once you got there. Skiing had been around for centuries but had not yet been widely adopted as a recreational sport, and while skating and curling were possibilities, many of those who were staying in St Moritz were looking for something new, a pastime that would satisfy their need for excitement and even a bit of danger.

It wasn't long before the local 'Schlitten' caught the eyes of the new arrivals. These were the heavy wooden sleds used by locals for hauling famer's loads and other produce along the streets of the town and on the roads outside. They could however be adapted to carry people and commandeered for a bit of sliding fun once the day's work was done. Soon the bored Brits were pushing the delivery boys off their schlitten in a desire to have a go themselves.

At first there were no dedicated ice runs. The tracks were simply the winding streets of the town or the roads between the villages down the valley. As more people joined in a competitive edge emerged with the entertainment committee of each hotel and then each resort organising races against each other along the public highways. As the sliding bug was caught down the Engadin Valley, pretty soon it was village against village.

Despite the increasing competitiveness of the new sport and its potential for injury and mayhem, a certain sense of decorum still prevailed amongst the exclusive clientele who took part in these races. Proper attire for example was de rigueur. For the women this usually meant long billowing dresses and showy bonnets, while the gentlemen would dress up in their best Sunday suits for the occasion. Often they would go down the course wearing a top hat.

The predominantly British guests brought with them the public school ethos of sporting rivalry and team loyalty. They formed themselves into clubs with their own regalia and sometimes even uniforms. Clubs meant rules and rules meant officials such as club secretaries to enforce them. It also meant a more systematic method of training its members in technique and the funding to ensure that what was evolving into a fully fledged sport could be supported in the future.

Remarkably for those times women fully participated in these races and often won them in mixed fields. This was despite the handicap of initially having to ride side saddle and wear skirts as big as boat sails. When one female rider had the temerity to lift her hem above the ice there was outrage. Later when the fashion of riding head first caught on the first woman to do so was met with shocked disbelief. She was of course American.

Women continued to ride the Cresta until the year 1929 when the club with its majority male membership voted to ban women from the run. The rather dubious excuse given was that it encouraged breast cancer. That of course, was patent nonsense. By that token no man should be let near a Cresta sled: what with all that banging about in front the testicular cancer rates would likely shoot right up. The real reason may have had more to do with men being alarmed at their wives and girlfriends facing injury and unladylike bruises, but perhaps that is too generous. More likely it was plain old misogyny. (Nevertheless, for a while some women continued to ride surreptitiously, dressed as men, or after the run had officially closed for the season at which time it was bulldozed to stop them going down it).

But back in the 1870's women were still fully engaged in the sledding league that had grown up down the valley. The main rivals were the villages of St Moritz and Davos. Generally they fought each other in the roads and tracks between the settlements. The earliest reported example of a proper ice run was one built in Davos in 1872. It required dragging the sledges to the top before freewheeling down to the bottom and then climbing back up to the top again. In 1876 Franklin Adams, an English guest in St Moritz improvised a track beside the Kulm hotel, all with the approval of its owner Johannes Badrutt who had not lost his flair for promotion. But Davos had the longer runs and the better talent at that time: they usually won.

Such dedicated runs were still the exception at that time but things were about to change. By the 1880's the authorities in St Moritz had became increasingly fed up by the carnage caused in its streets by upper crust yahoos knocking over the local citizens like skittles. Despite the introduction of the club ethos and some rules and regulations it was still basically the tobogganing equivalent of the Wild West. In addition St Moritz needed a proper run if it was ever to see off its great rival Davos. Something had to be done.

In December 1884 five guests of the Kulm Hotel,

all members of its, 'Outdoor Sports Committee', stepped outside into the snow and starting staking with pegs the outline of a track. It started just outside the hotel and ended in the village of Celerina in the valley below. They linked arms and with bandaged boots stamped their way down the course, after which they left the packed snow to harden with the frost. Nine weeks later they had created the original Cresta run and the first recognisable Bob-Skeleton track in the world.

The new run was revolutionary. For one thing it was not designed to be straight. It had numerous curves and banks, ten twists in all. Badrutt had engaged the services of a local geometrician Peter Bonorand to design the course in the hope that any local competitors would not be able to match the speeds generated by its snake like progression. Once it was finished they invited Davos to a return match. St Moritz lost again. Still, it is the Cresta run at St Moritz that still stands today and is world famous. Meanwhile in Davos the World Economic Forum meets every year, a much duller event.

The run was completely natural and has remained so. Every year between December and January it is created again from scratch, much to the same overall template but with slight modifications. Modern technology does not require boot stamping these days it but it still takes a couple of months for a twelve strong team of Italian and Portuguese constructors to build it. They use a wooden framework, earth banks, and piled snow as its foundation. The whole thing is liberally sprayed with water that instantly freezes and glues it all together. While in summer this is a quiet meadow peppered with wild flowers, in winter it is a place of life and possibly death. The Cresta is the world's only natural ice run- all the other Olympic and competition tracks are made out of reinforced concrete and are artificially refrigerated. That is why all the activity on the Cresta takes place early in the day. After noon the famous sunshine begins to pull at the run and the ice becomes even more lethal.

Building a dedicated run for the first time had the advantage of taking death off the streets and keeping it where it belonged: on the track itself. Now the sledding aficionados could ride their Schlitten without scaring the local populace. The technique however remained crude: they still sat upright on the sled and sometimes had to propel themselves along with the aid of sticks.

Then in 1887 scandal! A contemporary account in the local press marks the occasion of one rider's revolutionary leap of faith:

> *'Mr Cornish caused the chief excitement of the race by riding his toboggan head first. To do this he lay his body on the toboggan, grasping its sides well to the front, his legs alternating between a flourish in mid air and occasional contact with mother earth or rather farther ice and snow, for the purpose of controlling his course. To see him coming head first down the leap is what the Scotch call uncanny.'*

Soon everyone was doing it. The following year an Englishman, L P Child, introduced a whole new type of toboggan to the run. It looked nothing like the original heavy wooden Schlitten that riders first used. For one thing it had metal runners that made it much faster on the ice. It was a stripped down bare bones of a racing sled. It gained the nickname 'Skeleton'.

About this time someone had the bright idea of welding together a couple of 'skeletons' so that more than one rider could sit on it and the front man could 'steer' with a rope while the one at the back was the brakesman. It was thought that bobbing about in the sled would improve its speed. In the event this was wrong but the name stuck-henceforth it was called a Bob-Sleigh.

In 1902 Bob-Sleigh got its own track. Thus the sports of Luge, (sledding on your back), Bob-Sleigh and Cresta went their separate ways. One more innovation was to change the Cresta sled before the advent of the 1980's and what we know of today as the sport of Bob-skeleton, and that was the introduction of a sliding seat at the turn of the nineteenth century. The rules of the SMTC forbid any steering or breaking mechanism as such so the rider can only come forward on the sled for speed or hang back and bite into the ice with his raking boots to slow down. The sliding seat facilitates this technique. It was invented by an oarsman, Arden Bott.

And there the development pretty much stopped until the 1970's when the design of sleds came into the twentieth century at last. The more advanced Cresta riders may have moved on with their modern fibreglass and steel 'Flattops' but the 'Traditional' is what every beginner starts on. Essentially anyone new to the Cresta still runs it on a piece of kit the design characteristics of which are over a century old. Some traditions do not change at the St Moritz Tobogganing Club.

The SMTC was formed in 1887 from the same ice booting committee that trod out the first course just three years before. One of them, a Major William Henry Bulpett, would become its first president, starting a long line of mostly British military men and aristocrats who would oversee the organisation for the next 130 years.

From the start, the activities of the club were clearly stated: these were, 'The conduct of races and practice on the Cresta Run and the encouragement of tobogganing generally.' It was and remains strictly an amateur organisation, its members and all those involved seeking no remuneration apart from the glory of taking part. In the corporate minded world today of professional sports bankrolled by big business sponsorship, many regard that as a refreshingly different approach.

From its origins in St Moritz, the sport then known as 'Cresta' or just plain 'tobogganing', spread across the globe. It achieved Olympic recognition when its track was used in the 1928 winter games and again in 1948. The now exclusively male membership of the club was well represented on both occasions. In the 1928 Olympics the gold and silver medals were taken by two club members, the American brothers Jennison and Jack Heaton, while David Carnegie, better known as the 11th Earl of Northesk, took bronze. In 1948 it was the turn of local greengrocer and club member Nino Bibbia to claim the gold medal, one of over two hundred and thirty in competition in his lifetime. Before he died in 2013 he had ridden the Cresta more than anyone else-over 3,000 times in total.

But just as the sport appeared to be achieving a wider, global recognition, the St Moritz Tobogganing Club fell upon difficult times. After the 1948 games, chaos ensued. Sir Brian Williamson, a recent club secretary has been quoted as saying:

'The Cresta was handed over to the Olympic committee — which of course in those days was very, very small and very amateur — and they put a complete blight on the Cresta. There were no funds; they'd run out of money; there was a new secretary; the assistant secretary had resigned; the person in St. Moritz looking after everything had disappeared. The police couldn't find him, his mother couldn't find him, and the records of the club had been lost.'

Eventually the club was nursed back to health and would then go from strength to strength, although perhaps no longer at the centre of any international development of the sport. For the Olympic committee and the 'Fédération Internationale de Bobsleigh et de Tobogganing', (the body which was created to oversee all things sliding), the St Moritz Tobogganing Club was perhaps just a bit too Brit-centric and unique in its way of doing things. In 1954 'Cresta' was dropped from the Olympic programme. It didn't return for almost fifty years.

When it re-appeared it had evolved into something which looked a lot like 'Cresta' but was actually sophisticatedly different. The sport of Skeleton as it became known used fast, crowd pleasing bobsleigh tracks, not the narrower, low cornered Cresta run which tended to throw the riders out. The technique was also different: Cresta riders have rakes on their boots which can help in steering and can be used as a kind of brake, (the Skeleton rider has no brakes), and they use their weight and shifting body position to get round the corners and remain in the run. Skeleton riders on the other hand use the torque created by their head and shoulders to steer them safely to the finish.

The traditional Cresta sled with its sliding pad, flat board and looped runners is of course nothing like the

Skeleton sled used in international competition, a multi-million dollar research project of steel and carbon fibre, aerodynamically contoured to minimise drag. Even the Cresta Flattop, an advance on the 'traditional' that looks more like the solid sleek tray used by the Skeleton riders is not quite the same machine. It is fast, but not Olympic fast.

Undoubtedly the key to the survival of tobogganing as a competitive sport and the creation of modern Bob- Skeleton was the development of the sled. During the next three decades sleds were designed that could be used on the big refrigerated ice runs used by the Bob-Sleigh teams and the sport enjoyed a resurgence of popularity. So much so that it was re-instated as an Olympic event in the 2002 games at Salt Lake City which won the bid in 1995. After that, the money for development started piling in.

Well, perhaps not so much at first, at least in Britain. When Simon Timson, the first director of the British Skeleton programme was put in charge he had an *a*nnual budget of just £10,000. What he lacked in funds however he made up for in initiative, going as far as to bring back buckets full of Salt Lake water to test how the runners in the first generation of sleds he was developing would fare when all that liquid was frozen.

And he had a star: an exceptionally gifted athlete in the form of Alex Coomber, an army intelligence officer who eleven days after her first attempt came fifth in a World Cup race. While this may have been a niche sport in the late 1990's, (women's Skeleton had no official competition until the World Cup in December 1996 and the world championships were only started in 1999), Coomber had the right stuff *to* take it to the next level and knew what worked and didn't work for her on the track. She wasn't afraid to say so. According to Timson, Alex tried the new runners he had developed and promptly fell off her sled, following which she chucked them in the bin. A few years later she won a bronze medal at the 2002 Olympics.

While in Timson's words, 'The marriage of innovation with the human being,' was not always straightforward, it was apparent by that time that science as well as talent was in the driving seat when it came to Skeleton success. And Britain appeared to be at the forefront of such development.

It was a British PhD student, Kristan Bromley, the author in 1999 of a famous, (in the sliding world at any rate), thesis on Skeleton bobsleds, who first came up with a revolutionary sled. Like many others he found himself involved in Skeleton purely by accident, in his case while working for the aerospace company BAE Systems on the typhoon jet fighter.

'I just got hooked on the sport,' he told CNN many years later, 'I'd finished at university and was back at British Aerospace (now BAE Systems) and we were approached by the British Skeleton team to help with their performance. At the time, they were at the back of the field using second-hand equipment from whoever they could.'

According to Bromley, his first sled, 'Looked like something put together with a few nuts and bolts.' None of the British team would ride it. He had no choice but to get on it himself. In a few years he had twice won the men's overall Skeleton World Cup title and had become the first man in history to win the World Championship, European Championship and World Cup in the same season, as well as competing in four Olympics. Today his company is still working on cutting edge designs for the UK team, part of similar research that is going on all over the world involving such tools as computational fluid mechanics, laser scanning and aerodynamic simulation software as well as just simply sticking athletes in wind tunnels to see what happens, all with the aim of producing the best toboggan and racing line. It is a trade off apparently between 'stickiness' and manoeuvrability. The sled has to be stable but not like a 'snow plough.' You want to minimise drag but not let it take off. It is a tricky business. In a sport where tenths or hundredths of a second mean the difference between a gold medal or no medal at all, such advances are vital to competitive survival. Anyone who can reduce air resistance by say 5% is on to a winner.

In 2001 the British skeleton team were given a further boost when the artificial track was opened outside the city of Bath in the west of England, enabling Bob-Sleigh and Skeleton athletes to practice the run ups that are essential to produce winning times on the actual ice courses they compete on. This together with the other training and medical facilities at Bath university have made the sports complex on its campus the centre of British Winter Olympic war operations and have helped spark a run of Skeleton success. Since the 2010 games at Vancouver Britain has won gold at every Olympics and before that silver in Turin in 2016. Prior to Alex Coomber winning bronze at Salt Lake City in 2002 you have to go all the way back to 1948 for a medal. Britain's last golden moment apart from the epic win by its curling team in 2002 was in 1984 when ice dance skaters Jayne Torvill and Christopher Dean wowed the judges with their version of 'Bolero', which brought the house down at the Sarajevo Olympics.

Not that the British should be complacent. There are plenty of other nations competing for the top spot and they all know what the winning recipe is. Timson has been quoted as summing it up as follows:

'We put a very simple plan in place: to identify athletes with the potential to be the fastest starters in the world, put them on the ice every day - (because there used to be a big sliding deficit to the other nations) - employ the world's best coaches, and put them on cutting-edge equipment. Really for the last fourteen years, all the sport has done is ruthlessly and relentlessly pursue that formula.'

Amy Williams, gold medallist in the 2010 Olympics has said that success is down to a, 'Mixture of system and athletes,' while others talk about vision, efficient structure and transparency and the fact that once you are part of the Skeleton 'family', you always remain a part of it.

And that is what competitive tobogganing is like in the modern world: a huge well oiled machine that exists to propel the rider down an ice chute incrementally faster than the next man or woman. All this cutting edge technology and back up does not come cheap. In 2001 Team GB may have had £10,000 to play with, but today that is pocket money. The UK sporting authorities spent over £6.5 million alone in preparation for Bob Skeleton at the 2018 Olympics at Pyeongchang. That is a lot to shell out, detractors say, for one medal.

Nevertheless, you cannot really put a price on national pride or individual endeavour and besides you can't expect the riders to climb onto any old toboggan. This after all is a world where billions of people tune in to events like the winter Olympics, the TV rights for which sell for vast sums, where the pursuit of medals and the trouncing of opposition is financed at government level and in which joint research projects funded by aerospace companies and

Formula One teams lead to a NASA like exploration of the design characteristics of a piece of kit which although the size of a bath mat can cost more in development expenditure alone than many Ferrari sports cars.

This may seem a little bit crazy but that is what you need to do to keep on winning. The days of wooden Schlitten and women in bonnets going for a Sunday race in St Moritz have long gone. Nowadays sliding is a global industry. It's all a long way from sticking bones on your feet.

Epilogue

There is an old adage: *'You have to get back on the horse that threw you.'* That clearly does not apply to everyone on a toboggan. I never did saddle up on one again. No matter. In the end adventure travel is all about the experience and there is always something new around the corner to explore: the ghosts of your failures soon fade from memory. In fact once you have a taste for it there is no going back. One day you may find yourself on a beach in Antarctica being inspected by indignant penguins or even bobbing up and down in 'Shark Alley' off South Africa while a Great White patrols around the 'cage' that you hope will keep you in one piece.....so many adventures and so many places to visit. So go there. Write a book about it.

The Author

Is based in London and when not working likes to travel to many different parts of the globe, enjoying the sights and sounds and the prospect of being moderately scared, (or even on occasion terrified). Never returns to the same place twice. He has no interest in an all inclusive villa holiday.

TONY FOSGATE 2018.

Photo: 'Anasazi high fives' courtesy of Western River Expeditions

Bibliography and Sources

WHITEWATER

Addison, Graeme. 2000. **Whitewater Rafting: The essential guide to equipment and techniques**. New Holland Publishers, London.

Allan, Laura. *Creepy Things you didn't know about dying of thirst*. Ranker.com.

American Southwest website. 2018. *Slot Canyons*.

American Whitewater.com. *International scale of river difficulty, whitewater fatalities*.

Brody, Jane E. 2016. *Taking sports to the extreme*. Well blog, New York Times.

Deseret News. 1997. *Cataract Canyon rapids flipped 30 rafts, 134 people this season*.Deseret News Publishing Company, USA.

Fox News, US. 2014. *Ohio bowling alley worker crushed to death in pin setting machine.*

Foy, Catt. *Ancient rock art is still a mystery*. Article on DesertUSA.com website, Digital West Media, Inc.

Ghiglieri, Michael, Myers, Thomas. 2012. *Over the Edge: Death in Grand Canyon*. Puma Press, USA.

Hoffman, John. 1977, (text). *National Parkways Guide to Grand Canyon National Park*. National Parks Division of World-Wide Research and Publishing company, USA.

Hoops, Herm. 2009. *The history of rubber boats and how they saved rivers.* Westwater Canyon river rafting website.

Insurance Information Institute, USA. *Facts + Statistics: sports injuries*.

Lake Powell Resorts and Marinas website. 2018. Aramark, USA.

Lansing, David. 20.7.2010. *Brown Betty*. Online blog

Lonely Planet. 1999. *USA.* Lonely Planet Publications Pty Ltd, Australia.

National Geographic blog, Grand Canyon history. 2011. *Grand Canyon adventurers Glen and Bessie Hyde*.

National Parks Service website, Canyonlands National Park. *Park Statistics, American Indians,* (history and culture/native Americans.), *River incident reports, May 2000 Big Drop 2 incident report.*

Owen, David. 2017. *Where the water goes, life and death along the Colorado river*. Riverhead books, New York.

Raft Masters.com website. 2018. *10 whitewater rafting safety tips*.

Riverbrain.com site. 2018. Cataract Canyon/rapids.

Roberts, David. 2003. *Riddles of the Anasazi*. Smithsonian Magazine, USA.

Rocky Mountain National Park. 2015*. Nature's knife edge*. Plan your visit brochure, USA National Park Service.

Statista, statistics portal. 2018. *Number of recreational visitors to the Grand Canyon National Park*.Statista.com.

Slot canyons of the American Southwest. American Southwest.net website.2018

Greg Ward. *The Rough Guide to the Grand Canyon*, third edition May 2011. Rough Guides, Apa Publications Group London.

Utah.com travel website, hiking. 2018.*Black Hole of White Canyon*.

Ward, Greg, (Rough Guide). 2011, (third edition). *The Grand Canyon*. Rough Guides, (APA Publications), London.

Webb, Robert H, Belnap, Jayne, Weisheit, John S. 2004. **Cataract Canyon: A Human and Environmental History of the Rivers in Canyonlands.** University of Utah Press.

Weller, Sheila. 2011. *The ride of a lifetime: the making of Thelma and Louise*. Vanity Fair magazine, Conde Nast publications, USA.

Weinraub, Bernard. 1994. *Survival lesson for 'river director'*. New York Times.

White, Nick and D'Arrigo, Stephen. *Cataract Canyon Interpretation*. Notes uploaded BrianEssig.weebly.com.

Youngs, Yolonda, Buchanan, Mark. 2010. *Nature, culture and history at the Grand Canyon*. Arizona State University.

NORTH POLE

Aviation Safety Network. *2015 aircraft accident description, Antonov.*

Bartlett, Duncan. 2008. *Why dying is forbidden in the Arctic.* BBC News Channel online. UK.

Bennetts, Marc. 2015. **Murmansk: Life in a City without Sunlight**. Esquire article, Hearst magazines UK, London.

Bomann-Larsen, Tor. 1995*. Roald Amundsen*. History Press UK edition 2011, UK.

Dombrowski Jennifer. 2016. *Twelve facts you never knew about Longyearbyen*. Post on JohnnyJet.com website.

Explorersweb. 2007. **SOS from Barneo Arctic ice base: Hillary Clinton to the rescue for a false alarm.**

Hansen, Moreton T. 2011. *What it takes to win: Extreme lessons from Polar explorers*. Harvard Business Review online.

Ice Bears and Islands Expedition, press release 2015. *Kayakers complete World First Circumnavigation of Svalbard Archipelago.* Adventure Kayak magazine.

Jackson, Jeff. 2010. *Christian Stangl and the K2 hoax*. Rock and Ice, the climber's magazine online. Big Stone Publishing, USA.

Kayakers complete first circumnavigation of Svalbard archipelago. 2015*.* Adventure Kayak magazine online.

Lambert, Andrew. 2009. *Franklin, Tragic Hero of Polar Navigation*. Faber & Faber, London.

Larsen, Eric. 2016. **Alone on the ice**. Outside Online.

Lonely Planet. 1999. *The Arctic*. Lonely Planet Publications Pty Ltd, Australia.

Lopez, Barry. 1986*. Arctic Dreams.* Macmillan, London, (First edition).

Millar, Jamie. 2016. *The rise of technical fabrics in style*. Men's Health online.

Mcintosh, Audrey. 2015. *The North Pole marathon: the coolest marathon on earth*. Online blog.

Middleton,Nick. 2001. **Going to Extremes: Mud, Sweat and Frozen Tears**. Pan Macmillan. UK.

Midling, Anne Sliper. 2017*. Inside the Ice Caves on Svalbard*. Gemini Research News website.

Officer, Charles and Page, Jake. 2012, (second edition). *A Fabulous Kingdom, The Exploration of the Arctic.* Oxford University Press, Oxford.

Phllip's, 1996, (second edition). *Atlas of Exploration*. Philip's, (Octopus Publishing), London.

Pogorzelski, Robert. 2015. *Safety in a polar bear country*. Posted article, Robert Pogorzelski website.

Stack Exchange Network. 2017. *What are the considerations for landing on an ice runway?* Q&A submitted.

Statistics Norway. 2016. *This is Svalbard 2016: What the figures say, Accommodation tables.* Statistics Norway.

Woodhead, Patrick. 2015. *Ten things no one tells you before an Antarctic expedition*. The Telegraph online.

Zolfagharifard, Ellie. 2015. *Stay warm in synthetic spider's silk: North Face creates tough winter jacket using artificial proteins inspired by the creature*. Daily Mail online.

Arctic Info News Agency website. 2018. **Encyclopedia-Indigenous Peoples.** Arctic-Info.com. Russia.

Harding, Luke. 2009. **Yamal peninsula: The world's biggest gas reserves.** Guardian newspaper online. UK.

The Arctic website. 2018. **Population.** Arctic.Ru. Russia.

Dixon, Guy. 2010/2018. **New documentary recounts bizarre climate changes seen by Inuit elders.** Globe2Go website, The Globe and Mail, Canada.

Guardian Newspaper online. 2018**. Arctic has warmest winter on record: 'It's just crazy, crazy stuff'**

Green Facts website. 2018. **Arctic climate change**.

Harvey, Fiona. 2016**. Arctic ice melt could trigger uncontrollable climate change at global level.** The Guardian newspaper online.

Hours, Catherine. 2015. **Climate change: Inuit culture on thin ice.** Phys. org website. Science X News service.

National Snow and Ice Data Center. 2018. **Arctic sea ice maximum at record low for third straight year.**

Saunders, Ben. *The brain of a Polar explorer*. Your Amazing Brain.org website.

Serreze, Mark. 2018. **The melting Arctic shows that climate change is already upon us**. CityMetric, New Statesman magazine online, UK.

Taylor & Francis. 2014. [*Commercial Arctic Shipping through the Northeast Passage: Routes, resources, governance, technology and infrastructure.* Polar Geography.

CRESTA

Agile Lifestyle,net. Apergy Media LLC. (referred to in entry below).

Baer Drake. 2014. *How happiness, sun, parachutes, and other things make you make risky decisions*. Business Insider online, US.

Becker, Lars. 2018. **Sponsors of the Olympic Games: These are the Olympic funders.** ISPO.com website.

Brown, Eryn. 2015. *Why do extreme athletes like Dean Potter risk their lives?* Los Angeles Times online, US.

DiGiacomo, Michael. 2000, *Apparently Unharmed, (Riders of The Cresta Run).* Texere, New York.

Lemieux, Hannah. 2018. *Polo on snow, plenty of glamour and 1,400 bottles of champagne: behind the scenes in St Moritz.* Horse & Hound magazine online, UK.

Lonely Planet. 2000, (third edition). *Switzerland.* Lonely Planet Publications Pty Ltd, Australia.

Scott-Elliot, Robin. 2013. *Lizzy Yarnold: "The Bob Skeleton is petrifying and unnatural but I love it."* Independent newspaper online, UK.

St Moritz Gourmet festival programme. St. Moritz Gourmet Festival Association2018.

Tony Khuon. 2014.*What Skydivers and Jeff Bezos can teach us about leading fulfilling lives*. The Agile Lifestyle.net. Apergy Media LLC.

Time out website. 2015. **Ten of the wackiest Swiss Laws.** Time Out magazine, UK.

Wolchover, Natalie. 2011. *Why do people take risks?* Live Science website, US, UK.

Andrews, Crispin. 2016. *Sports Tech: Skeleton sledding* . E&T Engineering and Technology. UK...

Engineering Edge. 2012. *Athlete Engineered Technology Fine Tuned by Computational Fluid Dynamics.* Mentor, Siemens. USA.

Greenemeier, Larry. 2010. *U.S. Olympic Skeleton Team Studies Sled Forces in High-TechSimulator.* Scientific American magazine online. USA.

Hamilton Tom. 2018. *Just how did Team GB get so good at skeleton?* espn.co.uk/olympics/story

Hodgetts, Rob. 2014. *Lizzy Yarnold: Why do Britain do so well at skeleton?* BBC Sport website.

International Olympic Committee website. 2014. *SOCHI 2014 COVERAGE SETS NEW BROADCAST RECORDS.*

Kantar, Research, Data and Insight Consultancy. ***SOCHI 2014 GLOBAL BROADCAST & AUDIENCE REPORT.*** Published online.

Khuon Tony. 2014. ***What Sky divers and Jeff Bezos can teach us about leading fulfilling lives***. Agile Lifestyle,net. Apergy Media LLC.

Leaders Performance Institute website. 2017. ***My Biggest Mistake… With Simon Timson.***

Majendie, Matt. 2013. ***Kristan Bromley: Doctor Ice's quest for Olympic glory.*** CNN.

McCoy, Terrence. 2014***. The surprisingly simple way Egyptians moved massive pyramid stones without modern technology.*** The Washington Post, US.

Online Skeleton Scrapbook. Sven- Holger Design and Communications GmbH.

Pearson, James. 2018. ***The secret to Britain's skeleton success - no ice.*** Reuters Olympic news online.

Rensselaer Polytechnic Institute.2010.S***cience used to decode the secrets of Olympic skeleton sliding.*** Science Daily online. USA.

Reu, Lindsey. 2006. **What It Takes to Be an Olympic Athlete**. Fitness magazine website.

St Moritz Tourism website. 2018.

University of Bath, Team Bath website. 2018. ***Facilities, Sports Training Village.***

UK Sport. 2018. ***PyeongChang Olympic funding***

William O. Johnson. 20 Jan 1975 ***Every man has a mad streak***. Ssportsillustrated.cnn.com/vault/article/magazine.

Images and illustrations: unless specifically cited all photographs and maps are the work of the author of this publication.

Cover illustrations: stock images, permission granted for use

Printed in Great Britain
by Amazon